Technology, War and Independence

1901–Present Day

KS3 HISTORY FOURTH EDITION

TEA

Curriculum and Assessment Planning Guide

Aaron Wilkes   Lindsay Bruce

OXFORD

OXFORD
UNIVERSITY PRESS

Great Clarendon Street, Oxford, OX2 6DP, United Kingdom

Oxford University Press is a department of the University of Oxford.

It furthers the University's objective of excellence in research, scholarship, and education by publishing worldwide. Oxford is a registered trade mark of Oxford University Press in the UK and in certain other countries

British Library Cataloguing in Publication Data
Data available

978-019-849469-0

10 9 8 7 6 5 4 3 2

Paper used in the production of this book is a natural, recyclable product made from wood grown in sustainable forests.

The manufacturing process conforms to the environmental regulations of the country of origin.

Printed and bound by CPI Group (UK) Ltd, Croydon, CR0 4YY

Acknowledgements
The publisher would like to thank the following for permissions to use copyright material:

Cover illustration by Matthew Hollings

Artworks: Moreno Chiacchiera

Photos: p46: Underwood & Underwood/Getty Images; **p47:** The Royal Mint; **p70:** PRISMA ARCHIVO/Alamy Stock Photo; **p78:** Central Press/Hulton Archive/Getty Images; **p93:** Granger Historical Picture Archive/Alamy Stock Photo; **p128:** CSU Archives/Everett/Alamy Stock Photo; **p143:** Contraband Collection/Alamy Stock Photo; **p156:** ClassicStock/Alamy Stock Photo; **p159:** Flight Collection/Topfoto.

We are grateful for permission to reprint extracts from the following copyright texts.

David Cameron: Tribute to Margaret Thatcher, in *The Spectator,* 8 April 2013 used by permission of David Cameron via Curtis Brown Ltd, London.

David Douglass: 'Thatcher will never be forgiven for the devastation she caused in Sheffield', *The Star,* 9 April 2013, used by permission of the SWNS Media Group for The Star.

Boris Johnson: 'Churchill embodied Britain's greatness', *The Telegraph,* 23 Jan 2015, copyright © Telegraph Media Group Ltd 2015, used by permission of TMG Ltd.

Although we have made every effort to trace and contact all copyright holders before publication this has not been possible in all cases. If notified, the publisher will rectify any errors or omissions at the earliest opportunity.

Links to third party websites are provided by Oxford in good faith and for information only. Oxford disclaims any responsibility for the materials contained in any third party website referenced in this work.

From the authors Lindsay Bruce and Aaron Wilkes: Special thanks to the fabulous Kate Buckley at OUP, who has steered the creation of this handbook from beginning to end. Thanks also to the team at OUP – Janice Mansel-Chan, Alison Schrecker, Emma Jones, Melanie Waldron, Sarah Flynn, Georgia Styring, Marcus Bell and Jade Coyle.

Contents

Contents

Introduction

A unique approach

Oxford's *KS3 History* series by Aaron Wilkes has become one of the best-selling secondary school History series in recent years. This is its Fourth Edition, published in line with the latest National Curriculum framework. This new KS3 series also allows you to cater for the demands of the new GCSE History qualifications by ensuring that the relevant History content and skills needed to access the various question styles at a higher level are covered.

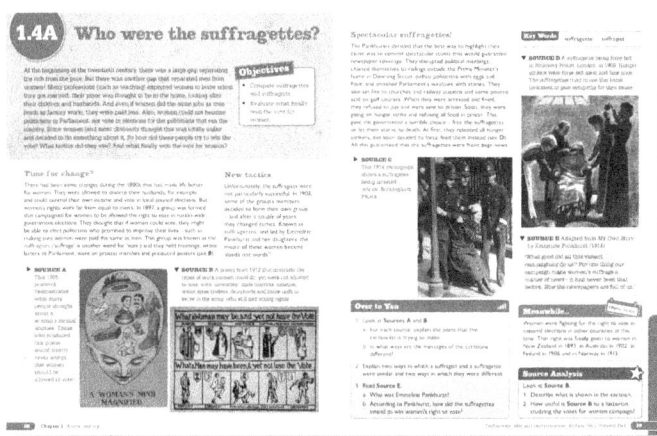

The series is based on the idea that any resources used with students should be as accessible and relevant as possible because children learn best when they are interested and engaged in activities that they think are both challenging and worthwhile. If a group of students are hooked early on in a lesson by an unusual picture, a curious title or a thought-provoking objective, a highly proactive learning environment can be created. Each topic in the *Student Book* aims to get the students involved, and keep them involved – through imaginatively presented double-page lessons with a clear route through them, headed by progressive learning objectives and finished off with an Over to You work section that aims to make the written part of any lesson as inspiring and as challenging as possible.

The *Student Book* contains differentiated activities and assessment opportunities, and essential historical vocabulary in the Glossary and in the Key Words feature. The *Kerboodle Lessons, Resources and Assessment* provides animations and film clips, summative and formative assessments, customisable differentiated worksheets, interactive activities, and more (see page 9). The accompanying *Curriculum and Assessment Planning Guide* (available in both print and digital format) provides further teacher support, including the key historical concepts and skills covered in each chapter, a brief introduction to each topic (ideal for those History departments where a non-specialist might teach), as well as further reading recommendations for both teachers *and* students, ideas for beyond the classroom, and answers guidance for each question.

A rich curriculum

KS3 History is not just a series of textbooks. The materials that accompany them make up a complete scheme of work for a comprehensive Key Stage 3 History course. However, the scheme is not meant to be prescriptive. Experienced teachers may want to plunder the materials for suitable resources and ideas, while supply teachers, non-specialists or those just starting out in the profession will soon understand why the series has been shown in recent research to inspire and motivate young historians[1].

This is a flexible two- or three-year course that matches the requirements of the KS3 History National Curriculum and lays the foundations for the rigours of further study in History. The series is based on the following curriculum principles:

- coherently planned and sequenced towards developing historical knowledge and understanding
- presenting subject matter clearly and making History engaging
- building a wide vocabulary to ensure students acquire the necessary language to access their learning and reduce the word gap[2]
- developing extended writing skills
- checking students' understanding systematically.

[1] The Oxford Impact Framework is a systematic approach to evaluating the impact of OUP products and services. It was developed through a unique collaboration between the National Foundation for Educational research (NFER) and is supported by the Oxford University Department of Education. A 2017 impact study (**www.oxfordsecondary.co.uk/ks3historyimpact**) found that the KS3 3rd Edition series motivates students, impacts positively on student preparedness for GCSE, helps students develop History exam skills and engages students of all abilities.

[2] The term 'word gap' is typically used to refer to pupils entering primary school with a vocabulary far below age-related expectations. However, we know that this issue affects a wider range of children. This word gap can be present throughout a child's education and beyond. The *Oxford Language Report* (2018) (**oxford.ly/wordgap**) found that half the 1,000 teachers surveyed reported that at least 40% of their pupils lacked the vocabulary to access their learning. Over 60% of secondary school teachers believe the word gap is increasing.

Guided by these principles, great emphasis has been placed on designing activities that help students understand key historical concepts and develop the skills needed to become excellent historians. We don't believe in teaching to the test but we understand that progression is a vital component of any good KS3 curriculum. We know that History teachers want their curriculum to be ambitious and designed to give all students the knowledge and cultural capital needed for success. We have tested this material with teachers during development to ensure it allows students to build substantive knowledge and skills to progress at a higher level. We have also benefited from a review from The Holocaust Educational Trust to ensure that we cover the Holocaust in line with the standards set by the International Holocaust Remembrance Alliance. Furthermore, we know that many History departments are planning KS3 with GCSE in mind. We've not overtly filled our *Student Book* full of GCSE references that might overwhelm students and put some off, but behind the scenes (in this guide) we've mapped our new resources carefully to basic GCSE requirements.

Developing knowledge and skills for young historians

The *Student Books* in this series are written in chronological order. With each book and accompanying *Kerboodle* package, students are encouraged to develop their historical understanding by using precise dates, correct vocabulary and chronological terms. A student's sense of chronology, sequence and duration is developed through the use of overviews, timelines, key date features such as 'Meanwhile' and 'Earlier/Later on…', and summative assessments. We have also ensured that there are numerous opportunities for students to demonstrate their understanding of second order historical concepts such as continuity and change, cause and consequence, similarity, difference and significance.

The series also provides a stimulating backdrop for promoting students' knowledge, and for encouraging their extended writing skills and their understanding of historical evidence. Some topics, such as *1.5 Did Emily Davison mean to kill herself?* and *5.9A/B Why is Sir Arthur Harris such a controversial figure?* encourage students to weigh evidence and analyse sources and interpretations of events and historical figures. Students are required to use strategies and enquiry techniques to arrive at reasoned conclusions. The *Student Book* also has specific lessons that are designed to help students develop insights into values, beliefs and culture of the time, as well as encouraging their understanding of key processes. For example, lessons 8.1 to 8.7 explore the post-war world from the fifties right up to the twenty-tens. These lessons focus on the second order concept of change and continuity. The concept of cause and consequence forms the central focus of lessons such as *2.1A/B Why did the First World War start?*, *7.4 Why did people*

migrate to Britain after the war? and *7.6 Multicultural Britain*. In *Chapter 5 The Second World War,* students are encouraged to explore the 'big picture' of the Second World War, and they are challenged to assess the significance of individuals and developments, identify the contribution of 'soldiers of Empire' and examine the journey to the 'Final Solution'. In the end-of-chapter assessment, students have the chance to compare two interpretations of one of the war's best-known leaders – Winston Churchill.

Progression throughout the curriculum

We have also ensured that the skills and concepts that are central to the development of excellent historians have been appropriately mapped.

● The skills and concepts covered in the *Student Book* have been audited and grids that map them throughout each chapter (question by question) have been included in this guide.
● You will see a star in the purple question boxes in many lessons. This indicates to you that the last question in the purple box is linked to GCSE in some way – it might be a genuine GCSE-style question, or simply part of a question that will help students build up to full questions as they make greater progress.

Significance

1 Read **Interpretation A**. According to this article, how significant was the work of Fleming, Florey and Chain in the history of medicine?

2 Explain the significance of Fleming's discovery of penicillin in 1928.

● You will also see a star in all of the end-of-chapter assessments, which show you that the assessments are based on GCSE exam-style question stems. There are grids showing exam-style questions covered in each chapter which identify questions linked to specific GCSE exam boards.

Literacy in History

A key curriculum principle in this *KS3 History* series is to build a historical vocabulary and close the word gap. With this in mind, each lesson contains a selection of vital Key Words. Students should be encouraged to look up their meanings in a dictionary and/or use the Glossary and Index at the back of the *Student Book*. The tasks will ask students to define and deploy these words with precision. Some of these words will be the vital substantive concepts, also known as 'first order concepts' (such as democracy, empire or revolution), that are essential for students to become familiar with as they progress through the subject. Also, it might be interesting to reference some of these concepts as you revisit them again during the course. For example, the same concept can have very different meanings when used in relation to different episodes, events and eras in History. For example, the concept of 'war' takes on different meanings in relation to the 'war on poverty' (with the Liberal Reforms and the Beveridge Report), the First World War and the Cold War.

Students are also asked to cover basic literacy competencies in the Over to You sections. They are taught to construct a proper paragraph, make a point, 'evidence it', and explain what they mean. There is also a range of activities that employ a variety of creative literacy strategies.

Schools now have a greater focus on learning key historical vocabulary and extended writing – the new 'Literacy Focus' activities at the end of each chapter will help with this. These activities will test students' abilities to spell and punctuate correctly, back up their views properly, and construct detailed paragraphs – essential skills for doing well in History.

kerboodle

Kerboodle Lessons, Resources and Assessment provides over 400 lively digital resources to help you deliver the content and skills needed for your KS3 curriculum and to prepare students for progression (see page 9 for more information). You can adapt many of these resources to suit you and your students' individual needs. You can upload your existing resources so everything can be accessed from one location – to help bring History to life in your classroom.

Assessment and progression

Each *Student Book*, and the accompanying *Kerboodle* package and *Curriculum and Assessment Planning Guide*, includes a ready-made set of formative and summative assessment tasks.

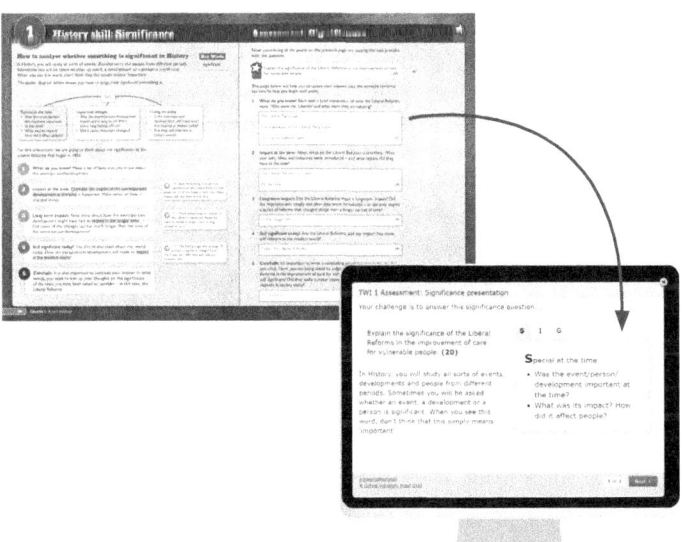

- The Over to You sections at the end of each lesson allow students to demonstrate their knowledge and understanding. These sections have been designed to get progressively more challenging as students work through the tasks, meaning we can successfully give all students the chance to demonstrate and apply their knowledge.

- The 'Have you been learning?' sections of each chapter contain 'Quick Knowledge Quizzes', which test students' knowledge, and 'Literacy Focus' activities, which help to improve students' essay-writing skills and grammar. This formative low stakes testing allows students one of many opportunities to recall and apply the knowledge they have acquired. These short activities allow you to check students' understanding systematically, identify misconceptions accurately, and provide clear, direct feedback.

- History skills assessments at the end of each chapter close with a 'big question' summative task, which has been designed to test students' understanding of historical concepts such as continuity and change, cause and consequence, similarity, difference and significance. Step-by-step guides model an approach to answering a challenging exam-style question. This is followed by a similar question that includes scaffolded support and coaching to help students write an extended answer. This guide contains guidance on how these tasks or assessments link to GCSE specifications, differentiated sample student answers, and a banded/graded mark scheme.

- Comprehensive assessment support on *Kerboodle* includes: step-by-step presentations for front-of-class use, differentiated worksheets, and auto-marked tests and quizzes.

- Baseline tests are included to help teachers try to establish the level of knowledge and learning that students have acquired in primary school.

The whole *KS3 History* package allows you to concentrate on delivering memorable History underpinned by a strong curriculum and a foundation of knowledge and skills that students will benefit from, whether they go on to study GCSE or not.

We sincerely hope that *KS3 History* helps you deliver the outstanding lessons that we all aspire to, and that the History series we've developed helps inspire and engage a new generation of students.

Aaron Wilkes   Lindsay Bruce

Using this guide

Curriculum and Assessment Planning Guide

This guide aims to help teachers design a coherent knowledge-rich curriculum with detailed guidance on assessment, key History knowledge and skills, and support for non-specialists.

Matched to each chapter of the *Student Book*, you'll find:
- Links to the KS3 History National Curriculum and to GCSE History curricula
- History skills and processes covered in the chapter

- Lesson sequence
- Exam-style questions covered in the chapter
- A brief history of the chapter topic, and a timeline
- Further reading for teachers and students, and activities that go beyond the classroom
- Answers guidance for all *Student Book* activities
- Comprehensive support for the end-of-chapter assessment, including a mark scheme and sample student answers.

You'll also find sample curriculum plans and support for different GCSE specifications throughout the guide.

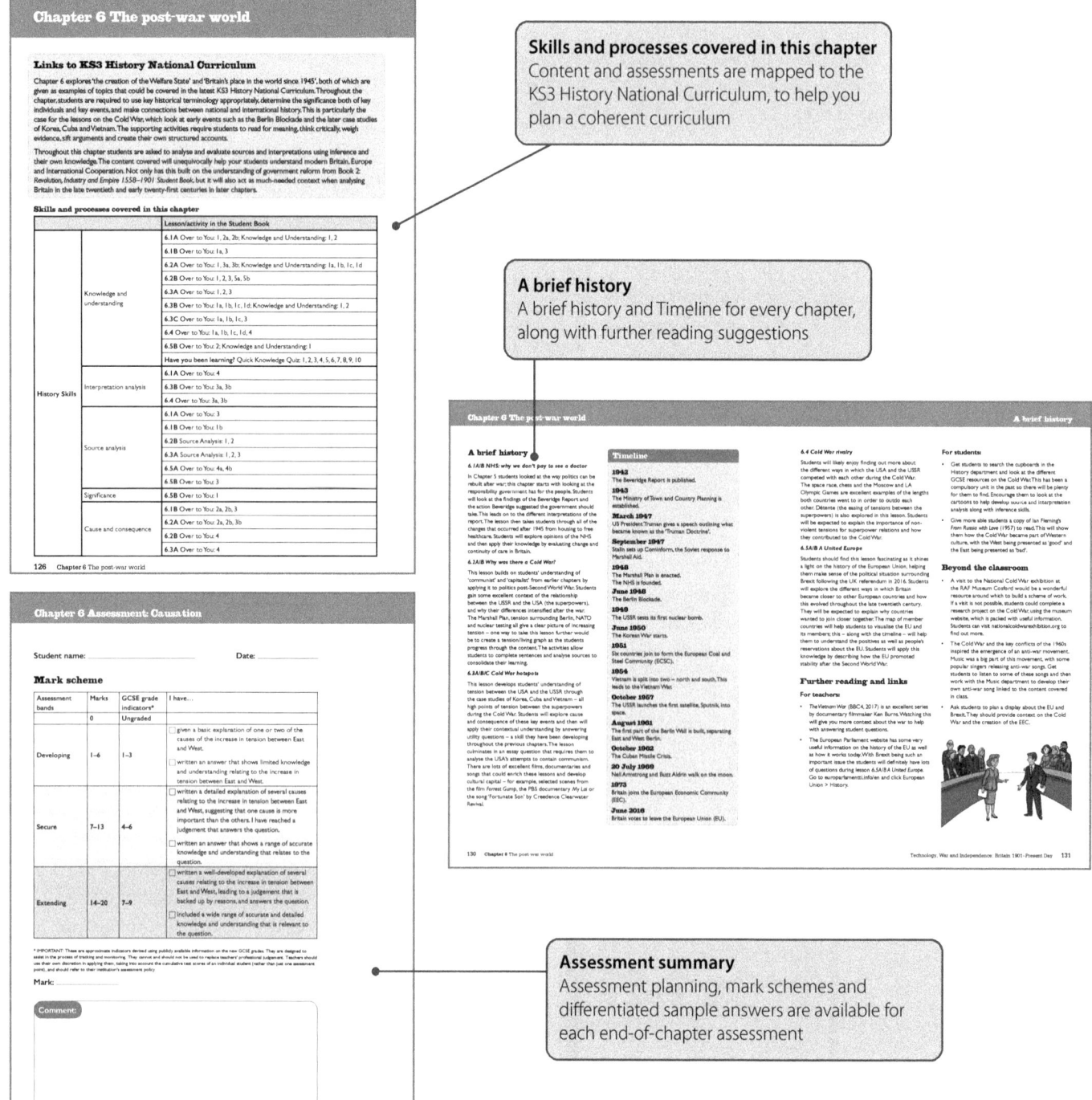

Skills and processes covered in this chapter
Content and assessments are mapped to the KS3 History National Curriculum, to help you plan a coherent curriculum

A brief history
A brief history and Timeline for every chapter, along with further reading suggestions

Assessment summary
Assessment planning, mark schemes and differentiated sample answers are available for each end-of-chapter assessment

kerboodle Lessons, Resources and Assessment (annual subscription)

978 019 839329 0

- An online package to support the *Student Book*

- Saves you time and enhances your lessons with over 400 ready-to-use resources, including **resource planners** for each lesson, **knowledge organisers, animations, film clips** (including selected clips from British Pathé), **history skills interactive activities, auto-marked quizzes** and much more

- Comprehensive support for assessment with **differentiated assessment worksheets, presentations, mark schemes and sample answers** to help your students as they progress through the curriculum

- **Digital version** of the *Student Book* can be used front-of-class, packed full of resources launching straight from the page

- Teacher access to the **digital** *Curriculum and Assessment Planning Guide* is included

- Regular updates to content and functionality to ensure you and your students are fully supported with the latest advice

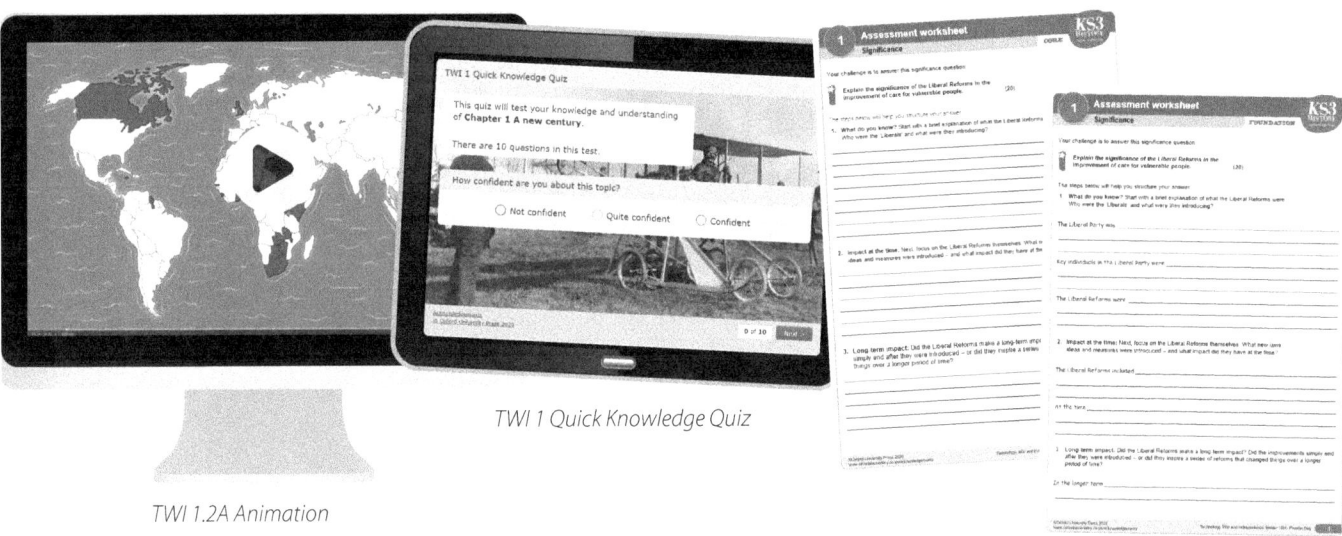

TWI 1.2A Animation

TWI 1 Quick Knowledge Quiz

TWI 1 Assessment worksheet: Significance

kerboodle Book (annual subscription)

978 019 839333 7

- **Student access** to the digital *Student Book*

- Includes **tools for annotation** and can be accessed on a **range of devices**

To find out more: **www.oxfordsecondary.co.uk/ks3history**

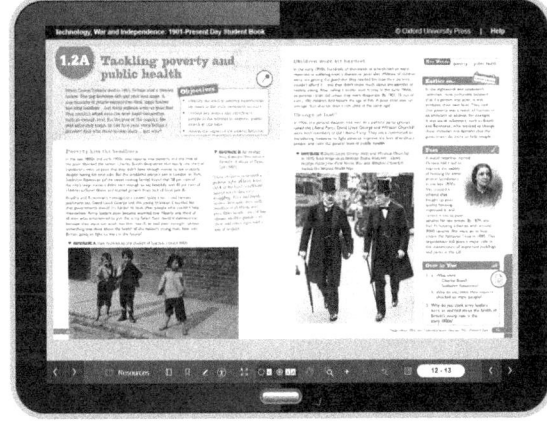

Technology, War and Independence: Britain 1901–Present Day Kerboodle Book

Scheme of Work

KS3 History Scheme of Work

This table shows all the lessons available in the *Technology, War and Independence Student Book*, in the *KS3 History* series, so that you can easily navigate through the book and supporting digital material on Kerboodle to select the key themes and topics that you might use to inform your own scheme of work.

> ### Key to resources
> SB – Student Book
>
> TG – Curriculum and Assessment Planning Guide (Teacher Guide)
>
> K – Kerboodle

Lesson title	Key Question	Resources	
Introduction			
Timeline from 1901 to the present day	What will we be learning this year in History?	• SB pp. 6–7	• TG p. 47
Chapter 1: A new century		• K TWI 1 Knowledge organiser	
1.1A Britain and the world in 1901	What was Britain's place in the world in 1901?	• SB pp. 8–9 • TG pp. 47, 49 • K TWI 1.1A Worksheet (Core): Interpretation • K TWI 1.1A Worksheet (Foundation): Interpretation	• K TWI 1.1A History skills: Knowledge and understanding • K TWI 1.1A End of lesson assessment
1.1B Britain and the world in 1901	What technological developments had been made in transport, communications and consumer goods?	• SB pp. 10–11 • TG p. 47, 49 • K TWI 1.1B Worksheet (Core): Knowledge and understanding • K TWI 1.1B Worksheet (Foundation): Knowledge and understanding	• K TWI 1.1B History skills: Change and continuity • K TWI 1.1B End of lesson assessment
1.2A Tackling poverty and public health	What was life like for Britain's poor?	• SB pp. 12–13 • TG pp. 47, 49 • K TWI 1.2A Worksheet (Core): Knowledge and understanding	• K TWI 1.2A Worksheet (Foundation): Knowledge and understanding • K TWI 1.2A Animation • K TWI 1.2A End of lesson assessment
1.2B Tackling poverty and public health	What changes were made to make life better for the poor in the early 1900s and what long-term impact did this have?	• SB pp. 14–15 • TG pp. 47, 49–50 • K TWI 1.2B Worksheet (Core): Source analysis • K TWI 1.2B Worksheet (Foundation): Source analysis	• K TWI 1.2B History skills: Cause and consequence • K TWI 1.2B End of lesson assessment
1.3 Who or what was to blame for the *Titanic* disaster?	What events led to one of the most well-known maritime disasters in history?	• SB pp. 16–17 • TG pp. 47, 50 • K TWI 1.3 Worksheet (Core): Cause and consequence	• K TWI 1.3 Worksheet (Foundation): Cause and consequence • K TWI 1.3 Film clip: Survivor • K TWI 1.3 End of lesson assessment
1.4A Who were the suffragettes?	What tactics were used in the fight to improve the rights of British women in the early twentieth century?	• SB pp. 18–19 • TG pp. 48, 50 • K TWI 1.4A Worksheet (Core): Source analysis	• K TWI 1.4A (Foundation): Source analysis • K TWI 1.4A History skills: Source analysis • K TWI 1.4A End of lesson assessment
1.4B Who were the suffragettes?	How did the suffragettes attempt to gain support for their campaign, and how successful were they?	• SB pp. 20–21 • TG pp. 48, 50–51 • K TWI 1.4B Worksheet (Core): Cause and consequence • K TWI 1.4B Worksheet (Foundation): Cause and consequence	• K TWI 1.4B Film clip: Suffrage • K TWI 1.4B History skills: Knowledge and understanding • K TWI 1.4B End of lesson assessment
1.5 History Mystery: Did Emily Davison mean to kill herself?	What event took place on 4 June 1913 and how does it relate to the women's rights campaign?	• SB pp. 22–23 • TG pp. 48, 51 • K TWI 1.5 Worksheet (Core): Source analysis	• K TWI 1.5 Worksheet (Foundation): Source analysis • K TWI 1.5 Film clip: Race • K TWI 1.5 End of lesson assessment
1 Have you been learning?	What can you recall from this chapter? How can sentences about the sinking of the Titanic be improved?	• SB pp. 24–25 • TG p. 51	• K TWI 1 Quick knowledge quiz

Lesson title	Key Question	Resources	
1 History skills and Assessment	Explain the significance of the Liberal Reforms in the improvement of care for vulnerable people.	• SB pp. 26–27 • TG pp. 52–56 • K TWI 1 Assessment: Significance worksheet (Core)	• K TWI 1 Assessment: Significance worksheet (Foundation) • K TWI 1 Assessment: Significance presentation
Chapter 2: The First World War		• K TWI 2 Knowledge organiser	
2.1A Why did the First World War start?	What were the short- and long-term causes of the First World War?	• SB pp. 28–29 • TG pp. 61, 64 • K TWI 2.1A Worksheet (Core): Cause and consequence • K TWI 2.1A Worksheet (Foundation): Cause and consequence	• K TWI 2.1A History skills: Interpretation analysis • K TWI 2.1A End of lesson assessment
2.1B Why did the First World War start?	Who was Archduke Franz Ferdinand and what role did his death play in the outbreak of war?	• SB pp. 30–31 • TG pp. 61, 64 • K TWI 2.1B Worksheet (Core): Interpretation analysis • K TWI 2.1B Worksheet (Foundation): Interpretation analysis	• K TWI 2.1B History skills: Cause and consequence • K TWI 2.1B End of lesson assessment
2.2 Joining up	How did the British government encourage men to sign up and fight for their country?	• SB pp. 32–33 • TG pp. 61, 64–65 • K TWI 2.2 Worksheet (Core): Source analysis	• K TWI 2.2 Worksheet (Foundation): Source analysis • K TWI 2.2 History skills: Source analysis • K TWI 2.2 End of lesson assessment
2.3A The First World War: an overview	What was trench warfare and where in the world did trench warfare take place?	• SB pp. 34–35 • TG pp. 61, 65 • K TWI 2.3A Worksheet (Core): Source analysis	• K TWI 2.3A Worksheet (Foundation): Source analysis • K TWI 2.3A History skills: Chronology • K TWI 2.3A End of lesson assessment
2.3B The First World War: an overview	What was it like for the soldiers fighting in the trenches?	• SB pp. 36–37 • TG pp. 61, 65 • K TWI 2.3B Worksheet (Core): Knowledge and understanding	• K TWI 2.3B Worksheet (Foundation): Knowledge and understanding • K TWI 2.3B Animation • K TWI 2.3B End of lesson assessment
2.4 Weapons of war	What role did science and technology play in First World War weaponry?	• SB pp. 38–39 • TG pp. 61, 65 • K TWI 2.4 Worksheet (Core): Change and continuity	• K TWI 2.4 Worksheet (Foundation): Change and continuity • K TWI 2.4 Film clip: Warfare • K TWI 2.4 End of lesson assessment
2.5A Why was Harry Farr killed?	What was 'shell shock' and how did the British Army deal with it at the time?	• SB pp. 40–41 • TG pp. 62, 65 • K TWI 2.5A Worksheet (Core): Knowledge and understanding	• K TWI 2.5A Worksheet (Foundation): Knowledge and understanding • K TWI 2.5A Film clip: Shell shock • K TWI 2.5A End of lesson assessment
2.5B Why was Harry Farr killed?	What were the reasons for Harry Farr's prosecution and what was his defence? What was eventually done to honour those who met with the same fate?	• SB pp. 42–43 • TG pp. 62, 65–66 • K TWI 2.5B Worksheet (Core): Interpretation analysis • K TWI 2.5B Worksheet (Foundation): Interpretation analysis	• K TWI 2.5B History skills: Interpretation analysis • K TWI 2.5B End of lesson assessment
2.6 How did the First World War change medicine?	How did the war lead to advances in medical science and treatment of casualties?	• SB pp. 44–45 • TG pp. 62, 66 • K TWI 2.6 Worksheet (Core): Significance • K TWI 2.6 Worksheet (Foundation): Significance	• K TWI 2.6 History skills: Change and continuity • K TWI 2.6 End of lesson assessment
2.7A Soldiers of Empire	Who was Khudadad Khan and what contribution did he and others like him make to the First World War?	• SB pp. 46–47 • TG pp. 62, 66 • K TWI 2.7A Worksheet (Core): Source analysis • K TWI 2.7A Worksheet (Foundation): Source analysis	• K TWI 2.7A History skills: Source analysis • K TWI 2.7A End of lesson assessment
2.7B Soldiers of Empire	How many soldiers joined the fight from around the Empire and where did they come from?	• SB pp. 48–49 • TG pp. 62, 66–67 • K TWI 2.7B Worksheet (Core): Knowledge and understanding • K TWI 2.7B Worksheet (Foundation): Knowledge and understanding	• K TWI 2.7B History skills: Knowledge and understanding • K TWI 2.7B End of lesson assessment

Lesson title	Key Question	Resources	
2.8 What was it like on the home front?	What role did the people who were left behind in Britain play in the First World War?	• SB pp. 50–51 • TG pp. 62, 67 • K TWI 2.8 Worksheet (Core): Change and continuity • K TWI 2.8 Worksheet (Foundation): Change and continuity	• K TWI 2.8 History skills: Cause and consequence • K TWI 2.8 End of lesson assessment
2.9 How did 'Poppy Day' start?	What brought about the end of the war? And how do we remember the conflict each year?	• SB pp. 52–53 • TG pp. 62, 67 • K TWI 2.9 Worksheet (Core): Cause and consequence • K TWI 2.9 Worksheet (Foundation): Cause and consequence	• K TWI 2.9 History skills: Cause and consequence • K TWI 2.9 Film clip: Veteran • K TWI 2.9 End of lesson assessment
2.10A How did countries try to avoid any more wars?	What ideas did the leaders of France, Britain and the USA have to maintain peace after the war? What was the Treaty of Versailles?	• SB pp. 54–55 • TG pp. 62, 67 • K TWI 2.10A Worksheet (Core): Cause and consequence	• K TWI 2.10A Worksheet (Foundation): Cause and consequence • K TWI 2.10 Film clip: Versailles • K TWI 2.10A End of lesson assessment
2.10B How did countries try to avoid any more wars?	What were some of the reactions to the Treaty of Versailles? Who were the League of Nations and what did they do?	• SB pp. 56–57 • TG pp. 62, 68 • K TWI 2.10B Worksheet (Core): Interpretation analysis • K TWI 2.10B Worksheet (Foundation): Interpretation analysis	• K TWI 2.10B History skills: Interpretation analysis • K TWI 2.10B End of lesson assessment
2 Have you been learning?	What can you recall from this chapter? How can sentences about the events leading to the outbreak of war be improved?	• SB pp. 58–59 • TG p. 69	• K TWI 2 Quick knowledge quiz
2 History skills and Assessment	1 Describe two features of everyday life for British soldiers serving in the trenches on the Western Front. 2 How useful are Sources A and B for an enquiry into everyday life for British soldiers serving in the trenches on the Western Front? Explain your answer, using both sources and your knowledge of the historical context. 3 How could you find out more about life in the trenches of the Western Front during the First World War? Name two sources (other than Sources A and B) you could use, and explain your reasons.	• SB pp. 60–63 • TG p. 70–75 • K TWI 2 Assessment: Source analysis (historic environment) worksheet (Core)	• K TWI 2 Assessment: Source analysis (historic environment) worksheet (Foundation) • K TWI 2 Assessment: Source analysis (historic environment) presentation
Chapter 3: Between the wars		• K TWI 3 Knowledge organiser	
3.1A Was the First World War worth winning?	What was Britain like in the years after the First World War?	• SB pp. 64–65 • TG pp. 79, 81 • K TWI 3.1A Worksheet (Core): Knowledge and understanding	• K TWI 3.1A Worksheet (Foundation): Knowledge and understanding • K TWI 3.1A History skills: Source analysis • K TWI 3.1A End of lesson assessment
3.1B Was the First World War worth winning?	What led to the 'General Strike'?	• SB pp. 66–67 • TG pp. 79, 81 • K TWI 3.1B Worksheet (Core): Change and continuity	• K TWI 3.1B Worksheet (Foundation): Change and continuity • K TWI 3.1B History skills: Chronology • K TWI 3.1B End of lesson assessment
3.2 The 'Roaring Twenties'	Why were the years after the war known as the 'Roaring Twenties'?	• SB pp. 68–69 • TG pp. 79, 81–82 • K TWI 3.2 Worksheet (Core): Source analysis • K TWI 3.2 Worksheet (Foundation): Source analysis	• K TWI 3.2 Film clip: Flapper • K TWI 3.2 History skills: Change and continuity • K TWI 3.2 End of lesson assessment

Lesson title	Key Question	Resources	
3.3 Independence in Ireland	How did the relationship between Britain and Ireland develop during the early twentieth century?	• SB pp. 70–71 • TG pp. 79, 82 • K TWI 3.3 Worksheet (Core): Knowledge and understanding	• K TWI 3.3 Worksheet (Foundation): Knowledge and understanding • K TWI 3.3 History skills: Chronology • K TWI 3.3 End of lesson assessment
3.4A The 'Hungry Thirties'	Who exactly were the 'hungry' and what was life like for them?	• SB pp. 72–73 • TG pp. 80, 82 • K TWI 3.4A Worksheet (Core): Interpretation analysis	• K TWI 3.4A Worksheet (Foundation): Interpretation analysis • K TWI 3.4A Animation • K TWI 3.4A End of lesson assessment
3.4B The 'Hungry Thirties'	What diverse experiences could be found in 1930s Britain?	• SB pp. 74–75 • TG pp. 80, 82–83 • K TWI 3.4B Worksheet (Core): Similarity and difference	• K TWI 3.4B Worksheet (Foundation): Similarity and difference • K TWI 3.4B History skills: Source analysis • K TWI 3.4B End of lesson assessment
3 Have you been learning?	What can you recall from this chapter? What are the key facts about Britain's role in the world after the First World War?	• SB pp. 76–77 • TG p. 83	• K TWI 3 Quick knowledge quiz
3 History skills and Assessment	How far do you agree with Interpretation A about the impact of the Depression on ordinary people in Britain?	• SB pp. 78–79 • TG pp. 84–89 • TWI 3 Assessment: Interpretation analysis worksheet (Core)	• TWI 3 Assessment: Interpretation analysis worksheet (Foundation) • TWI 3 Assessment: Interpretation analysis presentation
Chapter 4: Power in the early twentieth century		• K TWI 4 Knowledge organiser	
4.1 Democracy and dictatorship	What are the key differences between democracy and dictatorship?	• SB pp. 80–81 • TG pp. 94, 96 • K TWI 4.1 Worksheet (Core): Knowledge and understanding • K TWI 4.1 Worksheet (Foundation): Knowledge and understanding	• K TWI 4.1 History skills: Knowledge and understanding • K TWI 4.1 End of lesson assessment
4.2A Two types of dictatorship	What is communism and what happened in Russia in the late 1910s and early 1920s?	• SB pp. 82–83 • TG pp. 94, 96 • K TWI 4.2A Worksheet (Core): Knowledge and understanding • K TWI 4.2A Worksheet (Foundation): Knowledge and understanding	• K TWI 4.2A History skills: Knowledge and understanding • K TWI 4.2A End of lesson assessment
4.2B Two types of dictatorship	What is fascism and how did the Fascist party in Italy form?	• SB pp. 84–85 • TG pp. 94, 96–97 • K TWI 4.2B Worksheet (Core): Similarity and difference • K TWI 4.2B Worksheet (Foundation): Similarity and difference	• K TWI 4.2B History skills: Knowledge and understanding • K TWI 4.2B End of lesson assessment
4.3A What was Germany like in the 1920s?	How did Germany change in the 1920s?	• SB pp. 86–87 • TG pp. 94, 97 • K TWI 4.3A Worksheet (Core): Source analysis • K TWI 4.3A Worksheet (Foundation): Source analysis	• K TWI 4.3A History skills: Cause and consequence • K TWI 4.3A End of lesson assessment
4.3B What was Germany like in the 1920s?	Who was Adolf Hitler and what was the Nazi Party?	• SB pp. 88–89 • TG pp. 94, 97 • K TWI 4.3B Worksheet (Core): Change and continuity	• K TWI 4.3B Worksheet (Foundation): Change and continuity • K TWI 4.3B History skills: Source analysis • K TWI 4.3B End of lesson assessment
4.4 Why did Hitler become so popular?	Why did Hitler and the Nazi Party gain so many votes in the early 1930s?	• SB pp. 90–91 • TG pp. 94–95, 97 • K TWI 4.4 Worksheet (Core): Cause and consequence	• K TWI 4.4 Worksheet (Foundation): Cause and consequence • K TWI 4.4 Film clip: Officer • K TWI 4.4 End of lesson assessment
4.5A What was life like in Nazi Germany?	To what extent were Germans 'free, healthy and happy' under Hitler's rule?	• SB pp. 92–93 • TG pp. 95, 97–98 • K TWI 4.5A Worksheet (Core): Cause and consequence • K TWI 4.5A Worksheet (Foundation): Cause and consequence	• K TWI 4.5A History skills: Knowledge and understanding • K TWI 4.5A End of lesson assessment

Lesson title	Key Question	Resources	
4.5B What was life like in Nazi Germany?	How did Hitler use terror and fear to control people?	• SB pp. 94–95 • TG pp. 95, 98 • K TWI 4.5B Worksheet (Core): Source analysis	• K TWI 4.5B Worksheet (Foundation): Source analysis • K TWI 4.5B History skills: Source analysis • K TWI 4.5B End of lesson assessment
4.5C What was life like in Nazi Germany?	What was it like to grow up in Nazi Germany? How did Hitler keep control?	• SB pp. 96–97 • TG pp. 95, 98 • K TWI 4.5C Worksheet (Core): Source analysis	• K TWI 4.5C Worksheet (Foundation): Source analysis • K TWI 4.5C Film clip: Schoolgirl • K TWI 4.5C End of lesson assessment
4.6A Why was there another world war?	What was Hitler's attitude towards the Treaty of Versailles?	• SB pp. 98–99 • TG pp. 95, 98–99 • K TWI 4.6A Worksheet (Core): Source analysis	• K TWI 4.6A Worksheet (Foundation) Source analysis • K TWI 4.6A Animation • K TWI 4.6A End of lesson assessment
4.6B Why was there another world war?	What events led to the outbreak of war in 1939?	• SB pp. 100–101 • TG pp. 95, 99 • K TWI 4.6B Worksheet (Core): Interpretation analysis	• K TWI 4.6B Worksheet (Foundation): Interpretation analysis • K TWI 4.6B History skills: Cause and consequence • K TWI 4.6B End of lesson assessment
4 Have you been learning?	What can you recall from this chapter? In what ways have historians disagreed about the outbreak of war in 1939?	• SB pp. 102–103 • TG p. 99	• K TWI 4 Quick knowledge quiz
4 History skills and Assessment	Explain why Hitler emerged as Chancellor of Germany by 1933. You may use the following in your answer: • strengths of Hitler • the Great Depression. You must also use information of our own.	• SB pp. 104–105 • TG pp. 100–104 • K TWI 4 Assessment: Causation worksheet (Core)	• K TWI 4 Assessment: Causation worksheet (Foundation) • K TWI 4 Assessment: Causation presentation
Chapter 5: The Second World War		• K TWI 5 Knowledge organiser	
5.1A The Second World War: an overview	What were the key events in the early part of the Second World War?	• SB pp. 106–107 • TG pp. 110, 113 • K TWI 5.1A Worksheet (Core): Source analysis	• K TWI 5.1A Worksheet (Foundation): Source analysis • K TWI 5.1A Animation • K TWI 5.1A End of lesson assessment
5.1B The Second World War: an overview	What were the key turning points of the Second World War?	• SB pp. 108–109 • TG pp. 110, 113 • K TWI 5.1B Worksheet (Core): Cause and consequence • K TWI 5.1B Worksheet (Foundation): Cause and consequence	• K TWI 5.1B History skills: Cause and consequence • K TWI 5.1B Film clip: Pearl Harbor • K TWI 5.1B End of lesson assessment
5.1C The Second World War: an overview	What key events led to the end of the Second World War?	• SB pp. 110–111 • TG pp. 110, 113–114 • K TWI 5.1C Worksheet (Core): Chronology	• K TWI 5.1C Worksheet (Foundation): Chronology • K TWI 5.1C History skills: Source analysis • K TWI 5.1C End of lesson assessment
5.2A How should we remember Dunkirk?	What was the traditional view of Dunkirk at the time of the Dunkirk evacuation?	• SB pp. 112–113 • TG pp. 110, 114 • K TWI 5.2A Worksheet (Core): Source analysis • K TWI 5.2A Worksheet (Foundation): Source analysis	• K TWI 5.2A History skills: Source analysis • K TWI 5.2A End of lesson assessment
5.2B How should we remember Dunkirk?	What is the 'other' story about the events at Dunkirk?	• SB pp. 114–115 • TG pp. 110, 114–115 • K TWI 5.2B Worksheet (Core): Interpretation analysis • K TWI 5.2B Worksheet (Foundation): Interpretation analysis	• K TWI 5.2B History skills: Interpretation analysis • K TWI 5.2B Film clip: Military Policeman • K TWI 5.2B End of lesson assessment
5.3A Who were 'the Few'?	Why was the Battle of Britain such an important event?	• SB pp. 116–117 • TG pp. 110, 115 • K TWI 5.3A Worksheet (Core): Knowledge and understanding	• K TWI 5.3A Worksheet (Foundation): Knowledge and understanding • K TWI 5.3A Film clip: Beaten Back • K TWI 5.3A End of lesson assessment

Lesson title	Key Question	Resources	
5.3B Who were 'the Few'?	What happened during the Battle of Britain?	• SB pp. 118–119 • TG pp. 110, 115 • K TWI 5.3B Worksheet (Core): Significance • K TWI 5.3B Worksheet (Foundation): Significance	• K TWI 5.3B History skills: Cause and consequence • K TWI 5.3B End of lesson assessment
5.4 Soldiers of Empire	Who was Ulric Cross and what contribution did soldiers like him make during the Second World War?	• SB pp. 120–121 • TG pp. 110–111, 115 • K TWI 5.4 Worksheet (Core): Interpretation analysis • K TWI 5.4 Worksheet (Foundation): Interpretation analysis	• K TWI 5.4 History skills: Knowledge and understanding • K TWI 5.4 End of lesson assessment
5.5A Evacuation	Why were so many people evacuated from towns and cities and what was life like for both evacuees and hosts?	• SB pp. 122–123 • TG pp. 111, 115–116 • K TWI 5.5A Worksheet (Core): Interpretation analysis	• K TWI 5.5A Worksheet (Foundation): Interpretation analysis • K TWI 5.5A Film clip: Evacuation • K TWI 5.5A End of lesson assessment
5.5B Evacuation	Where were people moved to and what did this mean for the people who were moved?	• SB pp. 124–125 • TG pp. 111, 116 • K TWI 5.5B Worksheet (Core): Knowledge and understanding • K TWI 5.5B Worksheet (Foundation): Knowledge and understanding	• K TWI 5.5B History skills: Interpretation analysis • K TWI 5.5B End of lesson assessment
5.6 The home front	What impact did the war have on the people of Britain?	• SB pp. 126–127 • TG pp. 111, 116 • K TWI 5.6 Worksheet (Core): Change and continuity • K TWI 5.6 Worksheet (Foundation): Change and continuity	• K TWI 5.6 History skills: Similarity and difference • K TWI 5.6 End of lesson assessment
5.7 How did the Second World War change health and medicine?	What advances in medicine took place during the Second World War?	• SB pp. 128–129 • TG pp. 111, 116 • K TWI 5.7 Worksheet (Core): Knowledge and understanding • K TWI 5.7 Worksheet (Foundation): Knowledge and understanding	• K TWI 5.7 History skills: Knowledge and understanding • K TWI 5.7 End of lesson assessment
5.8 Penicillin and the war	How was penicillin discovered and what role did it play in the Second World War?	• SB pp. 130–131 • TG pp. 111, 116–117 • K TWI 5.8 Worksheet (Core): Significance	• K TWI 5.8 Worksheet (Foundation): Significance • K TWI 5.8 Animation • K TWI 5.8 End of lesson assessment
5.9A Why is Sir Arthur Harris such a controversial figure?	Why was the city of Dresden bombed and why did so many people die?	• SB pp. 132–133 • TG pp. 111, 117 • K TWI 5.9A Worksheet (Core): Knowledge and understanding • K TWI 5.9A Worksheet (Foundation): Knowledge and understanding	• K TWI 5.9A History skills: Cause and consequence • K TWI 5.9A Film clip: Dresden • K TWI 5.9A End of lesson assessment
5.9B Why is Sir Arthur Harris such a controversial figure?	What has the decision to bomb Dresden been so controversial?	• SB pp. 134–135 • TG pp. 111, 117 • K TWI 5.9B Worksheet (Core): Source analysis	• K TWI 5.9B Worksheet (Foundation): Source analysis • K TWI 5.9B History skills: Source analysis • K TWI 5.9B End of lesson assessment
5.10A Why is Winston Churchill on a £5 note?	Why was Winston Churchill chosen to feature on a £5 note?	• SB pp. 136–137 • TG pp. 111, 117 • K TWI 5.10A Worksheet (Core): Knowledge and understanding • K TWI 5.10A Worksheet (Foundation): Knowledge and understanding	• K TWI 5.10A History skills: Source analysis • K TWI 5.10A End of lesson assessment
5.10B Why is Winston Churchill on a £5 note?	Why has Winston Churchill not always been viewed in a positive way?	• SB pp. 138–139 • TG pp. 111, 117–118 • K TWI 5.10B Worksheet (Core): Knowledge and understanding • K TWI 5.10B Worksheet (Foundation): Knowledge and understanding	• K TWI 5.10B History skills: Knowledge and understanding • K TWI 5.10B End of lesson assessment

Lesson title	Key Question	Resources	
5.11A The journey to the 'Final Solution'	What was the build up to the 'Final Solution'?	• SB pp. 140–141 • TG pp. 111–112, 118 • K TWI 5.11A Worksheet (Core): Knowledge and understanding • K TWI 5.11A Worksheet (Foundation): Knowledge and understanding	• K TWI 5.11A History skills: Knowledge and understanding • K TWI 5.11A End of lesson assessment
5.11B The journey to the 'Final Solution'	What were the implications of the Wannsee Conference?	• SB pp. 142–143 • TG pp. 111–112, 118 • K TWI 5.11B Worksheet (Core): Change and continuity • K TWI 5.11B Worksheet (Foundation): Change and continuity	• K TWI 5.11B History skills: Knowledge and understanding • K TWI 5.11B Film clip: Aftermath • K TWI 5.11B End of lesson assessment
5.12 The war goes nuclear	How and why did the USA join the Second World War?	• SB pp. 144–145 • TG pp. 112, 118–119 • K TWI 5.12 Worksheet (Core): Interpretation analysis • K TWI 5.12 Worksheet (Foundation): Interpretation analysis	• K TWI 5.12 History skills: Significance • K TWI 5.12 Film clip: Hiroshima • K TWI 5.12 End of lesson assessment
5.13 A United Nations	What is the United Nations and how is it organised?	• SB pp. 146–147 • TG pp. 112, 119 • K TWI 5.13 Worksheet (Core): Knowledge and understanding • K TWI 5.13 Worksheet (Foundation): Knowledge and understanding	• K TWI 5.13 History skills: Knowledge and understanding • K TWI 5.13 End of lesson assessment
5 Have you been learning?	What can you recall from this chapter? How can the writing of historical narratives be improved?	• SB pp. 148–149 • TG p. 119	• K TWI 5 Quick knowledge quiz
5 History skills and Assessment	1 Interpretations A and B give different views about Winston Churchill. What is the main difference between the views? 2 Suggest one reason Interpretations A and B give different views about Churchill. 3 How far do you agree with Interpretation A about Winston Churchill? Explain your answer, using both interpretations and your own knowledge of the historical context.	• SB pp. 150–151 • TG pp. 120–125 • K TWI 5 Assessment: Interpretation analysis worksheet analysis presentation	• K TWI 5 Assessment: Interpretation analysis worksheet (Foundation) • K TWI 5 Assessment: Interpretation
Chapter 6: The post-war world		• K TWI 6 Knowledge organiser	
6.1A NHS: why we don't pay to see a doctor	What was the Beveridge Report and how did this lead to the welfare state?	• SB pp. 152–153 • TG pp. 130, 132 • K TWI 6.1A Worksheet (Core): Knowledge and understanding • K TWI 6.1A Worksheet (Foundation): Knowledge and understanding	• K TWI 6.1A History skills: Knowledge and understanding • K TWI 6.1A End of lesson assessment
6.1B NHS: why we don't pay to see a doctor	What is the National Health Service, what are its aims and what problems has it faced?	• SB pp. 154–155 • TG pp. 130, 132 • K TWI 6.1B Worksheet (Core): Change and continuity • K TWI 6.1B Worksheet (Foundation): Change and continuity	• K TWI 6.1B History skills: Interpretation analysis • K TWI 6.1B End of lesson assessment
6.2A Why was there a Cold War?	How did the allies of the Second World War become enemies?	• SB pp. 156–157 • TG pp. 130, 132 • K TWI 6.2A Worksheet (Core): Knowledge and understanding • K TWI 6.2A Worksheet (Foundation): Knowledge and understanding	• K TWI 6.2A History skills: Cause and consequence • K TWI 6.2A End of lesson assessment

Lesson title	Key Question	Resources	
6.2B Why was there a Cold War?	How was Germany divided after the Second World War and how did tensions result?	• SB pp. 158–159 • TG pp. 130, 133 • K TWI 6.2B Worksheet (Core): Source analysis	• K TWI 6.2B Worksheet (Foundation): Source analysis • K TWI 6.2B Film clip: Bomb Tests • K TWI 6.2B End of lesson assessment
6.3A Cold War hotspots	How did America attempt to contain communism in Korea?	• SB pp. 160–161 • TG pp. 130, 133 • K TWI 6.3A Worksheet (Core): Source analysis	• K TWI 6.3A Worksheet (Foundation): Source analysis • K TWI 6.3A Animation • K TWI 6.3A End of lesson assessment
6.3B Cold War hotspots	What was the Cuban Missile Crisis and which countries became involved in the crisis?	• SB pp. 162–163 • TG pp. 130, 133–134 • K TWI 6.3B Worksheet (Core): Chronology • K TWI 6.3B Worksheet (Foundation): Chronology	• K TWI 6.3B History skills: Knowledge and understanding • K TWI 6.3B End of lesson assessment
6.3C Cold War hotspots	Why did Vietnam become a Cold War focal point?	• SB pp. 164–165 • TG pp. 130, 134 • K TWI 6.3C Worksheet (Core): Cause and consequence	• K TWI 6.3C Worksheet (Foundation): Cause and consequence • K TWI 6.3C History skills: Chronology • K TWI 6.3C End of lesson assessment
6.4 Cold War rivalry	Why was there a space race and in what other ways were America and the USSR in competition?	• SB pp. 166–167 • TG pp. 131, 134 • K TWI 6.4 Worksheet (Core): Cause and consequence • K TWI 6.4 Worksheet (Foundation): Cause and consequence	• K TWI 6.4 History skills: Knowledge and understanding • K TWI 6.4 End of lesson assessment
6.5A A United Europe	How did European countries work to become a more peaceful place after the Second Word War?	• SB pp. 168–169 • TG pp. 131, 134 • K TWI 6.5A Worksheet (Core): Cause and consequence	• K TWI 6.5A Worksheet (Foundation): Cause and consequence • K TWI 6.5A History skills: Source analysis • K TWI 6.5A End of lesson assessment
6.5B A United Europe	How did membership of the European Union divide the British public?	• SB pp. 170–171 • TG pp. 131, 135 • K TWI 6.5B Worksheet (Core): Knowledge and understanding • K TWI 6.5B Worksheet (Foundation): Knowledge and understanding	• K TWI 6.5B History skills: Change and continuity • K TWI 6.5B End of lesson assessment
6 Have you been learning?	What can you recall from this chapter? How can an answer about the Beveridge Report be improved?	• SB pp. 172–173 • TG p. 135	• K TWI 6 Quick knowledge quiz
6 History skills and Assessment	'The main reason for the increase in tension between East and West from 1945 to 1949 was the issue of Berlin.' How far do you agree with this statement? Explain your answer.	• SB pp. 174–175 • TG pp. 136–140 • K TWI 6 Assessment: Causation worksheet (Core)	• K TWI 6 Assessment: Causation worksheet (Foundation) • K TWI 6 Assessment: Causation presentation
Chapter 7: From empire to Commonwealth		• K TWI 7 Knowledge organiser	
7.1 The decline of the British Empire	What caused Britain to slowly lose its Empire?	• SB pp. 176–177 • TG pp. 144, 146 • K TWI 7.1 Worksheet (Core): Source analysis	• K TWI 7.1 Worksheet (Foundation): Source analysis • K TWI 7.1 History skills: Source analysis • K TWI 7.1 End of lesson assessment
7.2 Independence for India	What events led to the partition of India?	• SB pp. 178–179 • TG pp. 144, 146 • K TWI 7.2 Worksheet (Core): Source analysis • K TWI 7.2 Worksheet (Foundation): Source analysis	• K TWI 7.2 History skills: Source analysis • K TWI 7.2 Film clip: On the Move • K TWI 7.2 End of lesson assessment
7.3A Independence in Africa	Why was so much of Africa colonised by 1901, and how did African nations gain their independence?	• SB pp. 180–181 • TG pp. 144, 146–147 • K TWI 7.3A Worksheet (Core): Source analysis • K TWI 7.3A Worksheet (Foundation): Source analysis	• K TWI 7.3A History skills: Source analysis • K TWI 7.3A End of lesson assessment

Lesson title	Key Question	Resources	
7.3B Independence in Africa	What impact did the Second World War have on independence for African Nations?	• SB pp. 182–183 • TG pp. 144, 147 • K TWI 7.3B Worksheet (Core): Interpretation analysis • K TWI 7.3B Worksheet (Foundation): Interpretation analysis	• K TWI 7.3B History skills: Cause and consequence • K TWI 7.3B Film clip: Uganda • K TWI 7.3B End of lesson assessment
7.4 Why did people migrate to Britain after the war?	Why did so many people migrate to Britain after the war?	• SB pp. 184–185 • TG pp. 144, 147 • K TWI 7.4 Worksheet (Core): Knowledge and understanding	• K TWI 7.4 Worksheet (Foundation): Knowledge and understanding • K TWI 7.4 Animation • K TWI 7.4 End of lesson assessment
7.5 Why should we remember the *Empire Windrush?*	What was the *Empire Windrush* and who are the 'Windrush generation'?	• SB pp. 186–187 • TG pp. 144–145, 147–148 • K TWI 7.5 Worksheet (Core): Change and continuity • K TWI 7.5 Worksheet (Foundation): Change and continuity	• K TWI 7.5 History skills: Interpretation analysis • K TWI 7.5 End of lesson assessment
7.6 Multicultural Britain	What does the term 'multicultural' mean and how has Britain benefitted from immigration?	• SB pp. 188–189 • TG pp. 145, 148 • K TWI 7.6 Worksheet (Core): Change and continuity	• K TWI 7.6 Worksheet (Foundation): Change and continuity • K TWI 7.6 History skills: Chronology • K TWI 7.6 End of lesson assessment
7 Have you been learning?	What can you recall from this chapter? What are the key facts about Indian independence?	• SB pp. 190–191 • TG p. 148	• K TWI 7 Quick knowledge quiz
7 History skills and Assessment	Which of the following was the more important reason why the British Empire declined after the Second World War: • the impact of two world wars • independence movements within the colonies? Explain your answer with reference to both reasons.	• SB pp. 192–193 • TG pp. 149–153 • K TWI 7 Assessment: Causation worksheet (Core)	• K TWI 7 Assessment: Causation worksheet (Foundation) • K TWI 7 Assessment: Causation presentation
Chapter 8: Into the modern world		• K TWI 8 Knowledge organiser	
8.1 The fifties	What were the key events, developments and ideas that influenced the 1950s?	• SB pp. 194–195 • TG pp. 157, 160 • K TWI 8.1 Worksheet (Core): Knowledge and understanding	• K TWI 8.1 Worksheet (Foundation): Knowledge and understanding • K TWI 8.1 Animation • K TWI 8.1 End of lesson assessment
8.2 The sixties	What were the key events, developments and ideas that influenced the 1960s?	• SB pp. 196–197 • TG pp. 157, 160 • K TWI 8.2 Worksheet (Core): Knowledge and understanding • K TWI 8.2 Worksheet (Foundation): Knowledge and understanding	• K TWI 8.2 History skills: Significance • K TWI 8.2 Film clip: Trends • K TWI 8.2 End of lesson assessment
8.3 The seventies	What were the key events, developments and ideas that influenced the 1970s?	• SB pp. 198–199 • TG pp. 157, 160 • K TWI 8.3 Worksheet (Core): Knowledge and understanding	• K TWI 8.3 Worksheet (Foundation): Knowledge and understanding • K TWI 8.3 History skills: Source analysis • K TWI 8.3 End of lesson assessment
8.4 The eighties	What were the key events, developments and ideas that influenced the 1980s?	• SB pp. 200–201 • TG pp. 158, 160 • K TWI 8.4 Worksheet (Core): Knowledge and understanding	• K TWI 8.4 Worksheet (Foundation): Knowledge and understanding • K TWI 8.4 History skills: Chronology • K TWI 8.4 End of lesson assessment
8.5 The nineties	What were the key events, developments and ideas that influenced the 1990s?	• SB pp. 202–203 • TG pp. 158, 160 • K TWI 8.5 Worksheet (Core): Knowledge and understanding • K TWI 8.5 Worksheet (Foundation): Knowledge and understanding	• K TWI 8.5 History skills: Knowledge and understanding • K TWI 8.5 End of lesson assessment
8.6 The noughties	What were the key events, developments and ideas that influenced the 2000s?	• SB pp. 204–205 • TG pp. 158, 160 • K TWI 8.6 Worksheet (Core): Knowledge and understanding	• K TWI 8.6 Worksheet (Foundation): Knowledge and understanding • K TWI 8.6 History skills: Chronology • K TWI 8.6 End of lesson assessment

Lesson title	Key Question	Resources	
8.7 The twenty-tens	What were the key events, developments and ideas that influenced the 2010s?	• SB pp. 206–207 • TG pp. 158, 160 • K TWI 8.7 Worksheet (Core): Change and continuity • K TWI 8.7 Worksheet (Foundation): Change and continuity	• K TWI 8.7 History skills: Knowledge and understanding • K TWI 8.7 Film clip: Decades • K TWI 8.7 End of lesson assessment
8.8A What is 'terrorism'?	What is terrorism – and why are acts of terrorism carried out?	• SB pp. 208–209 • TG pp. 158, 160 • K TWI 8.8A Worksheet (Core): Chronology	• K TWI 8.8A Worksheet (Foundation): Chronology • K TWI 8.8A History skills: Source analysis • K TWI 8.8A End of lesson assessment
8.8B What is 'terrorism'?	What methods have been used by terrorists?	• SB pp. 210–211 • TG pp. 158, 160–161 • K TWI 8.8B Worksheet (Core): Source analysis • K TWI 8.8B Worksheet (Foundation): Source analysis	• K TWI 8.8B History skills: Source analysis • K TWI 8.8B End of lesson assessment
8 Have you been learning?	What can you recall from this chapter? How can sentences about events in the post-war world be improved?	• SB pp. 212–213 • TG p. 161	• K TWI 8 Quick knowledge quiz
8 History skills and Assessment	Interpretations A and B both provide views on Prime Minister Margaret Thatcher. How do they differ, and what might explain the differences?	• SB pp. 214–215 • TG pp. 162–167 • K TWI 8 Assessment: Interpretation analysis worksheet (Core)	• K TWI 8 Assessment: Interpretation analysis worksheet (Foundation) • K TWI 8 Assessment: Interpretation analysis presentation
Chapter 9: The modern world: what changed?		• K TWI 9 Knowledge organiser	
9.1A How has Britain changed between 1901 and the present day?	What are some of the key changes that have taken place between 1901 and the present day?	• SB pp. 216–217 • TG pp. 170–171 • K TWI 9.1A Worksheet (Core): Change and continuity	• K TWI 9.1A Worksheet (Foundation): Change and continuity • K TWI 9.1A Animation • K TWI 9.1A End of lesson assessment
9.1B How has Britain changed between 1901 and the present day?	How much has Britain changed since 1901 and what benefits have these changes brought?	• SB pp. 218–219 • TG pp. 170–171 • K TWI 9.1B Worksheet (Core): Change and continuity • K TWI 9.1B Worksheet (Foundation): Change and continuity	• K TWI 9.1B History skills: Change and continuity • K TWI 9.1B End of lesson assessment
9 Have you been learning?	What can you recall from this chapter? What are some of the different views people have about the twentieth century world?	• SB pp. 220–221 • TG p. 171	• K TWI 9 Quick knowledge quiz
9 History skills and Assessment	How far do you agree that the way people communicate with each other has seen the greatest change between 1901 and the present day in Britain? Give reasons for your answer.	• SB pp. 222–223 • TG pp. 172–176 • K TWI 9 Assessment: Change and continuity worksheet (Core)	• K TWI 9 Assessment: Change and continuity worksheet (Foundation) • K TWI 9 Assessment: Change and continuity presentation

Curriculum planning

Curriculum planning: Ofsted inspection framework

A new Ofsted inspection framework has been used with schools from September 2019. The most notable change to this framework is that schools will be judged on the 'quality of education' – a judgement that is based around Ofsted's working definition of the 'curriculum'. Ofsted is clear that the new framework will credit schools that promote a rich and broad curriculum, and have announced that the main points of focus when assessing the quality of education will be related to the **'intent, implementation and impact'** of the curriculum. The aim of this section is to provide teachers, department leaders and faculty leaders with some guidance on how to ensure you are prepared for both the new framework, and, at the same time, delivering a *KS3 History* course that is coherently sequenced, ambitious, relevant and ideally placed to prepare students for study at a higher level. As educators, you will no doubt have given your *KS3 History* curriculum much thought up to this point. It is now even more important that your *KS3 History* curriculum helps to enhance the *whole-school* curriculum.

1 Reviewing your KS3 curriculum

Let's start by digging into what is meant when Ofsted say that the three main points of focus within the quality of education judgement will be 'intent, implementation and impact' – and think about where your History curriculum fits:

❝ Intent:

- *The curriculum is ambitious and designed to give* **all** *students the knowledge and cultural capital they need to succeed in life.*
- *The curriculum is coherently planned and sequenced towards cumulatively sufficient knowledge and skills for future learning and employment."*

As a department, your challenge here then is to ensure that the 'History diet' you offer in school earns its place in the whole school curriculum. It might be useful as a department to think about these questions relating to **curriculum intent:**

- ☐ What is the curriculum we offer? What knowledge, cultural capital and skills will be gained by a student undertaking our course?
- ☐ Why have we made those curriculum choices – and how are these choices 'ambitious'?
- ☐ How is our curriculum/scheme of work sequenced (and why was it sequenced this way)?
- ☐ How is progression built into the course/scheme of work?
- ☐ How does our curriculum/scheme of work help ensure students make progress?

- ☐ How can/will this curriculum/scheme of work be developed over time?

❝ Implementation:

- *Teachers have good knowledge of the subject and courses they teach.*
- *Teachers present subject matter clearly, promoting appropriate discussion about the subject matter being taught. They check students' understanding systematically, identify misconceptions accurately and provide clear, direct feedback.*
- *Over the course of study, teaching is designed to help students to remember in the long term the content they have been taught and to integrate new knowledge and concepts.*
- *Teachers and leaders use assessment well, for example to help students embed and use knowledge fluently or to check understanding and inform teaching.*
- *The resources and materials that teachers select reflect the school's ambitious intentions for the course and study and clearly support the curriculum."*

As you are reading some of these points, I am sure that you are thinking how well History as a subject promotes many of the curriculum ideas highlighted. It is a subject that invites discussion and allows us to embed and use knowledge fluently. You could consider these questions relating to **curriculum implementation**:

- ☐ How can the resources in the curriculum/scheme of work help us to present subject matter clearly?
- ☐ How can this curriculum/scheme of work help to reduce teacher workload (including, how does it help us with subject knowledge and knowledge of the course)?
- ☐ How is progression built into the course/scheme of work?
- ☐ How does our curriculum/scheme of work help to ensure students make progress?
- ☐ What assessments do we set and how do they help to form part of the process of evaluating progress and identifying next steps?
- ☐ Are there other ways that we establish what knowledge and skills students have gained?
- ☐ How does our KS3 curriculum contribute to the broader aims of the school in providing students with the cultural capital they need to succeed in life?

❝ Impact:

- *Students develop detailed knowledge and skills across the curriculum and, as a result, achieve well.*
- *Students are ready for the next stage of education".*

Any forward thinking, relevant, coherently planned History curriculum should be able to hit the two points above. History is a subject that allows students to develop detailed knowledge and skills while helping to build a comprehensive historical vocabulary, enhance their writing skills and generally prepare students for the rigours of further study. Again, it might be worth asking these questions around the **impact** of your own curriculum:

- ☐ How do our students develop detailed knowledge and skills, and how do we test this?
- ☐ How do we build strong literacy skills in our teaching (vocab, writing, etc.)?
- ☐ How do we prepare students for the rigours of further study from an early age?
- ☐ How do we measure impact?

2 How the Oxford *KS3 History* course can be part of your school's rich and ambitious curriculum

Our vision is a *KS3 History* series that helps teachers ensure that all students make progress and achieve their potential, and also allows teachers the flexibility to deliver a rich and broad curriculum that could be adapted to allow *all* students to develop as historians.

Supporting curriculum intent with coherently planned textbooks

Using the framework laid out in the KS3 History National Curriculum, the three textbooks in our *KS3 History* series chart the history of the British Isles as a coherent narrative. The topics in the books are sequenced chronologically (from pre-1066 to the present day) and the chapters are themed to help students accumulate sufficient knowledge. This helps you to teach both chronologically and thematically, which will ultimately help students grapple with the demands of History content at KS3 and beyond.

We focus on how people's lives have shaped this nation and how Britain has influenced and been influenced by the wider world. For example, in *Invasion, Plague and Murder 1066–1558* (**Book 1**) we explore the impact of William the Conqueror and his Norman Conquest, culminating in a lesson that assesses how life changed under the Normans. In later books we examine some of the great inventors and leaders that have made an influential and lasting impact on both this country and the world. As well as individuals, we look at key events, developments and ideas. In *Revolution, Industry and Empire 1558–1901* (**Book 2**), for example, we assess the Industrial Revolution – a significant aspect of world history – and the factors that made it happen, as well as the impact it made on both Britain and the wider world. Book 2 also looks at the expansion of the British Empire, with particular focus on India, while *Technology, War and Independence: 1901–Present Day* (**Book 3**) examines the decline of Britain's empire and the reasons behind this.

We ensure that all students are supported in the design of the curriculum with, for example:

- Over to You activities that are ramped in difficulty, so students can access and apply the key information.
- Engaging features like Fact boxes and Key Words which give all students the 'knowledge and cultural capital'.
- And in this guide, you can find further reading suggestions and activities for students to stretch and support those who will relish taking their learning 'beyond the classroom'.

Supporting curriculum implementation

By offering accessible, engaging content that builds into a solid body of historical knowledge and understanding, and by supporting the acquisition of key history skills, this *KS3 History* series can ensure that students develop a good knowledge and understanding of the subject. This will help them to 'remember in the long term the content they have been taught and to integrate new knowledge and concepts'.

Second-order concepts

Throughout the series we continually reference the second-order concepts that help us organise the process of studying history, such as continuity and change, cause and consequence, similarity, difference and significance. We use them to get students to make connections, draw contrasts, frame historically-valid questions and create their own structured accounts.

It is vital that students understand the methods of historical enquiry, including how evidence is used and how and why contrasting arguments and interpretations of the past have been constructed. In Book 1, for example, we look at the way actions of William the Conqueror have been interpreted, while in Book 2 students assess the reputation and legacy of Oliver Cromwell and get the chance to justify the sort of reputation they think Cromwell deserves. In Book 3, students examine how both the role of people (such as Winston Churchill and Arthur Harris) and events (such as the Dunkirk evacuation) have been interpreted.

Checking understanding systematically

Throughout the course we have built in regular opportunities for students to demonstrate the knowledge and understanding they have learned. This is done through a variety of assessments and activities. Every chapter and every lesson in each book follows a consistent approach, with features that have been successfully trialled and tested – Fact boxes, Over to You activities, and History Skills activities. Activities and assessments progress in difficulty as students work through the chapters and through the three textbooks.

Further, by offering a consistent mixture of low- and high-stakes assessment opportunities at the end of each chapter, we allow students to demonstrate progress and help them to retain knowledge in the long term. The mix of **summative** (Quick Knowledge Quizzes; Literacy Focus activities; auto-marked end-of-lesson self-assessments on Kerboodle) and **formative** assessments (end-of-chapter assessment questions with mark schemes and differentiated assessment worksheets on Kerboodle) help you to 'check understanding and inform teaching' so you can ensure that students 'embed and use knowledge fluently'.

Supporting curriculum impact

An impact study[3] on Oxford's *KS3 History* series (Third editions) was undertaken in order to gain an in-depth understanding of how teachers and Heads of History perceived the course had impacted both student motivation and preparedness for the next stage of education. Teachers who took part discussed the positive impact of the series and told us that this series:

OXFORD IMPACT
EVALUATED

- motivates students
- impacts positively on student preparedness for GCSE
- helps students develop History exam skills
- engages students of all abilities.

The chart below summarises some of the key questions you may have around the curriculum principles that inform this textbook series.

[3] *see* **Oxford University Press** *(2017) Impact Study: KS3 History by Aaron Wilkes 3rd Edition*

Key question	How OUP can help you:
What is the curriculum offered by this course (including what knowledge, cultural capital and skills will be gained)?	This is a flexible two- or three-year course that matches the requirements of the KS3 History National Curriculum and lays the **foundations** for the study of all GCSE History specifications. Our curriculum principles are to: • provide a coherently planned and sequenced curriculum towards developing historical knowledge and understanding • build a historical vocabulary and close the word gap • develop extended writing skills • present subject matter clearly and make History engaging • check students' understanding systematically • focus on how people's lives have shaped this nation and how Britain has influenced and been influenced by the wider world. This course has been proven (in its last edition) to engage and motivate KS3 students, and to support progression by preparing students for the rigours of further study in History.
Why were those curriculum choices made (including any research findings) and how are these choices 'ambitious'?	We understand that the teaching and learning landscape at KS3 and KS4 has changed in recent years. Almost 50% of schools[4] now offer a two-year KS3, mainly as a consequence of the view that the new GCSE is seen as extremely 'crowded' and it is difficult to get all the content in within a two-year framework. Also, many schools have changed the way they teach KS3 to provide **background knowledge** to GCSE topics and provide new understanding of history skills such as source/interpretation analysis[4]. In addition, there is clear evidence[5] of a significant **word gap** in UK schools: this is an increasing problem which is holding back children's learning. This OUP course has been ambitiously designed to reflect the new landscape by ensuring that each suggested topic in the KS3 History National Curriculum is covered, but we have also made sure that our content supports literacy and vocabulary development, and progression towards study beyond KS3. We have carefully designed the content and assessments to match the needs of students who will go on to study any of the GCSE History specifications (all of which offer vastly different question types and are different in scope of content).

Key question	How OUP can help you:
How is the course sequenced (and why is it sequenced this way)?	Topics are sequenced chronologically, from pre-1066 to the present day, and the chapters are themed. This ensures that schools can teach both chronologically and thematically in order to help students grapple with the demands of History content at KS3 and beyond. Every chapter and every lesson follow a consistent approach, with features that have been successfully trialled and tested such as Objectives, Fact boxes, Key Words, Over to You activities, and History Skills activities. Activities and assessments progress in difficulty as students work through the chapters and through the three textbooks.
How is progression built into the course?	This is done through a gradual ramping of level of activities for each lesson, as well as end-of-chapter assessment questions. Also, there are History Skills activities that deal with progressively more difficult question types through each book (and through all books). There are also regular low-stakes knowledge quizzes to check students' knowledge acquisition, and carefully designed literacy activities that support development in extended writing in History.
How does the course help ensure students make progress?	The series does this by offering accessible, engaging content that builds into a solid body of historical knowledge and understanding; by supporting the acquisition of key history skills; and by offering a consistent mixture of low- and high-stakes assessment opportunities that allow students to demonstrate progress.
What assessments does the course offer and how do they help form part of the process of evaluating progress and identifying next steps?	**Summative**: Quick Knowledge Quizzes; Literacy Focus activities; interactive auto-marked end-of-lesson self-assessments. Also, as stated, there is a set of activities at the end of each chapter that become progressively more challenging. **Formative**: end-of-chapter assessment questions with mark schemes and differentiated assessment worksheets (core and foundation). Teachers can also track performance.
How does this course ensure that students will know more?	This is done by presenting accessible, engaging content with regular progress checks (via the low- and high-stakes assessments) to assess knowledge and understanding.
How can/will this course be developed over time (includes adaptability)?	The *Kerboodle* package is continually reviewed and updated, likely with further assessment and auto-marked materials.
How can the resources in this course help teachers present subject matter clearly?	The *Student Books* are engaging and accessible, and easy to navigate. The accompanying *Curriculum and Assessment Planning Guides* map the course out with schemes of work, and support History departments with planning their assessments.
How can this course help reduce teacher workload (including how does it help teachers with their subject knowledge and knowledge of the course)?	The *Student Books* are clearly organised with a contents list and index, and they are supported by accompanying *Curriculum and Assessment Planning Guides* (in print and digital format). These teacher guides support curriculum planning, assessment planning and subject knowledge (including 'a brief history' and timeline features), and is ideal for non-specialists and NQTs. Answers guidance for *Student Books* activities and sample answers for assessment questions are available too, to help reduce teacher workload. The digital *Kerboodle* product provides the activities from the *Student Books* as printable and photocopiable differentiated worksheets and an assessment package that supports every lesson of every chapter.

[4] *data based on **Historical Association** survey (2018)*
[5] *based on the **Oxford Language Report** (2018), which surveyed over 1300 primary and secondary school teachers about their experiences of the word gap in schools*

Curriculum planning: building a historical vocabulary and closing the word gap

One of the curriculum principles in this *KS3 History* series is to build a historical vocabulary and close the word gap. This principle follows on from research from the *Oxford Language Report* (2018)[6], which found evidence of a significant word gap in UK schools. You may find the suggested activities and classroom strategies here and on pages 41–43 useful.

1 Building knowledge-rich vocabulary across year groups

Plan how you will teach key concepts and build them over time. Decide what students need to know by the end of KS3 or even GCSE, and work backwards to inform how you teach throughout key stages 3 and 4. Substantive knowledge and second-order concepts can therefore be planned throughout the five years. Here's an example:

Year 7	Year 8	Year 9 / GCSE
• Monarch – Norman invasion and medieval monarchs • Changes in Tudor and Stuart periods • Church – medieval England	• Introduce the concept of empire and how this had an effect on the monarchy in Victorian Britain.	• **Power and the people** – challenges to royal authority • Elizabethan systems of government
• Reformation • Revolution – English Civil War	• Use the Reformation for the context of the Troubles in Northern Ireland.	• **Elizabethan Church** and religious change
• French Revolution	• Apply the definition to a completely different kind of revolution – Industrial Revolution.	• **Germany in revolution** • American Revolution (context) • Revolution in 19th-century policing

This activity can be done as a department or with your classes. Share the bigger picture of what students are learning across the key stages – what is it leading to? Then try to break it down into big questions and then small questions. The learning is then mutually agreed, and students understand the context of their written work, which is more coherent and sustained as a result.

Our experience as a school of sharing knowledge-rich, big-picture planning with students is that it helps to democratise the learning process. Students become increasingly confident when articulating their ideas and their developing historical vocabulary is evident in their speaking, listening and writing.

[6] *report based on a survey of over 1,300 primary and secondary school teachers about their experiences of the word gap in schools*

2 Using word banks

Teacher notes

A word bank can be so much more than words on the wall; it can be a way to consolidate, test, apply and revisit knowledge. Research supports the idea that you need to teach vocabulary in the context of students' learning rather than in isolation.

Start with your KS3 curriculum, and group key words into themes such as academic words, question words or words that feature across topics. Try to avoid producing word banks with far too many words as this can be overwhelming for students.

You could adopt a knowledge-rich approach, and use knowledge organisers to embed and revisit key words (*Kerboodle* contains knowledge organisers for each chapter, to help save you time). The knowledge organisers can function as word banks which relate to the bigger picture – what students need to learn.

We were mindful that knowledge organisers could be a 'fad'. As Christine Counsell (2017) has observed, when we adopted them we did not expect or want them to be the full extent of students' learning, but to support their learning. Students use them at home to support their online homework or in class.

Also, try to provide an opportunity for students to hear the words spoken aloud, which can help to embed new vocabulary. Research suggests that students need to hear a word ten times before they become confident in understanding and applying it to different contexts (Schmitt, 2008).

Reference:

Counsell, C. (2017) 'I would call knowledge organisers a fad' in *Schools Week*, 28 November 2017.
Schmitt, N. (2008) Review article: Instructed second language vocabulary learning. *Language Teaching Research*, 12(3), 329–363.

Using the template below, students can test themselves or friends by folding the page over. Encouraging students to use the concept/term will help to push their responses into higher bands in the end-of-chapter *Student Book* assessments.

Content	Concept/term I expect to see
Transport	mass production, assembly line
Poverty	Liberal Reforms, free school meals
Dictatorship	Italy, Germany, fascism

This word bank could be used to introduce new vocabulary or as part of a knowledge organiser. Encourage students to write their own definitions or annotate existing definitions so that the words are meaningful on a personal level:

Key term	Definition
Militarism	the belief that a country should build and keep a strong military that they are prepared to use
Appeasement	keeping peace by letting someone get what they want, e.g. letting Hitler get away with taking over some countries in order to keep peace in Europe

Suggested strategies for using word banks

- **Highlight key words.** Use word banks to help students to assess their own written responses by highlighting key vocabulary in their work. This is a powerful visual tool to enable them to see how often they use key words, and to track their learning as they work.

- **Collaborate and compete.** Break a unit down into three parts and have three teams of students compete with each other to collate the most comprehensive word bank. For example a unit on fascism in the 1930s could be broken into: Great Depression, expansion and domestic policies. These word banks could then be evaluated and adapted by everyone. Consider using window crayons for easy reference when writing or discussing.

3 Model key vocabulary to all abilities

As teachers, we differentiate for our classes. I (Lindsay) had considered myself reasonably good at it: I stretched those who needed a challenge and supplied extra information for those needing more support. I later spoke to a friend who is developing literacy in his school, and he mentioned the Matthew effect (Cunningham & Stanovich, 2001). A little research revealed that I had not been helping the students who needed the most support: I had instead been depriving them of literacy and knowledge.

To interrogate how you model key vocabulary, record yourself teaching the same content to different ability levels. I found that I gave rich explanations to my higher-attaining students but simple, generic explanations to my lower-attaining students. I was in fact widening the word gap!

I now make a concerted effort to expose lower-attaining students to more advanced vocabulary in advanced texts and sources. I can emphasise and explain these as I read. Here are some suggestions:

- Annotate Big Questions (open-ended for exploratory discussion) to break down language without dumbing it down.

- Allow students to highlight and explore tier 2 words (skills words, many of which are command words) and tier 3 words (subject-specific, academic words), and use root words to decode meanings.

- Give students access to background knowledge and substantive knowledge, allowing them to build understanding.

Reference:

Cunningham A. E., & Stanovich, K. (2001) 'What Reading Does for the Mind' in *Journal of Direct Instruction*, Vol. 1 No. 2.

4 Knowledge-rich: the football net of words

To engage with the knowledge-rich approach to teaching, you can use the philosophy of building substantive knowledge over the course of your curriculum, giving students the chance to build on their subject knowledge and develop their vocabulary. A sensible departmental approach would include mapping out what key concepts, knowledge, and vocabulary students need to know by Year 11, and where this can be taught and revisited, starting from Year 7.

In *Why Closing the Word Gap Matters*, Jean Gross's football net analogy shows the importance of this in relation to vocabulary: some students can connect new words with words in their existing word net, whereas others struggle to do this because they have far fewer words available to them.

It is so important that first-order concepts (such as empire, parliament, war, monarchy, revolution) are taught and revisited to show that words/concepts can have multiple meanings. Giving time to building an understanding of concepts through knowledge should prevent students from feeling that they are repeatedly starting again.

- Expect students to make links and recall content from the previous unit, year, or key stage. By continually revisiting substantive knowledge, students will be able to retain a word's meaning.

- Allow students to discuss differences in key concepts and terms. Help them to make sense of how a word can mean the same thing in different contexts, but also to realise that this is not always the case.

Reference:
Oxford University Press (2018) *Why Closing the Word Gap Matters*, available online at: oxford.ly/wordgap

Curriculum planning: Sample curriculum plans

Sample curriculum plans for KS3

We know that History teachers want their KS3 curriculum to be ambitious and designed to give *all* students the opportunity to build substantive knowledge and develop the skills to progress at a higher level. We also understand that many History departments are planning KS3 with GCSE in mind, so what we provide on the following pages are suggested 'routes' through Oxford's *KS3 History* series that will help support progression towards all GCSE specifications. Each route takes into account both the requirements of the KS3 History National Curriculum *and* the demands of each of the main GCSE examination boards.

General note on curriculum planning

There are some issues to be taken into consideration when planning and constructing your KS3 History course so that it progresses seamlessly to your GCSE History specification. You can use the guidance and questions suggested in the *Curriculum planning: Ofsted inspection framework* section of this guide (pages 20–23) to help inform your planning.

Sample two-year and three-year routes

The sample curriculum plans in this section are intended purely as illustrations of possible course structures. Remember, there are many combinations for each GCSE History specification, so you have lots of flexibility to cater to the needs of both your staff and your students.

Visit these websites for more information on the specifications:

AQA www.aqa.org.uk

Edexcel qualifications.pearson.com

OCR www.ocr.org.uk

Eduqas www.eduqas.co.uk

WJEC www.wjec.co.uk

For AQA: a possible two-year route:

Year 7 Term 1		Term 2		Term 3	
Invasion, Plague and Murder (BOOK 1): Chapter 1 *1066 and all that* BOOK 1: Chapter 2 *The Norman Conquest*	BOOK 1: Chapter 4 *Life in the Middle Ages*	BOOK 1: Chapter 6 *Health and medicine* BOOK 1: Chapter 8 *Here come the Tudors*	BOOK 1: Chapter 9 *Medieval Britain: what changed?* **Revolution, Industry and Empire (BOOK 2):** Chapter 1: *Queen Elizabeth*	BOOK 2: Chapter 2 *Life in Tudor times* *This might be a good place to include the study of a* **historic environment** *such as the Globe Theatre or an Elizabethan country house. You can introduce the place's location, function, and design, the people connected with the site, and how important developments from the Tudor era are connected to the site.*	BOOK 2: Chapter 5 *The Restoration: the Merry Monarch* BOOK 2: Chapter 7 *The Industrial Revolution: from farming to factories*
Year 8 Term 1		Term 2		Term 3	
BOOK 2: Chapter 8 *Terrible towns* BOOK 2: Chapter 11 *India: a British Empire case study*	BOOK 2: Chapter 12 *From Tudor to Victorian Britain: what changed?*	**Technology, War and Independence (BOOK 3):** Chapter 1 *A new century* BOOK 3: Chapter 2 *The First World War* (depth study)	BOOK 3: Chapter 2 *The First World War* (depth study) continued BOOK 3: Chapter 4 *Power in the early twentieth century*	BOOK 3: Chapter 4 *Power in the early twentieth century* continued BOOK 3: Chapter 5 *The Second World War* (depth study)	BOOK 3: Chapter 8 *Into the modern world*

Many schools are now moving towards a two-year KS3. This route through the three textbooks helps to pick out some of the key content and themes for a school that has chosen the following topics from the AQA GCSE History specification:

☐ **Period study:** Germany 1890–1945: Democracy and Dictatorship

☐ **Thematic study:** Britain: Health and the People: c1000–Present Day

☐ **Wider world depth study:** Conflict and Tension 1918–1939: The Inter-War Years

☐ **British depth study:** Elizabethan England c1568–1603.

It is important that KS3 is not viewed purely as a 'feed' for KS4 – it is a programme of study in its own right and is vital in ensuring that schools deliver a coherently planned and sequenced curriculum that provides students with knowledge of the 'history of these islands as a coherent, chronological narrative, from the earliest times to the present day' (*DfE History Programmes of study: Key stage 3 National curriculum in England*).

This KS3 route begins in 'earliest times' and works through the Norman Conquest and the Middle Ages, towards the Tudors and Elizabethan England (as a focus point for this AQA specification route). The topic of Health is also highlighted in several places through this route when students focus on the Black Death (Year 7 Term 2), the Great Plague (Year 7 Term 3) and disease and public health in the topics covered in each of the terms in Year 8 (e.g. in Year 8 Term 1 when studying the 'public health heroes'). The rise of empire in the nineteenth century (something that students doing the Germany 1890–1945 topic will find helpful when studying the Kaiser's ambitions), the First World War and its impact, the rise of dictatorships in the 1930s, Hitler's Germany and the onset of the Second World War are also covered in Year 8, and will certainly help prepare those students studying Conflict and Tension 1918–1939 and Germany 1890–1945.

For AQA: a possible three-year route:

Year 7 Term 1		Term 2		Term 3	
BOOK 1: Chapter 1 *1066 and all that*	BOOK 1: Chapter 3 *How religious were people in the Middle Ages?*	BOOK 1: Chapter 4 *Life in the Middle Ages* continued	BOOK 1: Chapter 7 *England at war*	BOOK 1: Chapter 9 *Medieval Britain: what changed?*	BOOK 2: Chapter 3 *Exit the Tudors, enter the Stuarts*
BOOK 1: Chapter 2 *The Norman Conquest*	BOOK 1: Chapter 4 *Life in the Middle Ages* *This might be a good place to include the study of a **historic environment** such as a Norman castle or battle site.*	BOOK 1: Chapter 5 *Power in the Middle Ages*	BOOK 1: Chapter 8 *Here come the Tudors*	BOOK 2: Chapter 1 *Queen Elizabeth*	BOOK 2: Chapter 4 *From Civil War to Commonwealth*
Year 8 Term 1		**Term 2**		**Term 3**	
BOOK 2: Chapter 5 *The Restoration: the Merry Monarch*	BOOK 2: Chapter 7 *The Industrial Revolution: from farming to factories*	BOOK 2: Chapter 8 *Terrible towns*	BOOK 2: Chapter 10 *Britain versus France*	BOOK 2: Chapter 12 *From Tudor to Victorian Britain: what changed?*	BOOK 3: Chapter 1 *A new century*
BOOK 2: Chapter 6 *Exit the Stuarts, enter the Georgians*		BOOK 2: Chapter 9 *The slave trade*	BOOK 2: Chapter 11 *India: a British Empire case study*		BOOK 3: Chapter 2 *The First World War* (depth study)
Year 9 Term 1		**Term 2**		**Term 3**	
BOOK 3: Chapter 2 *The First World War* (depth study) continued	BOOK 3: Chapter 4 *Power in the early twentieth century*	BOOK 3: Chapter 5 *The Second World War* (depth study) continued	BOOK 3: Chapter 7 *From empire to Commonwealth*	*Many schools that have a three-year KS3 use the last term as a means of completing topics that have 'run over' a little – or as a place to introduce the GCSE topics/course, or even complete a depth study.*	
BOOK 3: Chapter 3 *Between the wars*	BOOK 3: Chapter 5 *The Second World War* (depth study)		BOOK 3: Chapter 8 *Into the modern world*		

This route through the three textbooks helps to pick out some of the key content and themes from a school that has chosen the following topics from the AQA specification:

☐ **Period study:** America 1920–1975: Opportunity and Inequality

☐ **Thematic study:** Britain: Power and the People c1170–Present

☐ **Wider world depth study:** Conflict and Tension: The First World War 1894–1918

☐ **British depth study:** Norman England c1066–c1100.

The links to the AQA Norman England topic are obvious – this route ensures that students have a basic understanding of the Norman Conquest and life in England at that time if they are to go on and study at a higher level. This route also puts slightly more emphasis on preparing students for the power Thematic study by, for example, covering topics such as Magna Carta, the Peasants' Revolt and the development of Parliament (Year 7 Term 2), the English Civil War (Year 7 Term 3), Chartism (Year 8 Term 3), the anti-slavery movement (Year 8 Term 2) and factory reform (Year 8 Term 1). There are also opportunities to do some vital groundwork in highlighting the development of America in preparation for a Period study of the USA (Year 7 Term 3 and Year 8 Term 2, for example). This route also covers the First World War as a distinct topic (Year 8 Term 3 and Year 9 Term 1) as well as subtly introducing some of the themes you will need to cover in that topic, such as empire (Year 8 Term 2, for example). As well as the beginnings of the British Empire and the contribution of it during the First World War, this route also explores the end of empire (Year 9 Term 2).

For Edexcel: a possible two-year route:

Year 7 Term 1		Term 2		Term 3	
BOOK 1: Chapter 4 *Life in the Middle Ages*	BOOK 1: Chapter 5 *Power in the Middle Ages* BOOK 1: Chapter 8 *Here come the Tudors*	BOOK 1: Chapter 8 *Here come the Tudors* continued BOOK 1: Chapter 9 *Medieval Britain: what changed?*	BOOK 2: Chapter 1 *Queen Elizabeth* BOOK 2: Chapter 2 *Life in Tudor times*	BOOK 2: Chapter 3 *Exit the Tudors, enter the Stuarts* BOOK 2: Chapter 4 *From Civil War to Commonwealth*	BOOK 2: Chapter 5 *The Restoration: the Merry Monarch* BOOK 2: Chapter 7 *The Industrial Revolution: from farming to factories*

Year 8 Term 1		Term 2		Term 3	
BOOK 2: Chapter 8 *Terrible towns* *This might be an opportunity to introduce students to the **historic environment** of Whitechapel, London. You might explore local sources relevant to the site.*	BOOK 2: Chapter 9 *The slave trade* BOOK 2: Chapter 10 *Britain versus France*	BOOK 2: Chapter 12 *From Tudor to Victorian Britain: what changed?* BOOK 3: Chapter 1 *A new century*	BOOK 3: Chapter 2 *The First World War* (depth study) BOOK 3: Chapter 3 *Between the wars*	BOOK 3: Chapter 4 *Power in the early twentieth century* BOOK 3: Chapter 5 *The Second World War* (depth study)	BOOK 3: Chapter 5 *The Second World War* (depth study) continued BOOK 3: Chapter 8 *Into the modern world*

This route through the three textbooks helps to pick out some of the key content and themes from a school that has chosen the following topics from the Edexcel specification:

☐ **Thematic study:** Crime and punishment in Britain c1000–Present *and* Whitechapel c1870–c1900

☐ **Period study:** British America 1713–1783

☐ **British depth study:** Early Elizabethan England 1558–1588

☐ **Modern depth study:** Weimar and Nazi Germany 1918–1939.

The focus of the route means that slightly more emphasis has been placed on preparing students for the changes (and continuities) relating to the crime and punishment Thematic study – from crime detention, trial and punishment in the Middle Ages (Year 7 Term 1) through to the infamous case of Jack the Ripper and more modern policing methods (Year 8 Term 1). This route also encompasses the coming of the Tudors and Elizabethan England through to British involvement in America from Elizabethan times to the late eighteenth century (Year 7 Term 3 and Year 8 Term 1, for example), as well as the rise the rise of dictatorships in the 1930s and Hitler's Germany, for example (Year 8 Terms 2 and 3).

For Edexcel: a possible three-year route:

Year 7 Term 1		Term 2		Term 3	
BOOK 1: Chapter 1 *1066 and all that*	BOOK 1: Chapter 3 *How religious were people in the Middle Ages?*	BOOK 1: Chapter 4 *Life in the Middle Ages* continued	BOOK 1: Chapter 7 *England at war*	BOOK 2: Chapter 1 *Queen Elizabeth*	BOOK 2: Chapter 3 *Exit the Tudors, enter the Stuarts*
BOOK 1: Chapter 2 *The Norman Conquest*	BOOK 1: Chapter 4 *Life in the Middle Ages*	BOOK 1: Chapter 5 *Power in the Middle Ages*	BOOK 1: Chapter 8 *Here come the Tudors*	BOOK 2: Chapter 2 *Life in Tudor times*	BOOK 2: Chapter 4 *From Civil War to Commonwealth*

Year 8 Term 1		Term 2		Term 3	
BOOK 2: Chapter 5 *The Restoration: the Merry Monarch*	BOOK 2: Chapter 7 *The Industrial Revolution: from farming to factories*	BOOK 2: Chapter 10 *Britain versus France*	BOOK 3: Chapter 2 *The First World War* (depth study)	BOOK 3: Chapter 3 *Between the wars*	BOOK 3: Chapter 5 *The Second World War* (depth study)
BOOK 2: Chapter 6 *Exit the Stuarts, enter the Georgians*	BOOK 2: Chapter 9 *The slave trade*	BOOK 2: Chapter 11 *India: a British Empire case study*		BOOK 3: Chapter 4 *Power in the early twentieth century*	*This might be an opportunity to introduce students to the **historic environment** of London during the Second World War. You might explore local sources relevant to the site.*

Year 9 Term 1		Term 2	Term 3
BOOK 3: Chapter 6 *The post-war world*	BOOK 3: Chapter 8 *Into the modern world* continued	*This time might be used to complete topics that have 'run over' a little.*	*This might be a place to introduce the GCSE topics/course, or complete a KS3 depth study.*
BOOK 3: Chapter 8 *Into the modern world*	BOOK 3: Chapter 9 *The modern world: what changed!*		

This route through the three textbooks helps to pick out some of the key content and themes from a school that has chosen the following topics from the Edexcel specification:

☐ **Thematic study:** Warfare and British society c1250–Present *and* London and the Second World War 1939–1945

☐ **Period study:** Superpower relations and the Cold War 1941–1991

☐ **British depth study:** Anglo-Saxon and Norman England c1060–1088

☐ **Modern depth study:** Weimar and Nazi Germany 1918–1939.

The route begins with a direct link to the Edexcel Anglo-Saxon and Norman England c1060–1088 topic. This route also puts slightly more emphasis on preparing students for the warfare Thematic study by, for example, covering topics such as the Hundred Years War (Year 7 Term 2), the English Civil War (Year 7 Term 3), the Napoleonic Wars (Year 8 Term 2), and the First and Second World Wars (Year 8 Terms 2 and 3). This route also covers the rise of dictatorships in the 1930s and Nazi Germany (Year 8 Term 3) and the Cold War (Year 9 Term 1).

For OCR B (SHP): a possible three-year route:

Year 7 Term 1		Term 2		Term 3	
BOOK 1: Chapter 1 *1066 and all that*	BOOK 1: Chapter 3 *How religious were people in the Middle Ages?*	BOOK 1: Chapter 4 *Life in the Middle Ages* continued	BOOK 1: Chapter 7 *England at war*	BOOK 1: Chapter 9 *Medieval Britain: what changed?*	BOOK 2: Chapter 3 *Exit the Tudors, enter the Stuarts*
BOOK 1: Chapter 2 *The Norman Conquest*	BOOK 1: Chapter 4 *Life in the Middle Ages*	BOOK 1: Chapter 5 *Power in the Middle Ages*	BOOK 1: Chapter 8 *Here come the Tudors*	BOOK 2: Chapter 1 *Queen Elizabeth*	BOOK 2: Chapter 4 *From Civil War to Commonwealth*
Year 8 Term 1		**Term 2**		**Term 3**	
BOOK 2: Chapter 5 *The Restoration: the Merry Monarch*	BOOK 2: Chapter 7 *The Industrial Revolution: from farming to factories*	BOOK 2: Chapter 8 *Terrible towns* continued	BOOK 2: Chapter 10 *Britain versus France*	BOOK 2: Chapter 12 *From Tudor to Victorian Britain: what changed?*	BOOK 3: Chapter 2 *The First World War* (depth study)
BOOK 2: Chapter 6 *Exit the Stuarts, enter the Georgians*	BOOK 2: Chapter 8 *Terrible towns*	BOOK 2: Chapter 9 *The slave trade*	BOOK 2: Chapter 11 *India: a British Empire case study*	BOOK 3: Chapter 1 *A new century*	
Year 9 Term 1		**Term 2**		**Term 3**	
BOOK 3: Chapter 3 *Between the wars*	BOOK 3: Chapter 4 *Power in the early twentieth century* continued	BOOK 3: Chapter 5 *The Second World War* (depth study) continued	BOOK 3: Chapter 7 *From empire to Commonwealth*	BOOK 3: Chapter 8 *Into the modern world* continued	*The final term might be an ideal opportunity to introduce the idea of the 'History Around Us' unit. Placing this at the end of KS3 gives you greater scope to select a historical site relevant to one of the topics you have covered.*
BOOK 3: Chapter 4 *Power in the early twentieth century*	BOOK 3: Chapter 5 *The Second World War* (depth study)	BOOK 3: Chapter 6 *The post-war world*	BOOK 3: Chapter 8 *Into the modern world*	BOOK 3: Chapter 9 *The modern world: what changed?*	

This route through the three textbooks helps to pick out some of the key content and themes from a school that has chosen the following topics from the OCR B specification:

☐ **Thematic study:** Migrants to Britain c1250–Present

☐ **Period study:** The Making of America 1789–1900

☐ **British depth study:** The Norman Conquest 1065–1087

☐ **Wider world depth study:** Living under Nazi Rule 1933–1945.

This route places slightly more focus on preparing students for a study of the Norman Conquest and life in England at that time (Year 7 Terms 1 and 2), early US history (Year 7 Term 3 and Year 8 Term 2), Migration (Year 9 Term 2), and Living under Nazi Rule (Year 9 Terms 1 and 2).

For Eduqas: a possible two-year route:

Year 7 Term 1		Term 2		Term 3	
BOOK 1: Chapter 4 *Life in the Middle Ages*	BOOK 1: Chapter 8 *Here come the Tudors*	BOOK 2: Chapter 1 *Queen Elizabeth*	BOOK 2: Chapter 4 *From Civil War to Commonwealth*	BOOK 2: Chapter 7 *The Industrial Revolution: from farming to factories*	BOOK 2: Chapter 8 *Terrible towns* continued
BOOK 1: Chapter 6 *Health and medicine*	BOOK 1: Chapter 9 *Medieval Britain: what changed?*	BOOK 2: Chapter 2 *Life in Tudor times*	BOOK 2: Chapter 5 *The Restoration: the Merry Monarch*	BOOK 2: Chapter 8 *Terrible towns*	BOOK 2: Chapter 12 *From Tudor to Victorian Britain: what changed?* *This might be an opportunity to introduce students to a* **historic environment** *such as a seaside resort.*
Year 8 Term 1		**Term 2**		**Term 3**	
BOOK 3: Chapter 1 *A new century*	BOOK 3: Chapter 2 *The First World War* (depth study) continued	BOOK 3: Chapter 4 *Power in the early twentieth century*	BOOK 3: Chapter 5 *The Second World War* (depth study) continued	BOOK 3: Chapter 6 *The post-war world* continued	BOOK 3: Chapter 8 *Into the modern world*
BOOK 3: Chapter 2 *The First World War* (depth study)	BOOK 3: Chapter 3 *Between the wars*	BOOK 3: Chapter 5 *The Second World War* (depth study)	BOOK 3: Chapter 6 *The post-war world*	BOOK 3: Chapter 7 *From empire to Commonwealth*	BOOK 3: Chapter 9 *The modern world: what changed?*

This route through the three textbooks helps to pick out some of the key content and themes from a school that has chosen the following topics from the Eduqas specification:

☐ **British depth study:** The Elizabethan Age 1558–1603

☐ **Period study:** The Development of the UK 1919–1990

☐ **Non-British studies in depth:** Germany in Transition 1919–1939

☐ **Thematic study:** Changes in Entertainment and Leisure in Britain c500–Present Day.

The Entertainment and Leisure in Britain topic is highlighted in several places through this route when students focus on leisure and entertainment in, for example, medieval times (Year 7 Term 1), the Tudor and Stuart era (Year 7 Term 2), the industrial age (Year 7 Term 3) and modern times (Year 8 Term 3). The Elizabeth Age (in Year 7 Term 2, for example), Germany in Transition (in Year 8 Terms 1 and 2) and the Development of the UK (in Year 8) are also key components of this route.

Assessment and progression to GCSE

The teaching and learning landscape at KS3 and KS4 has changed in recent years. According to the **Historical Association** survey (2018):

- 55% of secondary schools indicated that KS3 has been or was going to be shortened due to the new GCSE specifications, mainly as a consequence of the view that it is difficult to fit all the GCSE content in within a two year framework.
- 56% of schools have changed the way they teach KS3 to provide background knowledge to GCSE topics and provide new understanding of history skills such as source or interpretation analysis.

In addition, there is clear evidence from the *Oxford Language Report* (2018) of a significant word gap in UK schools, which can impede students' learning and success at KS3 and beyond.

As a result, we designed this *KS3 History* series to reflect the new landscape by ensuring that each suggested topic in the KS3 History National Curriculum is covered, but we have also made sure that our content supports literacy development and progression towards any of the GCSE History specifications.

This section provides: 1) a brief introduction to each of the GCSE exam board specifications and their key content; and 2) charts to show how our *Student Book* provides background context to the contents of different specifications.

AQA GCSE History specification

Introduction

The AQA GCSE History specification allows students to explore key themes in History, such as conflict and religion. AQA have included new topics to allow students to analyse the change and continuity of these themes – these topics can help students understand the world today. However, they have kept some of the more popular courses, for example Medicine through time (now known as Health and the People). The specification offers a good balance between political and social history, and there are no prohibited combinations, which allows departments to play to their strengths. Moreover, it builds nicely from well-established KS3 topics, and offers a firm foundation for further study in History.

AQA content	How *KS3 History: Technology, War and Independence* (Book 3) matches
Period study	
America 1840–1895: Expansion and Consolidation	*This topic is referenced in Book 2*
Germany 1890–1945: Democracy and Dictatorship	✓ **Chapter 4** Power in the early twentieth century
Russia 1894–1945: Tsardom and Communism	✓ **Chapter 4** Power in the early twentieth century
America 1920–1973: Opportunity and Inequality	*Book 3 provides a good foundation for this topic*
Wider world depth study	
Conflict and Tension 1894–1918	✓ **Chapter 2** The First World War
Conflict and Tension 1918–1939	✓ **Chapter 2** The First World War ✓ **Chapter 4** Power in the early twentieth century
Conflict and Tension between East and West 1945–1972	✓ **Chapter 5** The Second World War ✓ **Chapter 6** The post-war world
Conflict and Tension in Asia 1950–1975	✓ **Chapter 6** The post-war world
Conflict and Tension 1990–2009	✓ **Chapter 8** Into the modern world

Thematic study	
Health and the People c1000–Present	✓ **Chapter 1** A new century ✓ **Chapter 2** The First World War ✓ **Chapter 5** The Second World War ✓ **Chapter 6** The post-war world *Book 1 and Book 2 also provide a good foundation for this topic*
Power and the People c1170–Present	✓ **Chapter 1** A new century ✓ **Chapter 2** The First World War ✓ **Chapter 7** From empire to Commonwealth *Book 1 and Book 2 also provide a good foundation for this topic*
Migration, Empires and the People c790–Present	✓ **Chapter 6** The post-war world ✓ **Chapter 7** From empire to Commonwealth *Book 1 and Book 2 also provide a good foundation for this topic*
British depth studies including the historic environment	
Norman England c1066–c1100	*Book 1 provides a good foundation for this topic*
Medieval England: the Reign of Edward I 1272–1307	*Book 1 provides a good foundation for this topic*
Elizabethan England c1568–1603	*Book 1 and Book 2 provide a good foundation for this topic*
Restoration England 1660–1685	*Book 2 provides a good foundation for this topic*

The Over to You activities and the History Skills activities in each *Student Book* lesson, as well as the end-of-chapter History Skills and Assessments, are carefully mapped to command words from different exam boards, to help students familiarise themselves with the specialist vocabulary needed to succeed in further studies beyond KS3. You can also find in each chapter of this guide a detailed breakdown of **AQA exam-style questions** covered within that chapter. For example, see page 46 for the Chapter 1 chart.

Edexcel GCSE History specification

Introduction

Edexcel have built their GCSE specification on the feedback they have been given from the history subject community, combining the most popular modern topics, along with those favourites of the Schools History Project, and brand-new topics into a single specification. There are no prohibited options – you can pick any topic. Edexcel have made an effort to make their exam questions and mark schemes straightforward with the requirements for success made clear. They feel that their GCSE builds on KS3 content while giving students a chance to apply their contextual understanding to new topics.

Edexcel content	How *KS3 History: Technology, War and Independence* (Book 3) matches
Thematic study and historic environment	
Crime and Punishment in Britain c1000–Present *and* Whitechapel c1870–c1900: Crime, Policing and the Inner City	✓ **Chapter 1** A new century *Book 1 and Book 2 also provide a good foundation for this topic*
Thematic study and historic environment	
Medicine in Britain c1250–Present *and* The British Sector of the Western Front 1914–1918: Injuries, Treatment and the Trenches	✓ **Chapter 1** A new century ✓ **Chapter 2** The First World War ✓ **Chapter 5** The Second World War ✓ **Chapter 5** The post-war world *Book 1 and Book 2 also provide a good foundation for this topic*
Warfare and British Society c1250–Present *and* London and the Second World War 1939–1945	✓ **Chapter 2** The First World War ✓ **Chapter 5** The Second World War *Book 1 and Book 2 also provide a good foundation for this topic*
Period study	
Anglo-Saxon and Norman England c1060–1088	*Book 1 provides a good foundation for this topic*
The Reigns of King Richard I and King John 1189–1216	*Book 1 provides a good foundation for this topic*
Henry VIII and his Ministers 1509–1540	*Book 1 provides a good foundation for this topic*
Early Elizabethan England 1558–1588	*Book 1 and Book 2 provide a good foundation for this topic*
British depth study	
Spain and the 'New World' c1490–c1555	*Book 1 provides a good foundation for this topic*
British America 1713–1783: Empire and Revolution	*Book 2 provides a good foundation for this topic*
The American West c1835–c1895	*This topic is referenced in Book 2*
Superpower Relations and the Cold War 1941–1991	✓ **Chapter 6** The post-war world
Conflict in the Middle East 1945–1995	✓ **Chapter 8** Into the modern world
Modern depth study	
Russia and the Soviet Union, 1917–1941	✓ **Chapter 3** Between the wars
Weimar and Nazi Germany, 1918–1939	✓ **Chapter 3** Between the wars ✓ **Chapter 4** Power in the early twentieth century ✓ **Chapter 5** The Second World War
Mao's China, 1945–1976	*This topic is referenced in Book 3*
The USA, 1954–1975: Conflict at Home and Abroad	*This topic is referenced in Book 3*

The Over to You activities and the History Skills activities in each *Student Book* lesson, as well as the end-of-chapter History Skills and Assessments, are carefully mapped to command words from different exam boards, to help students familiarise themselves with the specialist vocabulary needed to succeed in further studies beyond KS3. You can also find in each chapter of this guide a detailed breakdown of **Edexcel exam-style questions** covered within that chapter. For example, see page 46 for the Chapter 1 chart.

OCR A GCSE History specification

Introduction

The key aim of the OCR A specification is to bring the subject to life and inspire students. Their specification is accessible and based on engagement with those in the History teaching community. OCR have a clear idea of what kind of students their specification produces: independent, articulate, and engaged. To assist teachers with this they offer a wide-range of support from the preparation stage to the delivery. As with previous exam boards, this Modern World option offers some of the old favourites and new exciting topics that are sure to engage students – moving away from a white, male dominated History.

OCR A content	How *KS3 History: Technology, War and Independence* (Book 3) matches
Period study and non-British depth study	
International Relations: the Changing International Order 1918–2001	✓ **Chapter 2** The First World War ✓ **Chapter 3** Between the wars ✓ **Chapter 4** Power in the early twentieth century ✓ **Chapter 6** The post-war world ✓ **Chapter 9** Into the modern world
China 1950–1981: The People and the State	*Book 3 provides a good foundation for this topic*
Germany 1925–1955: The People and the State	✓ **Chapter 3** Between the wars ✓ **Chapter 4** Power in the early twentieth century ✓ **Chapter 5** The Second World War
Poland 1956–1990: The People and the State	
Russia 1928–1964: The People and the State	*This topic is referenced in Book 3*
South Africa 1960–1994: The People and the State	*This topic is referenced in Book 3*
The USA 1919–1948: The People and the State	✓ **Chapter 3** Between the wars
The USA 1945–1974: The People and the State	✓ **Chapter 6** The post-war world
British thematic study	
Migration to Britain c1000–c2010	✓ **Chapter 7** From empire to Commonwealth *Book 1 and Book 2 also provide a good foundation for this topic*
Monarchy and Democracy in Britain c1000–2014	✓ **Chapter 1** A new century ✓ **Chapter 2** The First World War *Book 1 and Book 2 also provide a good foundation for this topic*
War and British Society c790–2010	✓ **Chapter 2** The First World War ✓ **Chapter 4** The Second World War ✓ **Chapter 6** The post-war world ✓ **Chapter 7** From empire to Commonwealth ✓ **Chapter 8** Into the modern world *Book 1 and Book 2 also provide a good foundation for this topic*
British depth study and a study of the historic environment	
The Impact of Empire on Britain 1688–c1730 with Urban Environments: Patterns of Migration	*Book 2 provides a good foundation for this topic*
The English Reformation c1520–c1550 with Castles: Form and Function c1000–1750	*Book 1 provides a good foundation for this topic*
Personal Rule to Restoration 1629–1660 with Castles: Form and Function c1000–1750	*Book 2 provides a good foundation for this topic*

The Over to You activities and the History Skills activities in each *Student Book* lesson, as well as the end-of-chapter History Skills and Assessments, are carefully mapped to command words from different exam boards, to help students familiarise themselves with the specialist vocabulary needed to succeed in further studies beyond KS3. You can also find in each chapter of this guide a detailed breakdown of **OCR exam-style questions** covered within that chapter. For example, see page 46 for the Chapter 1 chart.

OCR B GCSE History specification

Introduction

The ethos of OCR B echoes that of OCR A; however, this specification stays true to the principles of the Schools History Project by offering 'worthwhile and inspiring school history'. The course encourages students to ask questions of history through enquiry, and using pre-existing deep knowledge. The specification shows a commitment to diversity and the world around us. This specification offers new topics, but maintains some of the more popular courses from the Schools History Project. Improved teacher guidance aims to help with the implementation, delivery and results of the course.

OCR B content	How *KS3 History: Technology, War and Independence* (Book 3) matches
Thematic study	
The People's Health c1250–Present	✓ **Chapter 1** A new century ✓ **Chapter 2** The First World War ✓ **Chapter 5** The Second World War ✓ **Chapter 6** The post-war world *Book 1 and Book 2 also provide a good foundation for this topic*
Crime and Punishment c1250–Present	*Book 1 and Book 2 also provide a good foundation for this topic*
Migrants to Britain c1250–Present	✓ **Chapter 2** The First World War ✓ **Chapter 7** From empire to Commonwealth *Book 2 also provides a good foundation for this topic*
British depth study	
The Norman Conquest 1065–1087	*Book 1 provides a good foundation for this topic*
The Elizabethans 1580–1603	*Book 2 provides a good foundation for this topic*
Britain in Peace and War 1900–1918	✓ **Chapter 1** A new century ✓ **Chapter 2** The First World War ✓ **Chapter 3** Between the wars
Period study	
Viking Expansion c750–c1050	*Book 1 provides a good foundation for this topic*
The Mughal Empire 1526–1707	*This topic is referenced in Book 2*
The Making of America 1789–1900	*Book 2 provides a good foundation for this topic*
World depth study	
The First Crusade c1070–1100	*Book 1 provides a good foundation for this topic*
Aztecs and the Spanish Conquest 1519–1535	
Living under Nazi Rule 1933–1945	✓ **Chapter 3** Between the wars ✓ **Chapter 4** Power in the early twentieth century

The Over to You activities and the History Skills activities in each *Student Book* lesson, as well as the end-of-chapter History Skills and Assessments, are carefully mapped to command words from different exam boards, to help students familiarise themselves with the specialist vocabulary needed to succeed in further studies beyond KS3. You can also find in each chapter of this guide a detailed breakdown of **OCR exam-style questions** covered within that chapter. For example, see page 46 for the Chapter 1 chart.

Eduqas GCSE History specification

Introduction

The Eduqas specification makes clear links with the aims of the History National Curriculum by focusing on what kind of student the specification will produce. By the end of the GCSE course students will be able to ask questions, make judgements, and explain links between events, people, and outcomes. The specification focuses on key second order concepts while offering topics from across three compulsory time periods.

Eduqas content	How *KS3 History: Technology, War and Independence* (Book 3) matches
British study in depth	
Conflict and Upheaval: England 1337–1381	*Book 1 provides a good foundation for this topic*
The Elizabethan Age 1558–1603	*Book 1 and Book 2 provide a good foundation for this topic*
Empire, Reform and War: Britain 1890–1918	✓ **Chapter 1** A new century ✓ **Chapter 2** The First World War *Book 2 provides a good foundation for this topic*
Austerity, Affluence and Discontent: Britain 1951–1979	✓ **Chapter 7** From empire to Commonwealth
Non-British study in depth	
The Crusades c1095–1149	*Book 1 provides a good foundation for this topic*
The Voyages of Discovery and the Conquest of the Americas 1492–1522	*Book 1 provides a good foundation for this topic*
Germany in Transition 1919–1939	✓ **Chapter 2** The First World War ✓ **Chapter 4** Power in the early twentieth century
The USA: A Nation of Contrasts 1910–1929	✓ **Chapter 2** The First World War
Period study	
The Development of the USA 1929–2000	*Book 3 provides a good foundation for this topic*
The Development of Germany 1919–1991	✓ **Chapter 2** The First World War ✓ **Chapter 4** Power in the early twentieth century ✓ **Chapter 5** The Second World War ✓ **Chapter 6** The post-war world
The Development of the USSR 1924–1991	✓ **Chapter 6** The post-war world
The Development of the UK 1919–1990	✓ **Chapter 3** Between the wars ✓ **Chapter 5** The Second World War ✓ **Chapter 6** The post-war world ✓ **Chapter 7** From empire to Commonwealth ✓ **Chapter 8** Into the modern world
Thematic study	
Changes in Crime and Punishment in Britain c500–Present	✓ **Chapter 8** Into the modern world *Book 1 and Book 2 also provide a good foundation for this topic*
Changes in Health and Medicine in Britain c500–Present	✓ **Chapter 1** A new century ✓ **Chapter 2** The First World War ✓ **Chapter 5** The Second World War ✓ **Chapter 6** The post-war world *Book 1 and Book 2 also provide a good foundation for this topic*
The Development of Warfare in Britain c500–Present	✓ **Chapter 2** The First World War ✓ **Chapter 4** Power in the early twentieth century ✓ **Chapter 5** The Second World War ✓ **Chapter 6** The post-war world *Book 1 and Book 2 also provide a good foundation for this topic*
Changes in Entertainment and Leisure in Britain c500–Present	✓ **Chapter 8** Into the modern world *Book 1 and Book 2 also provide a good foundation for this topic*

The Over to You activities and the History Skills activities in each *Student Book* lesson, as well as the end-of-chapter History Skills and Assessments, are carefully mapped to command words from different exam boards, to help students familiarise themselves with the specialist vocabulary needed to succeed in further studies beyond KS3. You can also find in each chapter of this guide a detailed breakdown of **Eduqas exam-style questions** covered within that chapter. For example, see page 46 for the Chapter 1 chart.

WJEC GCSE History specification

Introduction

WJEC have developed a specification that allows teachers to develop their students as independent students who question and make links between the different topics studied. The specification builds on common KS3 topics and skills and concepts. As the course is linked to the Welsh Baccalaureate, there are opportunities to develop literacy and other skills that are being assessed through the Skills Challenge Certificate. The focus on the Welsh perspective, where possible, gives students the chance to see where they fit in to the wider UK, EU and world history.

WJEC content	How *KS3 History: Technology, War and Independence* (Book 3) matches
Wales/wider perspective study in depth	
The Elizabethan Age 1558–1603	*Book 2 provides a good foundation for this topic*
Radicalism and Protest 1810–1848	*Book 2 provides a good foundation for this topic*
Depression, War and Recovery 1930–1951	✓ **Chapter 3** Between the wars ✓ **Chapter 4** Power in the early twentieth century ✓ **Chapter 5** The Second World War ✓ **Chapter 6** The post-war world
Austerity, Affluence and Discontent 1951–1979	✓ **Chapter 7** From empire to Commonwealth ✓ **Chapter 8** Into the modern world
European/wider world study in depth	
Russia in Transition 1905–1924	*Book 3 provides a good foundation for this topic*
The USA: A Nation of Contrasts 1910–1929	✓ **Chapter 2** The First World War
Germany in Transition 1919–1939	✓ **Chapter 2** The First World War ✓ **Chapter 4** Power in the early twentieth century
Changes in South Africa 1948–1994	*This topic is referenced in Book 3*
Thematic study	
Changes in Crime and Punishment c1500–Present	✓ **Chapter 8** Into the modern world *Book 2 also provides a good foundation for this topic*
Changes in Health and Medicine c1340–Present	✓ **Chapter 1** A new century ✓ **Chapter 6** The post-war world *Book 1 and Book 2 also provide a good foundation for this topic*
The Development of Warfare c1250–Present	✓ **Chapter 2** The First World War ✓ **Chapter 4** Power in the early twentieth century ✓ **Chapter 5** The Second World War ✓ **Chapter 6** The post-war world *Book 1 and Book 2 also provide a good foundation for this topic*
Changes in Patterns of Migration c1500–Present	✓ **Chapter 7** From empire to Commonwealth *Book 2 also provides a good foundation for this topic*

The Over to You activities and the History Skills activities in each *Student Book* lesson, as well as the end-of-chapter History Skills and Assessments, are carefully mapped to command words from different exam boards, to help students familiarise themselves with the specialist vocabulary needed to succeed in further studies beyond KS3. You can also find in each chapter of this guide a detailed breakdown of **WJEC exam-style questions** covered within that chapter. For example, see page 46 for the Chapter 1 chart.

Progression to GCSE: closing the word gap

As mentioned in the Curriculum planning section of this guide (see pages 18–31), the research from the *Oxford Language Report* (2018) found evidence of a significant word gap in UK schools, which is holding back students' learning. As a result, we have included suggested activities and effective classroom strategies here that could help your school to close the word gap and support your students to succeed in progressing through KS3 and beyond.

1 Understanding vocabulary for exams/assessments

Teacher notes

The increased content demands of the current History GCSE specification has left us scrabbling for time to get students through the different units, and many schools have started to teach the KS3 curriculum over two years to allow more time for GCSE. In this context, it is easy to forget that students need time to practise applying their knowledge and skills to assessments, starting from KS3. We have all taught students who instinctively understand the demands of an exam-style question, but they are not in the majority.

We must help students to access the examination questions by making them become familiar with command words and giving them the confidence to break down unfamiliar vocabulary.

Consult with your exam board's examiner reports for more detail about the key words which specifically pose difficulties for students.

Work bank of command words

Command words used in GCSE History exams	AQA	Edexcel	OCR A	OCR B	WJEC Eduqas
account*	✓	✓	✓	✓	
accurate					✓
analyse	✓	✓	✓	✓	✓
change and continuity	✓	✓	✓	✓	✓
compare*		✓		✓	
connection			✓	✓	✓
convincing*	✓		✓	✓	
describe	✓	✓	✓	✓	✓
enquiry		✓			✓
evaluate		✓	✓	✓	✓
explain	✓	✓	✓	✓	✓
extent					✓
identify			✓	✓	✓
impact/change	✓		✓	✓	✓
importance*	✓		✓	✓	
inference		✓			✓
investigate			✓	✓	
judgement	✓	✓	✓	✓	✓
outline					✓
purpose					✓
significance	✓	✓			✓
summary			✓	✓	
utility*	✓	✓	✓	✓	✓

Words identified in recent examiner reports as posing difficulties for students.

Defining key words

Encourage students to engage with exam key words by creating their own annotated table of definitions and prompts:

Word	Definitions/prompts
infer	What can you learn from the information or what does it suggest?
critical/opposes	Against something
change	What impact or effect did it have?
similar	Can you find anything (features or reasons) that are the same, despite the time difference?
supports	In favour of something
account	A story or narrative that flows chronologically

2 Mining history articles and academic texts

Both academic and anecdotal research shows that for young people to develop their vocabulary and understand how to apply new vocabulary to their writing, they need time to read. When students read for pleasure, they develop a confidence that means they can make what they read 'mean something' to them; this is what gives them the confidence to give a tough question 'a go' in exams. This can help us in the History classroom when it comes to analysing and comprehending historical interpretations. Confident readers will be able to identify different opinions and attach those opinions to their contextual understanding, which is a skill vital for success at GCSE.

To promote reading in your classroom, gather different articles and books about a topic. For higher-tier vocabulary, you could make use of *BBC History* magazine, the Historical Association's articles, and *History Today*.

- Reading to students allows you to emphasise meaning and model how words can be used.
- Reading with students can lead to discussions about how vocabulary can be applied in their writing. This is a good exercise for identifying more advanced connecting words.

You can also use academic texts to help to extend students' vocabulary choices. For example, texts such as *The Age of Extremes: The Short Twentieth Century, 1914–1991* by Eric Hobsbawm (Abacus, 1995) can be used to teach how to compare arguments and to help students to widen their use of connectives to introduce new ideas. Students can

Checking confidence in key words

You could create a template similar to the one below to check students' confidence in using key words, using a scale from 1 to 5 (5 is most confident). Record the dates they use the words verbally or in their written work to show how their confidence rating changes:

Word	Confidence rating 1 to 5	Date used
communism	2	01/10/19
	4	09/01/20
appeasement	1	01/11/19
	5	20/01/20
uprising	1	09/01/20
censorship	4	20/01/20

highlight vocabulary used to compare historical concepts. They can then present the vocabulary they have chosen and explain what they thought of Hobsbawm's analysis, using his vocabulary. This activity can help students to be more able to compare arguments and ideas in exam settings.

- Give students a number of texts: GCSE, A Level, academic, or review articles. Give them a mind-map template (see page 43, and ask them to complete the mind-map in groups.
- Allow students several opportunities to read the academic texts, and make mind-maps with vocabulary as well as connections with prior vocabulary knowledge, before you expect to see any impact in their writing. This is about learning different writing styles – they need a chance to observe and understand a way of writing before they can apply it.
- Share good examples of new vocabulary to agree on ways that words, phrases, or style in general can be applied, and then get students to redraft their work.
- Develop low-stakes quizzes for matching definitions to new advanced vocabulary.
- As an alternative to classroom texts, share details of interesting broadsheet newspaper articles or satirical TV shows with your students.
- KS3 students might find the ***Teachit History*** resource *Handling challenging texts in history (19517)* a helpful starting point for looking at academic texts.

Mind-map template for analysing vocabulary in articles and academic texts

3 Organised writing

When analysing the demands of GCSE mark schemes, the top band always requires a clear, organised response with sustained judgements throughout. Some students will require writing frames and paragraph structures as a starting point for learning how to do this at the start of GCSE, while for others it is a skill they will have developed by the end of KS3, partly as a result of having a wide vocabulary.

- Modelling the use of connecting words such as conjunctions and tier three vocabulary (subject-specific academic words) can help students to incorporate more sophisticated language into their written work. We have built this modelling into this Oxford *KS3 History* series: for example, in the ***Technology, War and Independence 1901–Present* (Book 3) Chapter 5: Literacy Focus**

section, a linking words activity is included with a word bank to familiarise students with connectives.

- Using a visualiser, you can quickly model good language use before, during, and after writing tasks.
- Annotate articles to show where connections have been made, judgements given, and comparisons explained. When students have done this in their homework, you can use their work as a model of good practice.
- Use academic texts to show students how tier three language can be incorporated into their written work.
- Gradually remove essay-writing structures as students develop confidence in their own vocabulary range and writing style.

Chapter 1 A new century

Links to KS3 History National Curriculum

In this chapter students will explore the social and political changes in Britain before the First World War. The latest Key Stage 3 History National Curriculum states that students should be taught about the challenges for Britain, Europe and the wider world from 1901 to the present day. In order to assess this, it is essential to 'set up' where Britain stood as a nation at the beginning of the twentieth century. This chapter shows students what life was like for poor or vulnerable members of society at this time and how the government stepped in to bring about change through the Welfare State – a specific example from the National Curriculum. Another specific example explored is women's suffrage, allowing students to develop the skills of change and continuity.

In addition, the chapter provides several examples for students to pursue historically valid enquiries, for example *1.3 Who or what was to blame for the Titanic disaster?* and *1.5 History Mystery: Did Emily Davison mean to kill herself?* – which fit the demands of the National Curriculum to show how evidence can be used to build an enquiry. These examples also support students to create structured and evidentially supported accounts. Students are also given the opportunity to think carefully about historical concepts such as change and continuity, cause and consequence, similarity, difference and significance. The first order concepts of social reform, industry and the extension of the franchise are built upon and developed in this chapter.

Skills and processes covered in this chapter

		Lesson/activity in the Student Book
History Skills	Knowledge and understanding	1.1A Over to You: 2a, 2b
		1.1B Over to You: 1a, 1b, 1c, 2, 3a
		1.2A Over to You: 1a
		1.2B Over to You: 1
		1.3 Over to You: 1
		1.4A Over to You: 3a
		1.4B Over to You: 1
		1.5 Over to You: 4
		Have you been learning? Quick Knowledge Quiz: 1, 2, 3, 4, 5, 6, 7, 8, 9, 10
	Interpretation analysis	1.1A Interpretation Analysis: 1, 2
		1.4B Interpretation Analysis: 1, 2, 3, 4
		1.5 Over to You: 1a, 1b, 1c, 2, 3
	Sources analysis	1.1A Over to You: 1a, 1b
		1.2B Source Analysis: 1, 2, 3
		1.4A Over to You: 1a, 1b, 3b; Source Analysis: 1, 2
		1.4B Over to You: 3, 4a, 4b
		1.5 Over to You: 1a, 1b, 1c, 2, 3
	Significance	1 Assessment: Significance: 1, 2, 3, 4, 5
	Cause and consequence	1.1A Over to You: 2a, 2b
		1.2A Over to You: 1b, 2
		1.2B Over to You: 2, 3a, 3b, 3c, 3d

		Lesson/activity in the Student Book
		1.3 Over to You: 2a, 2b, 2c
		1.4B Over to You: 2
	Diversity/Similarity and difference	**1.1B** Over to You: 3a
		1.4A Over to You: 2
	Change and continuity	**1.1B** Over to You: 3b, 3c; Change: 1
Literacy and Numeracy	Literacy	**1.3** Over to You: 2c
		1.5 Over to You: 4
		Have you been learning? Literacy Focus: 1a, 1b, 1c, 1d, 2a, 2b, 2c, 2d, 2e, 2f, 2g, 3
	Numeracy	**1.2B** Source Analysis: 1

Lesson sequence

Lesson title	Student Book pages	Objectives
1.1A Britain and the world in 1901	pp 8–9	• Examine Britain's place in the world at the turn of the twentieth century.
1.1B Britain and the world in 1901	pp 10–11	• Explain how and why other countries were catching up with Britain in terms of industry, trade and empire.
1.2A Tackling poverty and public health	pp 12–13	• Identify the level of poverty experienced by many in the early twentieth century.
1.2B Tackling poverty and public health	pp 14–15	• Outline key events and significant people in the attempt to improve public health at this time. • Assess the impact of the Liberal Reforms.
1.3 Who or what was to blame for the *Titanic* disaster?	pp 16–17	• Explain why the *Titanic* is such a famous ship. • Judge who or what caused the *Titanic* disaster.
1.4A Who were the suffragettes?	pp 18–19	• Compare suffragettes and suffragists.
1.4B Who were the suffragettes?	pp 20–21	• Evaluate what finally won the vote for women.
1.5 History Mystery: Did Emily Davison mean to kill herself?	pp 22–23	• Examine the circumstances surrounding the death of Emily Davison. • Judge whether Emily Davison killed herself deliberately or not.
Chapter 1 Have you been learning?	pp 24–25	• Choose the correct answer from the given options for a quick recap. • Define and use key terms correctly. • Improve sentences by adding specific factual detail.
Chapter 1 History skill: Significance	p 26	• Define historical significance.
Chapter 1 Assessment: Significance	p 27	• Assess the significance of the Liberal Reforms in the improvement of care for vulnerable people.

Links to the GCSE curriculum

This chapter provides some historical context to the following:

AQA: Britain: Health and the People c1000–Present

AQA: Power and the People c1170–Present

Edexcel: Medicine in Britain c1250–Present

OCR A: The Changing International Order 1918–2001

OCR A: Monarchy and Democracy in Britain c1000–2014

OCR B: The People's Health c1250–Present

OCR B: Britain in Peace and War 1900–1918

Eduqas: The Development of Warfare in Britain c500–Present

Eduqas: Empire, Reform and War: Britain 1890–1918

Eduqas: Changes in Health and Medicine in Britain c500–Present

WJEC: Changes in Health and Medicine c1340–Present

Exam-style questions covered in this chapter

Exam board	Lesson/activity question location	Command words	History skills/concepts
AQA	1.1B Change: 1	In what ways...	Change and continuity
	1.2B Source Analysis: 3	How useful...	Source analysis
	1.4A Over to You	Explain two ways... similar/different	Similarity and difference
	1.4A Source Analysis: 2	How useful...	Source analysis
	1.4B Over to You: 2	What was the impact of...	Cause and consequence
	1.4B Interpretation Analysis: 3	How does... differ	Interpretation analysis
	1.4B Interpretation Analysis: 4	Which interpretation... more convincing	Interpretation analysis
Edexcel	1.1A Interpretation Analysis: 2	How far do you agree... interpretation...	Interpretation analysis
	1.2B Source Analysis: 3	How useful...	Source analysis
	1.4A Source Analysis: 2	How useful...	Source analysis
	1.4B Interpretation Analysis: 3	What is the main difference...	Interpretation analysis
OCR A	1.2B Source Analysis: 3	How useful...	Source analysis
	1.4A Source Analysis: 2	How useful...	Source analysis
OCR B	1.2B Source Analysis: 3	How useful...	Source analysis
	1.4A Source Analysis: 2	How useful...	Source analysis
	1.4B Interpretation Analysis: 3	How far do they differ...	Interpretation analysis
Eduqas	1.1A Interpretation Analysis: 2	How far do you agree... interpretation...	Interpretation analysis
WJEC	1.1A Interpretation Analysis: 2	How far do you agree... interpretation...	Interpretation analysis
	1.3 Over to You: 1	Complete the sentences...	Knowledge and understanding
	Have you been learning? Literacy Focus: 1a, 1b, 1c, 1d	Complete the sentences...	Knowledge and understanding

A brief history

1.1A/B Britain and the world in 1901

This lesson bridges content, themes and concepts from Book 2: *Revolution, Industry and Empire 1558–1901 Student Book* to show the fading legacy of the Industrial Revolution in Britain. Students will see that Britain no longer has the biggest empire, navy or industrial power, as the USA, Germany, Japan and Russia rise in power. The lesson then takes students away from the international – political – perspective, on to the diverse social history of the rich and poor in Britain at the turn of the century. Building on their understanding from Book 2 of what life was like for people by the end of the nineteenth century, students will explore the ways in which people's lives were beginning to change at the start of the twentieth century and the impact this had on society.

1.2A/B Tackling poverty and public health

This lesson leads with an enquiry on poverty and reform that will take the students from the problems for the industrial poor to the Liberal Reforms. Students will explore the issues facing the children of the poor – supported by statistics – and then the role of the individual in bringing about change, with a focus on Churchill and Lloyd George. The significance of the reforms is explored through the development of welfare up to the 1930s. The focus on dates and statistics would lend itself well to using call and response with students to ensure they can retain and recall facts. The students will apply this content by writing about how the reforms helped different groups. They will then study a graph that shows the impact of free school meals and then analyse its utility.

1.3 Who or what was to blame for the Titanic disaster?

This enquiry on the *Titanic* is often a popular topic with students. This lesson shows the importance of enquiry learning in a knowledge-rich curriculum – using evidence students will write a report for both the British and the US governments about the main cause of the sinking of the *Titanic*. The evidence presents the role everyone played in the disaster – this is an excellent example of the web of causation. Students will see the natural links between the causes so they can start to write a sustained analysis, which is the requirement for top grades at GCSE. To further support students with this they should be encouraged to include as many key terms, people, dates and statistics as they can.

Timeline

1876
The first telephone is invented.

1885
Karl Benz creates the first successful motor car.

1897
The suffragists are formed to campaign for the vote.

22 January 1901
Queen Victoria dies and her son becomes King Edward VII.

1903
The suffragettes are formed by the Pankhursts with a focus on 'deeds not words'.

1903
Orville Wright makes the first manned powered flight in an aeroplane.

1908
Henry Ford begins work on the Ford Model T motor car.

1906
The Free School Meals Act is passed.

1908
The Children's Charter (or Children's and Young Person's Act) is introduced.

14 April 1912
The *Titanic* sinks.

1913
Emily Davison is killed by the king's horse at the Epsom Derby.

1918
Women over 30 are given the right to vote.

1928
The voting age for women is reduced to 21 – in line with men.

A brief history continued

1.4A/B Who were the suffragettes?

Students will explore the creation of the women's suffrage movement in the late nineteenth century through to the changes in the movement under the Pankhursts. Sources are used to give students an understanding of the way many men viewed women at the time, especially their involvement in the world of politics. The focus on the role of the individual (for example, the Pankhursts), tactics and the turning point of war will give students the content they need to analyse why women got the vote. Students will go on to apply their knowledge of the movement by analysing interpretations. A way to extend this lesson could be to look at propaganda posters and cartoons for each side of the movement to analyse opinions of the time.

1.5 History Mystery: Did Emily Davison mean to kill herself?

The enquiry into the death of Emily Davison poses many questions that will spark students' interest. It is unlikely that they will get one clear answer, but the debates that follow would be a good opportunity to take the lesson further and to develop oracy in your classroom. Students are given two theories – much like a hypothesis they may receive in Science. They must investigate these theories and then come to a judgement in the style of a report, backing up all points with evidence. This will build towards 'write a narrative account' and 'how far do you agree' style questions, which feature in all GCSE specifications.

Further reading and links

For teachers:

- *Death in Ten Minutes: The forgotten life of radical suffragette Kitty Marion* by historian Fern Riddell (Hodder & Stoughton, 2018) offers an insight into the tactics used by the suffragettes. Riddell refers to the history of the suffragette movement as 'uncomfortable history'. Have a read to find out why.

- The National Archives has a great webpage on the *Titanic* that looks at individual stories and has podcasts and videos. Go to nationalarchives.gov.uk/ and search 'Titanic'.

For students:

- *Things a Bright Girl Can Do* by Sally Nicholls (Andersen Press, 2018) is a wonderful YA book about the suffragette movement that will offer a new perspective for students. They can watch an interview with the author on the Oxford Education YouTube page. Search 'Sally Nicholls author interview' to find it.

- BBC Teach has some fantastic videos on the Liberal Reforms. Go to bbc.co.uk/bitesize/subjects/ and click History > Higher History > Britain (1851–1951) to find useful clips.

Beyond the classroom

- Students could research suffrage movements in other countries, or could research when British women gained equal political, economic and social rights with men.

- Go to www.processions.co.uk and navigate to 'Make your banner' to access teaching resources and toolkits with activities about women's suffrage. You could use these resources to help you arrange a cross-curricular day with the Art and Textiles department and create suffrage banners and flags. The day could follow the oral history tradition where the stories of the women are shared as the children sew and make. These stories can then be shared again and again.

- Students could watch the film *Titanic* (1997) and act as the history consultant. Does the film explore all of the causes of the sinking? They could then create a presentation for the class about the accuracy of the film and how they would advise the creative team.

- Students could watch the most recent political debates such as the leaders' debate from the latest general election and use these as a model for structuring a debate about the Liberal Reforms. Some students could represent those in support of the reforms while others take on the role of the opposition party. This would be a good opportunity to link with your Politics, Citizenship and/or PSHE departments to make the cross-curricular links explicit.

Answers guidance

The answers provided here are examples, based on the information provided in the Student Book. There may be other factors which are relevant to each question, and students may draw on as much of their own knowledge as possible to give detailed and precise answers. There are also many ways of answering questions, including exam-style questions (for example, of structuring an essay). However, these exemplar answers should provide a good starting point.

Timeline from 1901 to present day

PAGES 6–7

Over to You

1a Answers will vary.

1b Answers will vary.

2 Students will identify inventions and explain which they think has had the greatest impact or made the biggest change.

1.1A Britain and the world in 1901

PAGES 8–9

Over to You

1a Answers will vary but will focus on the fact that Source B shows poor quality, crowded housing, while Source C has wider, paved streets, lighting, larger housing etc.

1b Answers will vary but will cover the fact that Source B shows people with poor quality clothing, in dark, dirty conditions, while Source C shows cleaner, wider, well-lit shows and more affluent housing.

2a Answers will vary but may include that people were better fed, better clothed, healthier and more educated than many people in other nations around the world. Cities were full of shops that contained a wide range of goods, either made in British factories or brought in from parts of the British Empire. Largest empire the world had ever seen – Britain controlled over a quarter of the world (about 450 million people).

2b Answers will vary but may include that Britain was under threat from other nations – USA was now making more goods than Britain, and Germany and Japan were quickly catching up. Japan, Germany, Russia and the USA were serious military rivals too.

Interpretation Analysis

1 The author is saying that Britain's empire was huge ('vast') and at its height ('peak') around 1900. But other nations were looking for supremacy too.

2 Students should generally agree that there was a large divide between the rich and the poor at this time. The wealthier people of Britain lived a life of luxury. They owned land and homes, and many didn't have to work at all because they made so much money out of investments and rents. But this was not the way the vast majority of people lived. Many earned just enough to get by, often working in factories, mills or shipyards.

1.1B Britain and the world in 1901

PAGES 10–11

Over to You

1a Model T: car produced by Ford.

1b Baby Grand: plane created by the Wright Brothers.

1c Phonograph: device for playing music.

2 As a result of mass production and the assembly line – this allowed cars to be made quickly and at lower cost, so cars were cheaper.

3a Student posters will vary but will reflect the information on these pages and match the criteria.

3b Student posters will vary but will reflect Britain and the world today.

3c Answers will vary, but there will be similarities in some areas (e.g. we have telephones and still watch films and enjoy consumer goods) but there will be differences too (e.g. the differences in telephones). For example, the changes in travel (more cars, plane use), the different ways people watch films (online) etc.

Change

1 Student answers will cover speed of travel (travel got faster), modes of transport (cars, improved railway network), consumer goods more readily available (wristwatches, telephones, cameras), film more widely watched.

1.2A Tackling poverty and public health

PAGES 12–13

Over to You

1a • Booth investigated the lives of the poor in London.
• Rowntree investigated the lives of the poor in York.

1b People (including politicians) did not realise things were so bad.

2 Nearly one third of all men who volunteered to join the army failed their medical examination, so army leaders worried there might not be enough quality recruits to fight wars.

1.2B Tackling poverty and public health

PAGES 14–15

Over to You

1 Liberal Reforms: a series of new laws, ideas and measures to help some of the most vulnerable people in society.

2 Answers might include free medical checks and treatment, and detail from the Children's Charter.

3a Answer should include job centres and unemployment pay.

3b Answer should include sickness pay.

3c Answer should include banning the building of overcrowded back-to-back housing.

3d Answer should include pensions.

1 Weight increases during school time, e.g. during the first month of free school meals the average weight increased by about 1kg.

2 It went down.

3 It shows historians the impact of change, as it is first-hand data from the time.

1.3 Who or what was to blame for the *Titanic* disaster?

PAGES 16–17

Over to You

1 • Belfast
   • the evening of Sunday 14 April 1912
   • 2200, 704
   • Edward Smith
   • Atlantic, 1985

2a Examples might include: i) Smith = ignored ice warnings; ii) shipbuilders = poor quality materials; iii) Andrews = reduced height of watertight compartments; iv) Lord = ignored distress flares; v) Ismay = pressure on Smith to go fast, reduced lifeboat numbers.

2b Answers will vary but students should attempt to justify their order based on the hints in the question.

2c Answers will vary but should satisfy the criteria laid out in the Student Book in that students have started their report with a brief introduction to the disaster, outlined the role in the sinking of each factor under investigation and written a conclusion.

1.4A Who were the suffragettes?

PAGES 18–19

Over to You

1a Source A argues that women do not think about 'serious'

issues, and their minds are full of unimportant issues – so they should not have the right to vote because they are incapable of the sort of serious thought needed in politics. Source B makes the point that women can do worthy things in society yet not vote, while men can do things of no value to society and still vote.

1b The messages differ in that one (A) argues that women are capable of contributing to society, so should have the vote, while the other (B) argues that women are not capable of thinking about serious issues so shouldn't be allowed to vote.

2 They are similar in that they both seek to put pressure on government to grant women the right to vote, yet the tactics are different – suffragettes are more radical/extreme in approach whereas suffragists seek to put pressure on government in a non-violent way.

3a Leader of the suffragettes.

3b The violent campaigning would get national attention in the media, bringing the issue of votes for women to the masses.

1 Image shows all the worthy jobs women can do but not have the right to vote; it also shows the worthless things that men can do yet still be able to vote.

2 Answers will vary, but should mention that it shows the tactics of a particular group, the arguments they were using and the underlying philosophy of the movement.

1.4B Who were the suffragettes?

PAGES 20–21

Over to You

1 The suffragettes lost many supporters who did not want

to be associated with such destructive and dangerous tactics.

2 • The campaign of violence was called off and they asked their supporters to help the war effort as much as possible instead. The war brought women unexpected opportunities.
   • With more and more men leaving to become soldiers, women could 'fill in' for the men and do jobs they had never done before – bus drivers, police officers, car mechanics and road menders.

3 Women made a great impact on weapon production, mostly in line with men. They also had an impact on the Prime Minister who recognised their contribution.

4a 100 years since the WSPU, led by Emmeline Pankhurst, was formed and the government wanted to officially recognise the part played by them in the votes for women campaign.

4b Students' coins will vary but should reflect the votes for women campaign.

1 The author writes that the suffragette campaign did more harm than good, that the violence turned people against their cause and made Parliament more determined not to grant the right to vote.

2 This author argues that the suffragette campaign and what happened to them in prison gained lots of support for their cause from people who had not really cared about the issue before.

3 One (J) claims that the suffragette campaign made no (or even a negative) impact, whereas the other (K) claims that the suffragette campaign raised the profile of the cause.

4 Answers will vary, but both interpretations should be mentioned before the student argues which one they support.

1.5 History Mystery: Did Emily Davison mean to kill herself?

PAGES 22–23

Over to You

1a Answers will vary, but some students might say because she was going to pin them to things and wanted two in case one was confiscated; others might say to make sure, even in death, people knew she was a suffragette.

1b Answers will vary, but some students might say that she didn't tell anyone 'in case someone tried to stop her' or because she 'wasn't sure what she was going to do yet'.

1c Answers will vary.

2 Answers will vary, but students will probably put H in the 'trying to kill herself' category.

3 Answers will vary, but students will probably put E and G (the return train ticket) in the 'not trying to kill herself' category.

4 Student reports will vary, but they should cover the basic outline of the categories in the Student Book: they should give a basic outline of Davison's death, including details of Davison herself and the events before she was killed, then state clearly if they think she planned to make a protest or whether she planned to kill herself – or if they are not sure, state why – and back up any of their conclusions with evidence.

Chapter 1 Have you been learning?

Answers guidance

Chapter 1 Have you been learning?

Quick Knowledge Quiz

PAGE 24

1 c 1901
2 a her son, Edward, who became King Edward VII
3 b Model T
4 c Louis Bleriot
5 a Charles Booth
6 c the Liberal Reforms
7 b 1912
8 a Atlantic
9 a the suffragettes
10 b 1928

Literacy Focus

PAGE 25

Defining key words and terms

1a poor people in York.
1b Winston Churchill and David Lloyd George.
1c Children's Charter.
1d job centres (labour exchanges).
2b Consumer goods
  • New inventions that people bought such as electric irons.
  • After 1901 people started to buy new electrical inventions such as vacuum cleaners and electrical irons. People also bought goods for fun such as cameras and phonographs.

2c Assembly line
  • A system in a factory to make goods in stages.
  • A system in a factory to make goods in different stages. This was a success for Henry Ford who mass produced his Model T car this way.

2d Children's Charter
  • Liberal reforms to protect young people.
  • Liberal reforms that protected children in 1908. It stated that children under 14 were not allowed in pubs and that parents could be prosecuted for neglect.

2e Suffragists
  • A group formed in 1897 to campaign for the vote.
  • A group formed in 1897 that led a campaign for women to get the vote in general elections. They held meetings, wrote letters to MPs and went on marches.

2f Suffragettes
  • Formed in 1903 to use militant methods to get the vote.
  • Formed in 1903 as the suffragists were not successful. They were led by Emmeline Pankhurst and her daughters. They used violent tactics

2g 'Deeds not words'
  • The motto of the suffragettes.
  • The motto of the suffragettes that matched their tactics of chaining themselves to railings and setting fire to buildings.

Writing in detail

1 Example: The *Titanic* was a large passenger liner that sank in the middle of the Atlantic Ocean in April 1912. There were just over 2200 people on board, but only 704 were rescued. Nearly 1500 people died. There were several different factors that caused the ship to sink. For example… [here the students should mention some of the factors discussed on pages 16–17 of the Student Book].

Chapter 1 Assessment: Significance

Assessment summary

The assessments in this textbook have been carefully designed and tested with History teachers to support student progression throughout the course. This specific assessment is written to support Year 8 or Year 9 students in tackling questions relating to the significance of key events or people.

> Explain the significance of the Liberal Reforms in the improvement of care for vulnerable people. (20)

Students will build a picture of historical significance by firstly identifying who the Liberals were and what the Liberal Reforms were (Question 1). Then they will focus on the impact the reforms had at the time (Question 2) by considering how they changed things. The focus will then turn to the long-term impact of the Liberal Reforms (Question 3), before students consider their significance today (Question 4). This will lead to a conclusion where students make an overall judgement on their significance (Question 5).

Sentence starters, prompt questions and tips about the impact of the reforms are provided to support students with this assessment.

For the mark scheme, see page 54.

A note about the end-of-chapter assessments

There is an assessment for each Student Book chapter. Each is structured like a GCSE exam-style question, with scaffolding steps to support KS3 students. Each assessment has a total of 20 marks, and is designed to be completed in a typical lesson – each has been written with a time allowance of about 30 minutes.

There is a mark scheme for each assessment. You can choose how to give student outcomes: a mark out of 20; a percentage; a performance indicator (we use a three-stage indicator – 'Developing', 'Secure', 'Extending' – but you could adapt to match any performance indicators used in your school); or a GCSE grade indicator. To convert raw marks to a performance or GCSE grade indicator, use this table:

Raw marks			
0	1–6	7–13	14–20
GCSE grade (9–1) indicators*			
U	1–3	4–6	7–9
Performance indicator			
Ungraded	Developing	Secure	Extending

*Please appreciate that these are approximate grades based on grade boundaries from recent GCSE exam papers. If a student achieves a Grade 7 in one of these assessments, it is not the equivalent of a Grade 7 at GCSE. Instead it is an indicator of the grade the student could expect to get if they continue on their flight path through KS3 and GCSE. Please note:
- the raw-mark boundaries are based on but do not match precisely those for recent GCSE exam papers: this is because our assessments are focused around one exam-style question, likely to be done at the end of a chapter (topic) rather than at the end of the course. Secondly, we provide carefully considered scaffolded steps to allow KS3 students to tackle high level questions and gain confidence through the deliberate practice of building up detailed answers.
- the assessments for Student Book 3 are progressively more demanding in that they use higher-order command words and provide less scaffolded support – if you set one of them for Year 8 students, please take that into account when awarding GCSE grade indicators.

Entering student outcomes into the Kerboodle Markbook

The Kerboodle Markbook records scores and percentages to allow for quick comparison of performance. If you want to use the Markbook to record student outcomes, you will need to enter the appropriate values given in the raw marks row of the table above.

Links to GCSE

By the end of KS3, students should be familiar with the History skill of considering significance. At GCSE, most exam boards specifically ask students to consider the significance of an event, person or movement. For example:

AQA:

*   Explain the significance of… in/for… (8)

Edexcel:

*   How far do you agree with Interpretation 2 about the significance of…? (20)

OCR A:

*   How significant was…? (14)

Eduqas:

*   Arrange the [bullet points] in order of their significance in… Explain your choices. (9)

Links to KS3 History resources

Student Book

This assessment question links to these lessons:

1.2A/B Tackling poverty and public health

Kerboodle

Support for this assessment question on Kerboodle:

TW1 1 *Assessment presentation: Significance*
TW1 1 *Assessment worksheet (Core): Significance*
TW1 1 *Assessment worksheet (Foundation): Significance*

Curriculum and Assessment Planning Guide

Support for this assessment question in this guide:

1 Assessment mark scheme – page 54
1 Assessment sample student answers – pages 55–56

Student name: _____   Date: _____

Mark scheme

Assessment bands	Marks	GCSE grade indicators*	I have...
	0	Ungraded	
Developing	1–6	1–3	☐ given some basic information about the Liberal Reforms. ☐ supported my answer with examples of limited knowledge of Liberal Reforms.
Secure	7–13	4–6	☐ given a detailed description of the Liberal Reforms and attempted to explain one aspect of significance (short term, long term, or relevance today). ☐ supported my answer with accurate knowledge and understanding that is mostly relevant to the question.
Extending	14–20	7–9	☐ given a well-developed explanation and analysis of the significance of the Liberal Reforms at the time, their long-term impact, and their relevance in today's world. ☐ supported my answer with a range of accurate knowledge and understanding that is fully relevant to the question. ☐ concluded my answer with a judgement that gives my opinion about the significance of the Liberal Reforms.

* IMPORTANT: These are approximate indicators devised using publicly available information on the new GCSE grades. They are designed to assist in the process of tracking and monitoring. They cannot and should not be used to replace teachers' professional judgement. Teachers should use their own discretion in applying them, taking into account the cumulative test scores of an individual student (rather than just one assessment point), and should refer to their institution's assessment policy.

Mark: _____

Comment:

Sample student answers

Assessment: Significance

STUDENT BOOK PAGE 27

 Explain the significance of the Liberal Reforms in the improvement of care for vulnerable people. (20)

 ### Sample Developing band answer

The Liberal Party won the 1906 general election. They wanted to improve people's lives. David Lloyd George and Winston Churchill were both members of the Liberal Party. The Liberals brought in new laws which were to help the poor, one being the School Meals Act of 1906. Their reforms went on to improve the health of children.

 ### Sample Secure band answer

The Liberal Party came to power after the 1906 general election. They were a party who believed in helping the poor and improving the health of the nation. They introduced a series of reforms from 1906 which became known as the Liberal Reforms. The health of Britain was not good – this was highlighted when men went to join the army and they weren't fit enough to pass the medical test. The Liberals introduced reforms such as the School Meals Act of 1906 to combat the poor health of children. This meant that by 1914 over 158,000 children were having a free school meal each day. The Liberals also created a Children's Charter to protect young people. All of this meant that children became healthier, life expectancy started to rise and infant mortality rates dropped. This shows the impact of the Liberal Reforms because Britain became healthier in the long term and it was a big step in the government taking responsibility for helping the poor and improving the lives of people.

Sample Extending band answer

The Liberal Party was elected in 1906 and was a party that was committed to bringing in measures to fight poverty, improve the lives of ordinary people and raise the general level of public health. In the late 19th and early 20th centuries two reports had been published on the lives of the poor in Britain. These reports shocked people and made them feel that something had to be done to improve the health of the nation. Key individuals in the Liberal Party were Winston Churchill and David Lloyd George, who both later went on to become Prime Minister of Great Britain.

The Liberal Reforms were introduced from 1906 and included the School Meals Act which provided free school meals for the poorest children. By 1914, 158,000 children were having a free meal every day. This had a positive impact on the health of these children. The Liberal Reforms also helped other vulnerable people in society such as those who could not work due to injury or ill-health, and elderly people. Unemployment benefit, sick pay and pensions were all introduced to help people stay out of poverty.

At the time, the Liberal Reforms did not solve all of society's problems, but they did show that it was the government's responsibility to look after people who could not look after themselves. In the longer term the reforms did improve the health and welfare of Britain's poor. Life expectancy increased by eleven years for both men and women by 1930 and infant mortality rates started to drop too. The Children's Charter continued to protect children and parts of it still apply today. In conclusion the Liberal Reforms were significant for the improvement in the care of vulnerable people because they protected children and saved poor people from falling into more poverty. They were the foundation stones of further welfare and public health measures, and they led to many more reforms by future governments.

Links to KS3 History National Curriculum

Chapter 2 is a depth study of the First World War and the peace settlement, which is a specific example of subject content from the latest KS3 History National Curriculum. Students will, among other things, be required to read for meaning, understand and use historical terminology appropriately, place events in chronological order, and select and combine information from sources to complete tasks. They will analyse short- and long-term timescales and causes and explain the relationships between them.

The 'Meanwhile' feature enriches the content being delivered and gives students context and a real sense of period. The focus on the individual stories of war will allow students to see the humanity instead of being focused solely on the number of casualties – the scale is often too big for many students to comprehend. The enquiry questions that are built into this chapter also meet the demands of the National Curriculum where students are expected to be able to understand 'methods of historical enquiry, including how evidence is used rigorously to make historical claims, and discern how and why contrasting arguments and interpretations of the past have been constructed'.

Skills and processes covered in this chapter

		Lesson/activity in the Student Book
History Skills	Knowledge and understanding	2.1A Over to You: 1, 2a
		2.2 Over to You: 1, 2; Causation: 1, 2
		2.3A Over to You: 1a, 1b, 1c, 1d
		2.3B Over to You: 1a, 1b, 2, 3; Knowledge and Understanding: 1, 2
		2.4 Over to You: 1, 2; Knowledge and Understanding: 1
		2.5A Over to You: 1, 2, 3
		2.5B Over to You: 1a, 1b, 1c
		2.6 Over to You: 1, 2
		2.7A Over to You: 1a, 1b
		2.7B Over to You: 1a, 1b, 1c, 1d, 1e, 2; Consequences: 1
		2.8 Over to You: 1
		2.9 Over to You: 1a, 1b, 1c, 3a, 3b
		2.10A Over to You: 1, 2, 3a
		2.10B Over to You: 1a, 1b, 1c
		Have you been learning? Quick Knowledge Quiz: 1, 2, 3, 4, 5, 6, 7, 8, 9, 10
	Interpretation analysis	2.1B Interpretation Analysis: 1, 2
		2.2 Over to You: 4a, 4b
		2.5B Interpretation Analysis: 1, 2
		2.7B Over to You: 3a, 3b
		2.10B Interpretation Analysis: 1, 2
	Source analysis	2.2 Over to You: 3
		2.3A Source Analysis: 1, 2
		2.7A Over to You: 1c, 2a, 2b, 2c, 2d; Source Analysis: 1, 2
		2.8 Over to You: 3

		Lesson/activity in the Student Book
		2.10A Source Analysis: 1, 2
		2.10B Over to You: 2a, 2b, 2c, 2d
		2 Assessment Source Analysis (historic environment): 1, 2, 3
	Significance	
	Cause and consequence	**2.1A** Over to You: 2b, 2c, 3a, 3b, 3c
		2.1B Over to You: 1a, 1b, 1c, 1d, 2, 3, 4a, 4b
		2.2 Causation: 3
		2.3B Over to You: 3
		2.4 Over to You: 3
		2.5B Over to You: 1d, 2, 3
		2.6 Over to You: 3; Consequences: 1, 2
		2.7A Over to You: 1c
		2.7B Consequences: 2
		2.8 Over to You: 2, 4
		2.9 Over to You: 3a
		2.10A Over to You: 3b, 4
		2.10B Over to You: 1d
	Diversity/Similarity and difference	
	Change and continuity	**2.8** Change: 1
Literacy and Numeracy	Literacy	**2.6** Over to You: 2
		Have you been learning? Literacy Focus: 1, 2
	Numeracy	**2.9** Over to You: 2a, 2b

Lesson sequence

Lesson title	Student Book pages	Objectives
2.1A Why did the First World War start?	pp 28–29	• Identify short- and long-term causes of the First World War. • Explain how an assassination led to the outbreak of war.
2.1B Why did the First World War start?	pp 30–31	
2.2 Joining up	pp 32–33	• Outline the reasons why men chose to fight. • Define 'propaganda' and explain how the government used it to attract more volunteers.
2.3A The First World War: an overview	pp 34–35	• Examine the typical experience of a soldier in the trenches. • Identify the main areas of conflict and the main features of trench warfare.
2.3B The First World War: an overview	pp 36–37	
2.4 Weapons of war	pp 38–39	• Explain why the weapons used in the First World War were so deadly. • Judge which weapons were most effective.

Lesson title	Student Book pages	Objectives
2.5A Why was Harry Farr killed?	pp 40–41	• Examine how victims of 'shell shock' were treated during the First World War.
2.5B Why was Harry Farr killed?	pp 42–43	• Decide whether Harry Farr was a coward or the victim of cruel injustice.
2.6 How did the First World War change medicine?	pp 44–45	• Examine and explain the links between war and medical progress. • Assess the impact of the First World War on surgery, health and medicine.
2.7A Soldiers of Empire	pp 46–47	• Examine why soldiers from the British Empire fought for Britain.
2.7B Soldiers of Empire	pp 48–49	• Judge the contribution of these 'soldiers of Empire'.
2.8 What was it like on the home front?	pp 50–51	• Describe how the First World War affected everyday life in Britain. • Assess the effect of the First World War on the lives of women in Britain. • Explain how and why British civilians were at risk between 1914 and 1918.
2.9 How did 'Poppy Day' start?	pp 52–53	• Outline how the war came to an end in 1918. • Explain how and why 11 November is remembered today.
2.10A How did countries try to avoid any more wars?	pp 54–55	• Explain who the 'Big Three' were and how they contributed to the peace settlement.
2.10B How did countries try to avoid any more wars?	pp 56–57	• Judge whether the League of Nations was a success or a failure. • Examine opinions about the League of Nations.
Chapter 2 Have you been learning?	pp 58–59	• Choose the correct answer from the given options for a quick recap. • Ensure correct spellings and chronological order of events. • Categorise historical vocabulary and check understanding.
Chapter 2 History skill: Source analysis (historic environment)	pp 60–61	• Define historic environment. • Consider questions relating to historic environment.
Chapter 2 Assessment: Source analysis (historic environment)	pp 62–63	• Describe features in sources relating to trench warfare. • Assess the usefulness of sources relating to trench warfare.

Links to the GCSE curriculum

This chapter provides some historical context to the following:

AQA: The First World War 1894–1918

Edexcel: Crime and Punishment in Britain c1000–Present

Edexcel: The British Sector of the Western Front 1914–1918: Injuries, Treatment and the Trenches

Edexcel: Warfare and British Society c1250–Present

OCR A: The Changing International Order 1918–2001

OCR A: Monarchy and Democracy in Britain c1000–2014

OCR A: War and British Society c790–c2010

OCR B: Migrants to Britain c1250–Present

OCR B: Britain in Peace and War 1900–1918

Eduqas: Germany in Transition 1919–1939

Eduqas: Changes in Crime and Punishment in Britain c500–Present

Eduqas: Empire, Reform and War: Britain 1890–1918

Eduqas: The Development of Germany 1919–1991

Eduqas: The Development of Warfare in Britain c500–Present

WJEC: Germany in Transition 1919–1939

WJEC: Changes in Crime and Punishment c1500–Present

WJEC: The Development of Warfare c1250–Present

Exam-style questions covered in this chapter

Exam board	Lesson/activity question location	Command words	History skills/concepts
AQA	2.3A Source Analysis: 2	How useful…	Source analysis
	2.3B Knowledge and Understanding: 2	Describe…	Knowledge and understanding
	2.4 Knowledge and Understanding: 1	Describe…	Knowledge and understanding
	2.6 Consequence: 2	How far do you agree?	Cause and consequence
	2.8 Change: 1	In what ways…	Change and continuity
	2.10A Source Analysis: 2	How useful…	Source analysis
	2.10B Interpretation Analysis: 1	How does… differ from…	Interpretation analysis
Edexcel	2.3A Source Analysis: 2	How useful…	Source analysis
	2.2 Causation: 3	Explain why…	Cause and consequence
	2.3B Knowledge and Understanding: 2	Describe…	Knowledge and understanding
	2.4 Knowledge and Understanding: 1	Describe…	Knowledge and understanding
	2.6 Consequences: 1	Explain why…	Cause and consequence
	2.6 Consequences: 2	How far do you agree?	Cause and consequence
	2.10A Source Analysis: 2	How useful…	Source analysis
OCR A	2.2 Causation: 3	Explain why…	Cause and consequence
	2.3A Source Analysis: 2	How useful…	Source analysis
	2.3B Knowledge and Understanding: 2	Describe…	Knowledge and understanding
	2.4 Knowledge and Understanding: 1	Describe…	Knowledge and understanding
	2.5B Interpretation Analysis: 2	Do you think this interpretation…	Interpretation analysis
	2.6 Consequences: 1	Explain why…	Cause and consequence
	2.6 Consequences: 2	How far do you agree?	Cause and consequence
	2.7B Consequence: 2	Explain the part…	Cause and consequence
	2.10A Source Analysis: 2	How useful…	Source analysis
OCR B	2.1B Over to You: 2	Why do you think…	Cause and consequence
	2.3A Source Analysis: 2	How useful…	Source analysis
	2.6 Consequences: 1	Explain why…	Cause and consequence
	2.6 Consequences: 2	How far do you agree?	Cause and consequence
	2.10A Source Analysis: 2	How useful…	Source analysis
Eduqas	2.1B Interpretation Analysis: 2	Does the interpretation support…	Interpretation analysis
	2.2 Causation: 3	Explain why…	Cause and consequence
	2.4 Knowledge and Understanding: 1	Describe…	Knowledge and understanding
	2.7A Source Analysis: 2	What was the purpose…	Source analysis
	2.10B Over to You: 2d	What can be learned from…	Source analysis
WJEC	2.2 Causation: 3	Explain why…	Cause and consequence
	2.4 Knowledge and Understanding: 1	Describe…	Knowledge and understanding
	2.6 Consequences: 1	Explain why…	Cause and consequence
	2.7B Over to You: 1	Complete the sentences…	Knowledge and understanding

A brief history

2.1A/B Why did the First World War start?

The lesson starts with the context for the name: Great War. Students will then explore the long-term causes of the war by exploring the first order concepts of: militarism, nationalism and imperialism. The concept of the alliance system is consolidated with some map work that allows the students to see why this system would contribute to the start of the war. Next is the short-term cause: the spark of war. The students will be expected to read about the events of June–August 1914, before the outbreak of war, and link them to the domino theory. This is a great activity for showing students how events influence each other. They will then apply their knowledge and the skills developed in an 'explain' question that requires students to evaluate all the causes of the war.

2.2 Joining up

Students are introduced to the key terms of 'propaganda' and 'censorship'. The terms are given life with two excellent examples of propaganda posters from the time that each present war and the enemy in a particular way. They will then explore patriotism in all its guises, how this was used to encourage men to join the war effort and why it was not enough for some men who believed war was wrong under any circumstances (conscientious objectors). Students will consider the advantages and disadvantages of pals battalions on both the men and the wider community. You could encourage them to think about what it would be like to join up with their friends and if this would encourage them to do what many men did during the First World War.

2.3A/B The First World War: an overview

This lesson gives the students a solid understanding of the scale of the Western Front and a sense of how this was a global war by giving an overview of the different fronts and the nationalities of those fighting in key battles. They will explore the key details of trench warfare through photographs and artwork, which extends cultural capital. They will then analyse sources, applying their own knowledge. Further context is offered with a timeline of key battles on the Western Front and a labelled diagram of a trench showing conditions and layout. The diagram will help students to describe the features of trench warfare.

2.4 Weapons of war

Students will compare the different weapons available during the First World War using this visual spread

Timeline

28 June 1914
Archduke Franz Ferdinand is assassinated.

July 1914
The First World War begins.

1914
The First Battle of the Marne.

1915
The Women's Land Army is set up.

1915
Shell shock is diagnosed as an illness.

1916
Conscription is introduced to get more men to fight.

1916
The Battle of Jutland.

1916
The Battle of Verdun.

1917
The Third Battle of Ypres.

1918
The Battle of Amiens.

11 November 1918
The First World War ends.

January 1919
The Big Three meet at Versailles.

1920
The League of Nations is set up to try to avoid another war.

1921
Poppies are sold as an act of remembrance for the first time.

of information cards. The weapons are ranked for defensive ability, range and killing power, which provides an opportunity for you to link to the previous lesson on the nature of trench warfare. Students will consolidate their learning by completing a table that requires them to select statistics and relevant information about each weapon – this is a great exercise for summarising. The activities allow students to make a judgement on the ability of weapons to defend or attack; more able students should be encouraged to link back to the features of the trench system, layout and conditions.

A brief history continued

2.5A/B Why was Harry Farr killed?

This lesson starts by introducing shell shock, which was first defined as an illness in 1915 – your PSHE or RSE department will be able to offer you resources and support information around mental health. Students will work through a list of reasons why soldiers might have been put in front of the firing squad, before exploring the case study of Harry Farr who was shot for cowardice. Students will be expected to read transcripts from the court martial of Farr building their evidence for the enquiry. The second part of the lesson reveals the remaining evidence that they will use to make their judgement. Prepare for some heated debate!

2.6 How did the First World War change medicine?

Students will explore a positive consequence of war through this lesson on the development of medicine. This is a theme that has been explored in each book of the series so there is scope for change and continuity both within and across time periods. Students should use their prior learning on trench warfare to help them rank the developments in medicine in order of the impact they had on saving soldiers' lives. The final activity allows them to apply their knowledge of the different developments to make a judgment on the impact of the war on medicine.

2.7A/B Soldiers of Empire

The focus on people and their stories in this lesson will help the students engage in this necessary topic of the empire soldiers. Previous learning on the British Empire has been based around what Britain took from the colonies, but now we focus on the contribution of the men and women who lived in countries that were part of the empire. The map of the British Empire showing the work of other nations during the war will help students visualise the extent of this contribution. Sources provide further context and students are given the opportunity to analyse them. The lesson requires students to process lots of dates, statistics and names. The activities give them scope to consolidate this information, which they can then apply when explaining the part played by the empire troops in the First World War.

2.8 What was it like on the home front?

After learning about the developments of war on the front lines, this lesson will show students the impact of the war on civilians in Britain. Rationing, women's contribution to the war and the Defence of the Realm Act are all excellent areas for showing the various ways war can impact on the home front. The loss of men and the effect this has on communities will probably shock students. It will also provide context for the next lesson on remembrance and why it is so widespread. Students will be given the opportunity to use sources to describe the role of women during the war. They will then be expected to describe the ways Germany directly attacked British civilians during the war. This focus on different social groups during the war will enable them to develop a richer context and to show how lives changed during and because of the First World War.

2.9 How did 'Poppy Day' start?

Students will learn about the end of the war and will be invited to reflect on the impact the war has had. They will use the map to examine the number of war deaths for different nations and apply this information in a numeracy activity. Acts of remembrance are then explored. Students will read about why poppies started being sold in 1921 and how there came to be a two-minute silence every year in Britain to commemorate the end of the war. They will then explain why the poppy became a symbol of the First World War, which leads into discussion and debate around wearing the poppy.

2.10A/B How did countries try to avoid any more wars?

The lesson starts with the aims of the Big Three at Versailles after the war. This will not only build breadth and depth for KS3 but also links to many GSCE specifications whether directly or as context. Students will then evaluate reactions to the Treaty of Versailles and analyse sources focusing on these. Finally, they will be given the opportunity to explore the work of the League of Nations and give a judgement on whether it was a success or not. Further application is offered with a cartoon analysis exploring membership issues of the League of Nations and then with comparisons of interpretations about the Paris Peace Conference.

Further reading and links

For teachers:

- *1917* (2019) by Sam Mendes is a film set in the trenches of the First World War. Watching this will give you more of an insight into the trench system, the differences between the German and British trenches, and the different nationalities fighting. This will undoubtedly enrich the descriptions you can offer your students.

- The recent Centenary of the First World War means that there are lots of excellent resources available on this topic. This resource pack from the Red Cross focuses on volunteers and refugees. Visit redcross.org.uk and search 'World War One centenary'. The Red Cross also runs fantastic school workshops about refugees and asylum seekers if you want to link to current refugee crises.

- The novel *The Well of Loneliness* by Radclyffe Hall (1928) offers a diverse view of the war as the main character, a lesbian, tries desperately to join the war effort and goes to the Western Front as a mechanic.

For students:

- Students could read *All Quiet on the Western Front* (1929). It offers an insight into life in the German Army, the daily routine of the trenches, the battles, weapons and impact on the community at home. Once they have read it there are many other novels set during the First World War that you could recommend.

- BBC Bitesize have various clips about the First World War. In particular, the clip 'The impact of J R R Tolkien's experiences in the Somme in 1916' may offer students a new perspective on the war. Go to bbc.co.uk/bitesize/clips/ and click History > KS3 > World War One (in Modern World History section) > Class clips and search for the Tolkien clip.

Beyond the classroom

- There are many obvious suggestions for enrichment opportunities – battlefield tours or a trip to the Imperial War Museum, for example. But often, local museums do some 'outreach' work that might entail one of their education officers coming into your school with parts of uniform, weaponry, 'trench art', posters and so on. A call to your local museum might be really worthwhile.

- Local war memorials are a rich source of material, and an examination of and research project into one is a wonderful way of bringing tales of 'a corner of a foreign field' to your locality. Something as simple as a student seeing their surname on a memorial can engage them in a way that is not possible in the classroom.

- Students could research their local pals battalion. How many men joined and what was their fate?

- Ask students to read Carol-Anne Duffy's poem 'The Christmas Truce'. They should then create a display board about the Christmas Truce in 1914 and link it to elements of the poem.

Answers guidance

The answers provided here are examples, based on the information provided in the Student Book. There may be other factors which are relevant to each question, and students may draw on as much of their own knowledge as possible to give detailed and precise answers. There are also many ways of answering questions, including exam-style questions (for example, of structuring an essay). However, these exemplar answers should provide a good starting point.

2.1A Why did the First World War start?
PAGES 28–29

Over to You

1 • militarism: to take great pride in your country's armed forces.
   • alliances: groups of nations that agree to back each other up in a war.
   • imperialism: to gain control of land and people around the world and build an empire.
   • nationalism: to love your country and think it is superior to others.
2a • Triple Alliance: Germany, Austria-Hungary, Italy
   • Triple Entente: Britain, France, Russia
2b Russia could help France by forcing Germany and Austria-Hungary to split its forces in half because Germany would have to fight in two different areas.
2c Austria-Hungary could also attack Russia from another angle, forcing the Russians to fight on a wider front.
3a All would join together to help and prevent an accident.
3b All the countries would fall together because they are tied together.
3c The alliance system was like a rope that tied countries together and there was a danger that they could all get dragged into something.

2.1B Why did the First World War start?
PAGES 30–31

Over to You

1a Austria-Hungary blamed Serbia for killing Archduke Franz Ferdinand.
1b Russia had promised to protect Serbia against attack.
1c Belgium refused to let German troops pass through Belgium to attack France, so Germany simply attacked Belgium.
1d Britain had a deal to protect Belgium from attack (dating back to 1839).
2 When dominoes knock into each other there is little that can stop them, and the alliance system ensured that the outbreak of war was like this.
3 Answers will vary, but there should be some discussion of long-term and short-term causes.
4a Answers will include long-term causes (e.g. militarism, imperialism) and short-term causes (e.g. the assassination, breakdown of alliance system).
4b Long-term causes will include militarism, imperialism; short-term causes will include the assassination, breakdown of alliance system.

Interpretation Analysis

1 The author makes the point that it was not as big a cause as other causes. He states that it is not really as genuine as others. He thinks that the assassination was used by countries as an excuse to do what had been brewing up for many years.
2 Student answers will vary, some might agree that the assassination was the 'spark' that started something that had been building up for years; others might disagree and claim that war had been avoided for many years before

the assassination, so might have continued to be avoided if it were not for the assassination.

2.2 Joining up
PAGES 32–33

Over to You

1 • propaganda: false or misleading information used to spread a certain point of view.
   • conscription: government policy of forcing men to join the armed forces in wartime.
   • pals battalions: a group of friends or co-workers who enlisted to fight in the First World War together.
   • conscientious objectors: people who believe war is wrong and refuse to fight.
2 Answers may vary, but advantages include the increased likelihood of more men joining as a group, and that recruits were with friends. Disadvantage was that whole communities were robbed of men if that particular group of soldiers were involved in heavy fighting.
3 • A = proud British people, keen to defend the country. B = both men and women – to inspire anger. Women to get men to join and men to get revenge on the Germans.
   • A = appealing to pride and willingness to defend country. B = make people angry at the Germans.
   • Answers will vary, but both probably successful – and the fact that so many men joined perhaps supports this.
4a White feathers – a symbol of cowardice – were handed out to any man who seemed fit enough to fight, but was not in military uniform. This sort of public humiliation was enough to make some men join.
4b The humiliation and pressure from the soldier made Lang join up.

Causation

1 Over 1 million
2 2.5 million
3 A mixture of reasons – pride in country, anger at Germans, the propaganda campaign (e.g. posters), pals battalions – and, after 1916, conscription.

2.3A The First World War: an overview

PAGES 34–35

Over to You

1a True
1b False – fighting took place in other areas, such as Africa and the Pacific.
1c True
1d False – the Western Front stretched for over 640km through France and Belgium from the English Channel to Switzerland.

Source Analysis

1 Answers will vary but should mention weapons, defending the trenches from enemy attack, communication among soldiers.
2 Answers should reflect that it helps picture the fighting, gives detail on uniforms, weaponry etc., done at the time so should reflect what it was like.

2.3B The First World War: an overview

PAGES 36–37

Over to You

1a Questions will vary.
1b Answers will vary.
2 Answers will vary but should reflect the rules of censorship – that the government closely controlled information that might damage morale back home, lead to fewer people joining up to fight, or alert the enemy to British troops' movements.
3 Answers will vary, but students may mention the fact that detail has disappeared.

Knowledge and Understanding

1 Student definitions might vary but an example is: a type of combat in which opposing troops fight from trenches facing each other. (14 words)
2 Answers will vary, but students might refer to the fighting being done from heavily defended trenches dug into the ground where each side attacks each other. They might mention that a feature was the weaponry used to defend the trenches – barbed wire, machine guns etc.

2.4 Weapons of war

PAGES 38–39

Over to You

1 Answers will vary, based on students' own interpretations, but an example might be:
Weapon: Flamethrower
Range: Short range
Killing power: Low/medium killing power
Attack, defence or both?
Mainly used when attacking an enemy trench, but could be used in defence.
2 Answers will vary, but machine guns and artillery are commonly chosen, based on the casualties incurred by them.
3 Answers will vary, but most students tend to go for defence, based on the fact that it was hard to carry some of the weapons with you (e.g. machine gun) so they were static, which suited defending a place with the enemy coming towards you.

Knowledge and Understanding

1 Answers will vary, but should focus on the use of the latest technology and the high killing power of most of the weapons.

2.5A Why was Harry Farr killed?

PAGES 40–41

Over to You

1 • desertion: illegally leaving a military position without permission.
 • court martial: military court for trying soldiers accused of breaking the rules.
 • cowardice: lack of courage.
2 306
3 Answers will vary, but most students write that Haking seems to have tried to help Farr and Farr resisted, so Haking had to arrest him. They may say that Farr seems 'difficult' and didn't do as he was told, disobeying orders.

2.5B Why was Harry Farr killed?

PAGES 42–43

Over to You

1a To go against or say the opposite of what someone else is doing or saying.
1b Students should pick out the differences in the way Haking presents his case as an attempt to help Farr, with Farr becoming difficult, while Farr says how aggressive Haking was, and how threatening he was – which Haking does not mention.
1c Same basic outline of events: Farr not where he should be, Haking finds him, sends him to dressing station, then finds him again not where he should be – arrest.
1d People have their own version of the events they witness, they concentrate on different details, and sometimes lie about things.
2 To set an example, firmness needed to stop others doing the same.
3 Student opinions will vary, but they should be justified.

1 While there are genuine cases of shell shock, some soldiers perhaps make it up to get something out of it. And that the nation should not 'reward' cowards.

2 Student answers will vary but will probably reflect that the writer seems harsh and unsympathetic in thinking that the men are simply looking for compensation. Students will likely feel that there were genuine cases (like Harry Farr) and will not think the interpretation is a fair comment.

2.6 How did the First World War change medicine?
PAGES 44–45

Over to You

1 • shell shock: a nervous condition suffered by some soldiers exposed to the noise and chaos of battle.
   • blood transfusions: replacing lost blood with blood from a donor.
   • skin graft: taking a healthy piece of skin and attaching it to an injured place on a patient's body.

2 Student letters will vary but should briefly explain how the latest scientific and technological developments have helped surgeons. For example, advances in blood storage have meant that blood can get to patients quicker and large stores can be kept, which means fewer soldiers die from blood loss.

3 Answers will vary, but students should be able to justify the order.

Consequences

1 Answers will vary, but may include: governments of fighting countries spend lots of money on developing ways to get their injured soldiers back 'fighting fit' as soon as possible.

Doctors and surgeons work incredibly hard in wartime, often in battlefield situations, to develop their ideas in order to treat the injured. The huge numbers of wounded soldiers give them more opportunity to try new techniques.

2 Answers should agree with the quote to a large extent, and use several examples to illustrate this. For example, the First World War made a huge impact in the field of what is now known as plastic surgery. The war gave Harold Gillies, an army doctor, the opportunity to perform skin grafts on patients injured during the war. Queens Hospital in Kent opened in 1917 and provided over 1000 beds for soldiers with severe facial wounds by 1921. Over 5000 servicemen had been treated by 1921.

2.7A Soldiers of Empire
PAGES 46–47

Over to You

1a An Indian soldier (born in what is now Pakistan) who fought in the trenches in the First World War and won the Victoria Cross for bravery.

1b A soldier from a country in the British Empire who fought for Britain.

1c From B: to be loyal and show gratitude to Britain, to defend the king, not fighting was a sin. From C: for the honour of their country, as well as to maintain promises the country has made, to stand up for freedom. Sense of duty.

2a 'old lion' = Great Britain. 'young lions' = the colonies within the empire.

2b Colony nations – Canada, India etc.

2c The colony nations need to defend their father – the idea of family sticking together to fight a common enemy.

2d Answers will vary, but students may say very successful, and the numbers of recruits support this.

1 Australia

2 To get men to join the army to fight in the war, by telling them that their country has made a promise to Britain so must keep that promise and provide more recruits.

2.7B Soldiers of Empire
PAGES 48–49

Over to You

1a 2.5
1b Africa
1c India
1d Anzacs
1e West Indian

2 Answers will vary but might include: lack of education on it; if you don't live in the country, you tend not to know about things in other countries; most films/documentaries in Britain tend to show only the British side.

3a The empire's contribution was vital, it helped Britain win, and there was an idea that the empire relied on Britain – but in fact, during the war, Britain relied on the empire.

3b Answers will vary, but most students will agree and use examples from the book about the contribution of the empire.

1 Answers will include: Canada, Australia, Aboriginal and Torres Strait Islander people New Zealand, Māori and Pacific Islanders, Caribbean (including Jamaica, Trinidad and Tobago, Barbados, the Bahamas, Grenada, St Lucia and St Vincent), South Africa, India, Africa (including Nigeria, Gambia, Gold Coast (now Ghana), Kenya and Sierra Leone).

2 Answers will summarise the part played by a variety of colonies, with examples. For example, around 15,000 West Indians joined up, including nearly 10,000 from Jamaica. Soldiers also joined up from other places in the region, including Trinidad and Tobago, Barbados, the Bahamas, Grenada, St Lucia and St Vincent. West Indian troops were mainly used as labourers – carrying ammunition, digging trenches, building roads and loading ships and trains. And around 1.4 million Indians volunteered as both soldiers and labourers – the largest volunteer army the world had yet seen. Indian soldiers fought on the Western Front, in the Middle East and alongside British and Anzac troops during the Gallipoli campaign in Turkey.

2.8 What was it like on the home front?

PAGES 50–51

 Over to You

1 The civilian population and activities of a nation whose armed forces are engaged in a war abroad.

2 The 'Defence of the Realm Act' – the government thought it necessary to introduce rules and laws to protect sensitive information, improve production and preserve vital supplies.

3 In 1915, a Women's Land Army was created so women (known as Land Girls) could work in farming, replacing men called up to the military, as shown in Source B. Source C shows female engineers. With so many men away fighting, women were needed to do men's jobs.

4 The Germans flew huge inflatable airships – called Zeppelins – over the eastern parts of Britain, dropping bombs on towns and cities there. By the end of the war, over 50 Zeppelin air raids had

dropped over 5000 bombs, killing 557 people and injuring over 1300. German bomber planes attacked Britain too, and German battleships shelled seaside towns such as Scarborough and Whitby.

Change ⭐

1 Answers should focus on the new roles women had, and the opportunities that the war provided that were not available before wartime.

2.9 How did 'Poppy Day' start?

PAGES 52–53

Over to You

1a One major nation left (Russia) and another joined in (USA), bringing fresh troops and new equipment to the front.

1b 11am, 11 November 1918.

1c We buy and wear poppies, raising money for those affected by war, we have a two minutes' silence on Remembrance Sunday, a day which marks the anniversary of the end of the war.

2a Student charts will reflect the figures from major countries shown in the table.

2b Around 8 million.

3a US teacher Moina Michael campaigned to make the poppy a symbol of remembrance of those who had died in the war. Her idea caught on and by 1921 artificial poppies were sold in Britain to raise money for war widows and injured soldiers.

3b Answers will vary.

2.10A How did countries try to avoid any more wars?

PAGES 54–55

Over to You

1 The leaders of the most powerful winning countries – David Lloyd George, Prime Minister of Great Britain; Georges Clemenceau, Prime

Minister of France; Woodrow Wilson, President of the USA.

2 They were the leaders of the most powerful winning countries, and as world powers had more influence.

3a Answers will vary.

3b Answers will vary, but most students will likely say Clemenceau, based on the fact that Germany was treated harshly and this was what he wanted. Student answers should mention each of the three, though.

4 Germany was punished severely, had to take the blame, lost land and had severe limits placed on armed forces, making it weak. The reparations were crippling too – and Germany felt it was no more guilty of starting the war than any other nation.

Source Analysis

1 Student inferences will vary, but examples might be that the Germans felt that the treaty was wrong and they had been treated badly – they call it 'disgraceful'; the Germans felt that they were once one of the great nations – because the article mentions that the 'German people will *reconquer* their place among nations to which it is entitled'; there was a politically motivated anti-treaty media in Germany at this time that was concerned with reflecting key events of the time.

2 Answers will vary but should reference the fact that both are useful regarding the feelings within the media about German reactions, and the fact that the media often reflects public opinion. Shows historians who the Germans felt were responsible for the punishments and how the Germans felt about their nation ('the German people will reconquer their place among nations to which it is entitled').

2.10B How did countries try to avoid any more wars?

PAGES 56–57

Over to You

1a Clemenceau wanted the treaty to be much tougher on Germany, perhaps splitting it into smaller states. Wilson thought the treaty was too harsh (and even said that, if he were a German, he wouldn't sign it!). Lloyd George, despite coming home from France to a hero's welcome, wrote that if Germany 'feels unfairly treated she will find a way of getting revenge'.

1b The League hoped to solve any disputes by discussion rather than war. If one nation declared war on another, all the other member nations would stop trading with the invading country until a lack of supplies would bring the dispute to an end.

1c No army of its own, fewer than half the countries in the world joined – Germany wasn't allowed, and politicians in the USA voted against it – so this made it weaker.

1d Answers will generally be positive, and use examples from the list of successes provided (although better answers should mention problems it failed to deal with).

2a USA

2b An important part of a bridge that holds all the other stones in position, supporting their weight.

2c USA didn't join.

2d Britain thought the League would be weaker as a result of the USA's failure to join.

Interpretation Analysis

1 E: The treaty wasn't that bad – Germany lost after all. The reparations were tough, but Germany didn't pay them, the treaty was not properly enforced. F: The treaty should have either destroyed Germany or helped them recover – but it did neither and left them angry.

2 E writes that the peace settlement wasn't too bad, Germany lost and was punished – but the reparations were not all collected. F says that the peacemakers had the chance to either destroy Germany or help Germany, but did neither so left Germany 'humiliated and resentful' (something E makes no reference to).

Answers guidance

Chapter 2 Have you been learning?

Quick Knowledge Quiz

PAGE 58

1 **c** 1914 to 1918
2 **b** Germany, Austria-Hungary and Turkey
3 **b** conscientious objector
4 **a** men who joined up together with their friends and ended up in the same group in the army
5 **a** the Western Front
6 **c** no man's land
7 **c** poison gas
8 **b** Harold Gillies
9 **a** 2.5 million
10 **b** Treaty of Versailles

Literacy Focus

PAGE 59

Chronology and spelling

1
- Archduke Franz Ferdinand and Sophie arrived at Sarajevo train station at 9:28am.
  - They were driven towards the town hall to meet the mayor. Crowds lined the streets and the car drove slowly so that the royal couple could wave to the people.
- Seven Black Hand assassins waited for the car by the Cumurja Bridge. As the car passed, one of the Serbians threw a bomb at the royal couple. The bomb missed its target and exploded beneath the car behind, injuring several people.
- The Archduke's car sped off to the town hall. The Archduke cancelled the rest of his visit, but decided to check on those injured by the bomb before he went home.
- At 11:00am, he again got into the car – but it drove much faster this time! As it passed Schiller's Café, the driver was informed that he'd taken a wrong turn. He stopped to turn around.
- By coincidence, one gang member – 19-year-old Gavrilo Princip – was standing outside the café. He took out a pistol, walked towards the car and fired two shots.

Vocabulary check

2b Answers may vary but students may identify France, as the others are part of the trench system.
2c Answers may vary but students may identify conscientious objector, as the others are associated with joining the army whereas a conscientious objector was concerned with *not* joining.
2d Answers may vary but students may identify bayonet, as the others are related to explosives.
2e Answers may vary but students may identify mud, as the others are weapons.
2f Answers may vary but students may identify Jutland, which was fought at sea whereas the others were fought on land.
2g Answers may vary but students may identify Austria-Hungary, as the others are Allied nations fighting for the British Empire.

Assessment summary

The assessments in this textbook have been carefully designed and tested with History teachers to support student progression throughout the course. This specific assessment is written to support Year 8 or Year 9 students in tackling questions relating to source analysis (historic environment).

1   Describe two features of everyday life for British soldiers serving in the trenches on the Western Front. (4)
2   How useful are **Sources A** and **B** for an enquiry into everyday life for British soldiers serving in the trenches on the Western Front? Explain your answer, using both sources and your knowledge of the historical context. (12)
3   How could you find out more about life in the trenches of the Western Front during the First World War? Name two sources (other than **Sources A** and **B**) you could use, and explain your reasons. (4)

▼ **SOURCE A** A British look-out in a captured German trench in 1916; note the other soldiers asleep in the trench.

▼ **SOURCE B** Adapted from an article written by Robert Donald for the British newspaper the *Daily Chronicle*, August 1915. Donald was the paper's editor and visited the Western Front several times, reporting back on his findings.

'The soil is soft clay, suitable for building trenches, tunnelling, and mine warfare – when it is dry. As an outside observer, I do not see why the war in this area should not go on for a hundred yeasrs, without any decisive result. What is happening now is precisely what happened last year. The only difference is that the trenches are deeper, dug-outs better made, tunnels are longer, and the charges of explosives heavier.

> Everywhere there are trenches, barbed wire, machine guns where they are least expected, and all the complicated arrangements for defence. The trenches are very deep, very narrow, and very wet. Streams of water run at the bottom.
>
> You are allowed to peer through an observation post towards the German trenches a few hundred yards away. You see absolutely nothing but a mass of broken trees, hanging branches and barbed wire.'

Students will start by describing features of everyday life in the trenches (Question 1). This will then lead to an analysis of the two sources to show utility (Question 2), before students consider the source limitations by naming other sources that could provide more information about everyday life in the trenches (Question 3).

For the mark scheme, see page 73.

A note about the end-of-chapter assessments

There is an assessment for each Student Book chapter. Each is structured like a GCSE exam-style question, with scaffolding steps to support KS3 students. Each assessment has a total of 20 marks, and is designed to be completed in a typical lesson – each has been written with a time allowance of about 30 minutes.

There is a mark scheme for each assessment. You can choose how to give student outcomes: a mark out of 20; a percentage; a performance indicator (we use a three-stage indicator – 'Developing', 'Secure', 'Extending' – but you could adapt to match any performance indicators used in your school); or a GCSE grade indicator. To convert raw marks to a performance or GCSE grade indicator, use this table:

Raw marks			
0	1–6	7–13	14–20
GCSE grade (9–1) indicators*			
U	1–3	4–6	7–9
Performance indicator			
Ungraded	Developing	Secure	Extending

* Please appreciate that these are approximate grades based on grade boundaries from recent GCSE exam papers. If a student achieves a Grade 7 in one of these assessments, it is not the equivalent of a Grade 7 at GCSE. Instead it is an indicator of the grade the student could expect to get if they continue on their flight path through KS3 and GCSE. Please note:
  * the raw-mark boundaries are based on but do not match precisely those for recent GCSE exam papers: this is because our assessments are focused around one exam-style question, likely to be done at the end of a chapter (topic) rather than at the end of the course. Secondly, we provide carefully considered scaffolded steps to allow KS3 students to tackle high level questions and gain confidence through the deliberate practice of building up detailed answers.
  * the assessments for Student Book 3 are progressively more demanding in that they use higher-order command words and provide less scaffolded support – if you set one of them for Year 8 students, please take that into account when awarding GCSE grade indicators.

Entering student outcomes into the Kerboodle Markbook

The Kerboodle Markbook records scores and percentages to allow for quick comparison of performance. If you want to use the Markbook to record student outcomes, you will need to enter the appropriate values given in the raw marks row of the table above.

Links to GCSE

By the end of KS3, students should be familiar with the History skill of analysing sources. At GCSE, most exam boards specifically ask students to analyse sources. In some cases, the sources can relate to a specific place (historic environment). For example:

Edexcel:

- Describe two features of... (4)

- How useful are Sources A and B for an enquiry into...? Explain your answer, using Sources A and B and your knowledge of the historic context. (8)

- How could you follow up Source A to find out more about...? In your answer, you must give the question you would ask and the type of source you could use. (4)

OCR A:

- Study Sources D and E. Which of these sources is more useful to a historian studying...? (10)

OCR A:

- How useful are Sources B and Interpretations C and D for a historian studying...? In your answer, refer to the source and the two interpretations as well as your own knowledge. (15)

Links to KS3 History resources

Student Book

This assessment question links to these lessons:

2.3A/B *The First World War: an overview*
2.4 *Weapons of war*
2.5A/B *Why was Harry Farr killed?*

Kerboodle

Support for this assessment question on Kerboodle:

TWI 2 *Assessment presentation: Source analysis (historic environment)*
TWI 2 *Assessment worksheet (Core): Source analysis (historic environment)*
TWI 2 *Assessment worksheet (Foundation): Source analysis (historic environment)*

Curriculum and Assessment Planning Guide

Support for this assessment question in this guide:

2 *Assessment mark scheme – page 73*
2 *Assessment sample student answers – pages 74–75*

Student name: _____   Date: _____

Mark scheme

Assessment bands	Marks	GCSE grade indicators*	I have...
	0	Ungraded	
Developing	1–6	1–3	☐ identified one feature of everyday life for British soldiers serving in the trenches on the Western Front, without describing it in detail. ☐ completed one thing learned for each source from these categories: content, caption and context. ☐ given a basic description of the usefulness of each source. ☐ identified one new source to follow up, without providing reasons.
Secure	7–13	4–6	☐ described one feature of everyday life for British soldiers serving in the trenches on the Western Front in some detail, or identified two features without describing them. ☐ completed some (perhaps two of the three – but not all) of the boxes for each source relating to content, caption and context. ☐ concluded about the usefulness of each source, with some relevant supporting knowledge. ☐ identified two new sources to follow up, with basic explanations of why they're useful.
Extending	14–20	7–9	☐ described two features of everyday life for British soldiers serving in the trenches on the Western Front with precise, detailed supporting knowledge. ☐ described two things learned from each source from *each* of these categories: content and caption, *and* explained one thing I already know about everyday life for British soldiers serving in the trenches on the Western Front (context) that relates to each source. ☐ concluded about the usefulness of each source with detailed accurate, relevant supporting knowledge. ☐ identified two new sources to follow up, with clear, detailed explanation of why they are useful.

* IMPORTANT: These are approximate indicators devised using publicly available information on the new GCSE grades. They are designed to assist in the process of tracking and monitoring. They cannot and should not be used to replace teachers' professional judgement. Teachers should use their own discretion in applying them, taking into account the cumulative test scores of an individual student (rather than just one assessment point), and should refer to their institution's assessment policy.

Mark: _____

Comment:

Sample student answers

Assessment: Source analysis (historic environment)

STUDENT BOOK PAGES 61–63

1 Describe two features of everyday life for British soldiers serving in the trenches on the Western Front. (4)
2 How useful are **Sources A** and **B** for an enquiry into everyday life for British soldiers serving in the trenches on the Western Front? Explain your answer, using both sources and your knowledge of the historical context. (12)
3 How could you find out more about life in the trenches of the Western Front during the First World War? Name two sources (other than **Sources A** and **B**) you could use, and explain your reasons. (4)

 Sample Developing band answer

1 Soldiers repaired the trenches.

2 Source A is useful for an enquiry into everyday life in the trenches as it shows that the men had to do guard duty. Source B is useful as it shows the trenches were full of water which the men had to stand in.

3 I would find out more about everyday life in the trenches from soldiers who kept diaries or wrote about their experiences.

 Sample Secure band answer

1 The men had to do guard duty. They also had to repair any damaged trenches.

2 Source A is a photograph of a captured German trench taken in 1916. The source provides information about the daily routine of the men in the trenches. From the content I have learned that men had to do guard duty but that if they were not on duty they could sleep. This is useful because it shows two sides of everyday life in the trenches. Although there was a lot of fighting, the men did get time to relax and would write letters home and play games. Source B is a British newspaper report from 1915, by a journalist who had visited the Western Front many times. The source provides information on the conditions of the trenches – for example, it tells us how the weather affected the trenches. From the content I have learned that the men would have to live in trenches with water running down the middle. This is useful because it shows how they got trench foot.

3 I would find out more about everyday life in the trenches with the novel *All Quiet on the Western Front*. This would give me more perspective of the day-to-day routine in the trenches and would provide insight into how the men felt. Another source I would also use is the court martial notes of Harry Farr who was killed for cowardice.

Sample Extending band answer

1   Trenches were built quickly, and were often damaged by shells, which meant the men had to spend some of their time repairing and rebuilding them. Another feature of everyday life in the trenches was that the men's health was at risk because of the poor conditions. Lice and rats were a big problem, and as the weather could be cold and wet, the men would often develop illnesses such as bronchitis.

2   Source A is a photograph of a captured German trench in 1916. It shows one soldier on guard duty, watching the enemy, while the rest of the men sleep. The source shows the reality of everyday life in the trenches – for much of the time there was a lot of waiting around. The source is also useful as it shows the terrible conditions in the trenches due to the wet weather. One thing I already know is that soldiers slept in the trenches in dugouts, and this makes the source useful because it shows the reality of trench life. Source A is quite useful for someone studying everyday life in the trenches as it shows both sides of trench life – solders on and off duty – and gives an insight into the conditions of the trenches. However as it is a photograph of the British after capturing a German trench we might need to be cautious as it could be used as propaganda in some way.

Source B is from an article written by Robert Donald who was a British journalist. He wrote the article in 1915 but he had visited the Western Front many times reporting on his findings. The source is useful as it gives detailed descriptions of the conditions in the trenches. It mentions how the trenches have got better but that they are at their best when it is dry, not when it is wet. This is useful as it shows us that the soldiers had to deal with the weather on top of everything else. The source goes on to say that there was a stream of water running down the middle of the trench – this is useful as we know that this is what caused trench foot and other conditions which made everyday life difficult. One thing I already knew about everyday life in the trenches was that the men had to do guard duty. This is supported by the source when it mentions the observation post. This makes the source very useful as it talks about a key feature of trench design but also the jobs and routines of trench life. However, as with Source A, it is a report for a British newspaper which may mean it was written to sound more positive than in reality.

3   I would find out more about everyday life in the trenches from the novel *All Quiet on the Western Front*. I would use this source as although it is fiction it is based on the real experience of soldiers, in this case a German soldier. It gives details of daily routine, trench structure and the personal opinions of those fighting.

Another source I would use for information is the court martial trial of Harry Farr who was killed by a firing squad for cowardice. This would tell us about the impact of everyday life on the soldiers and would give us details of attacks and the mental, not just physical, health of those fighting.

Chapter 3 Between the wars

Links to KS3 History National Curriculum

Life for different groups after the First World War changed dramatically and this chapter shows students how society changed for women, workers and the people of Ireland. The events studied offer context to key developments in the decade after the war such as the roaring twenties and the onset of the Great Depression. The latest KS3 History National Curriculum mentions the inter-war years and the Great Depression as possible areas of study. This chapter focuses on Britain at this time and students are given the opportunity to think deeply about the process of change, cause and consequence, and similarity and difference. They are invited to assess Britain's place in the wider world and are asked to make links between events and show how one event can lead to another: for example, the Wall Street Crash leading to the Great Depression and the impact that had on the shipbuilders of Jarrow.

The study on Ireland shows how Britain's empire is changing and gives the students a new sense of revolution and rebellion with the Easter Rising and the eventual Wars of Independence. This is essential context for the period but also subsequent chapters on Ireland. This, along with the growing influence of the United States, links with the National Curriculum demands that students should study a 'significant society or issue in world history and its interconnections with other world developments'.

The chapter introduces new key terms such as 'nationalist' and 'unionist' and has a focus on source analysis and writing to support judgements.

Skills and processes covered in this chapter

		Lesson/activity in the Student Book
History Skills	Knowledge and understanding	3.1A Over to You: 1a
		3.1B Over to You: 1a; Change: 1
		3.2 Over to You: 1a, 1b, 1c, 1d, 2, 3
		3.3 Over to You: 1a, 1b, 2a, 2b, 3
		3.4A Over to You: 1a, 3a; Interpretation Analysis: 1
		3.4B Over to You: 2, 3a
		Have you been learning? Quick Knowledge Quiz: 1, 2, 3, 4, 5, 6, 7, 8, 9, 10
	Interpretation analysis	3.1A Over to You: 2a, 2b
		3.1B Over to You: 2a, 2b
		3.4A Interpretation Analysis: 2, 3
		3.4B Interpretation Analysis: 1, 2
		3 Assessment: Interpretation analysis: 1, 2, 3
	Source analysis	3.1A Over to You: 3
		3.2 Source Analysis: 1, 2
		3.4A Over to You: 2a, 2b, 3a, 3b
	Significance	
	Cause and consequence	3.1A Over to You: 1b
		3.1B Over to You: 1b, 1c
		3.2 Over to You: 3
		3.3 Over to You: 1b, 2c, 3
		3.4A Over to You: 1b, 3a, 3b
		3.4B Over to You: 1, 3b, 3c

		Lesson/activity in the Student Book
	Diversity/Similarity and difference	3.1B Over to You: 3a, 3b
	Change and continuity	3.1A Over to You: 2
		3.1B Change: 2
Literacy and Numeracy	Literacy	**Have you been learning?** Literacy Focus: 1

Lesson sequence

Lesson title	Student Book pages	Objectives
3.1A Was the First World War worth winning?	pp 64–65	• Examine the state of Britain in the decade after the First World War ended.
3.1B Was the First World War worth winning?	pp 66–67	• Judge the extent to which Britain changed.
3.2 The 'Roaring Twenties'	pp 68–69	• Define the term 'Roaring Twenties'. • Outline why and how society changed for some people in the 1920s.
3.3 Independence in Ireland	pp 70–71	• Define a 'nationalist' and 'unionist'. • Analyse how and why Ireland was divided.
3.4A The 'Hungry Thirties'	pp 72–73	• Define the term 'Hungry Thirties'.
3.4B The 'Hungry Thirties'	pp 74–75	• Assess the diverse range of experiences of ordinary British citizens in the 1930s.
Chapter 3 Have you been learning?	pp 76–77	• Choose the correct answer from the given options for a quick recap. • Write down the important words from sentences to practice note-taking.
Chapter 3 History skill: Interpretation analysis	p 78	• Explore how to analyse an interpretation.
Chapter 3 Assessment: Interpretation analysis	p 79	• Assess an interpretation of the impact of the Depression on ordinary people in the 1930s. • Judge how far you agree with an interpretation of the impact of the Depression on ordinary people in the 1930s.

Links to the GCSE curriculum

This chapter provides some historical context to the following:

AQA: Power and the People c1170–Present

OCR A: The Changing International Order 1918–2001

OCR A: The USA 1919–1948: The People and the State

OCR B: Britain in Peace and War 1900–1918

Eduqas: The Development of the UK 1919–1990

WJEC: Depression, War and Recovery 1930–1951

Exam-style questions covered in this chapter

Exam board	Lesson/activity question location	Command words	History skills/concepts
AQA	3.1B Over to You: 2b	How useful…	Interpretation analysis
	3.2 Over to You: 3	In what ways…	Change and continuity
	3.2 Source Analysis: 2	How useful…	Source analysis
Edexcel	3.1B Over to You: 2b	How useful…	Interpretation analysis
	3.2 Source Analysis: 2	How useful…	Source analysis
	3.3 Over to You: 3	Explain why…	Cause and consequence
OCR A	3.1B Over to You: 2b	How useful…	Interpretation analysis
	3.2 Source Analysis: 2	How useful…	Source analysis
	3.3 Over to You: 3	Explain why…	Cause and consequence
OCR B	3.1B Over to You: 2b	How useful…	Interpretation analysis
	3.2 Source Analysis: 2	How useful…	Source analysis
	3.3 Over to You: 3	Explain why…	Cause and consequence
	3.4A Interpretation Analysis: 3	If you were asked… interpretation…	Interpretation analysis
Eduqas	3.1B Change: 2	How far did…	Change and continuity
	3.4B Interpretation Analysis: 2	To what extent…	Interpretation analysis
WJEC	3.2 Over to You: 1	Complete the sentences…	Knowledge and understanding
	3.3 Over to You: 3	Explain why…	Cause and consequence

A brief history

3.1A/B Was the First World War worth winning?

At the start of the lesson students are reminded about the human loss of the war and how this affected communities. However, the lesson then focuses on the diverse history post-war with some groups benefiting and others who did not. Students will find the image and details about unemployed ex-soldiers questioning the war very thought-provoking. The positive changes after the war will be recognisable as the foundations for the welfare state we have today. Case studies on the lives of women and the General Strike give much needed context to the inter-war period. The activities allow students to evaluate change and continuity in this period.

3.2 The 'Roaring Twenties'

How people spent their leisure time has featured in every book of the series. Students will enjoy seeing how young people responded after the war to be part of the 'Roaring Twenties'. To fully understand the phenomenon of the 'flapper', students must consider how women's roles changed through the war and then after – this is good practice for exam questions in all GCSE specifications. The influence of the United States on culture is an exciting opportunity to play music and show film clips to give the students an even deeper sense of period. The source analysis activity gives students a chance to apply what they have learned about seaside resorts. Higher ability students could include content from Book 2 (*12.5B How did people have fun in Victorian times?*) on the rise of people spending their time at the seaside in the late 1800s.

3.3 Independence in Ireland

This lesson starts with the much-needed context of the relationship between Britain and Ireland. The key terms of 'nationalist' and 'unionist' are important and students must be encouraged to use them when discussing and writing about the period. This will help them when they write about the divisions in Ireland. The Easter Rising is an engaging story that is a real turning point in Irish history. There are some great individuals in this story who should not be overlooked, for example Countess Markievicz, a Sinn Fein politician who was the first woman to be elected as a British MP, in 1918, but she refused to take her seat as a protest. You could set students a research task to find out more about the key players in the movement for Irish independence. This knowledge would enrich the application activities where students explain different interpretations of the Easter Rising.

Timeline

1916
The Easter Rising in Ireland. A group of nationalists take control of Dublin.

1918
The Education Act sets the minimum school leaving age to 14.

1918
The Representation of the Peoples Act gives women over 30 the right to vote, as long as they own property.

1919
The Irish Republican Army is created.

Ministry of Health set up.

1921
Two million people are unemployed in Britain.

December 1921
The Anglo-Irish Treaty is signed, which divides Ireland.

1922
The BBC is set up to 'educate, inform and entertain'.

1926
The General Strike lasts for nine days.

1928
All women over 21 are given the right to vote.

1929
The Wall Street Crash leads to the Great Depression.

1936
The Jarrow March takes place.

A brief history continued

3.4A/B The 'Hungry Thirties'

The diverse voices of the 1930s will show students what life was like for different people in the decade. The students will be introduced to the Great Depression and its impacts. A focus on the Jarrow March highlights the issues people faced in industry after the Depression and how this affected women and families, not just the men who worked. The lesson then goes on to look at the people who prospered in the 1930s in the new industries such as car manufacturing. The students also get a sense of regional divides, something that they can still relate to Britain today. More able students could make this comparison when they are asked to summarise an interpretation about British industry in the 1930s.

Further reading and links

For teachers:

- The historian Diarmaid Ferriter's book *A Nation and Not a Rabble: The Irish Revolution 1913–1923* (Profile Books, 2015) offers an insight into the role of women and other key individuals during the Irish revolution.

- The National Archives have fantastic resources designed for A-Level students that give more detail on legislation surrounding the General Strike. Go to nationalarchives.gov.uk/ and search 'Cabinet papers', then click A-level resources > The General Strike.

For students:

- Read the novel *Star by Star* by Sheena Wilkinson (Little Island Books, 2017). This follows the life of a suffragette who is orphaned by the Spanish Flu after the First World War. The book gives a fascinating insight into the changing role of women in the 1920s, regional differences after the war and the life of ex-soldiers.

- BBC Teach has a fantastic video of a student from Jarrow finding out more about the march. It gives more detail of what happened once the marchers reached London. Go to bbc.co.uk/teach/ and click on Class Clips > Secondary > History 14–16 > Exploring the Past: The history of protest in the UK > The Jarrow March.

Beyond the classroom

- A trip to Dublin to Kilmainham Gaol will add depth to the history of the Easter Rising as students can see the cells that those involved were kept in and how the British treated them.

- Many living museums have exhibitions and displays of life in your local area in the 1920s and 1930s. A trip to your local museum can give students a real sense of what life was like for different groups, how people spent their free time and the problems they faced.

- Students could link up with the Geography department and look at housing areas in a local town or city. Which areas were built during the 1920s and 1930s? The Geography department will almost certainly be able to show you a 'land use model' that includes inter-war developments.

- A cross-curricular day with the English department would be a great opportunity to explore 1920s fiction. The day could revolve around the students presenting the historical context for their English teachers and the literature to their History teachers.

- Get students to research the industry linked to their local area. They should find figures for production before, during and after the First World War and then create a whole year assembly to show the impact war, changing society and the Great Depression had on their area.

Answers guidance

The answers provided here are examples, based on the information provided in the Student Book. There may be other factors which are relevant to each question, and students may draw on as much of their own knowledge as possible to give detailed and precise answers. There are also many ways of answering questions, including exam-style questions (for example, of structuring an essay). However, these exemplar answers should provide a good starting point.

3.1A Was the First World War worth winning?
PAGES 64–65

Over To You

1a A person who wishes to work but is unable to get a job.

1b Industries that had done well in Britain during the war – coalmining, ship-building and steel-making – were not doing as well now the war was over, since there was less demand for their products, so fewer workers were needed. Also, countries such as Japan and the USA had started to make the things that Britain had traditionally made – so other nations often bought from these rivals, rather than Britain, so again, the factories needed fewer workers.

2 Answers might include: School-leaving age raised to 14, children with SEN were recognised, pensions were increased, work found for ex-soldiers and new laws protected tenants. Teachers' and farm workers' wages increased and a 'Ministry of Health' created to improve healthcare. 200,000 new homes were built that could be rented from local councils. (49 words)

3 Student answers will vary but most will probably say that this man did not think the war was worth winning because, despite being awarded the medals he proudly shows, he is still starving.

4 While some things were not completed (such as the amount of housing), the most important change was in the way politicians thought. The changes laid the foundations for future change.

3.1B Was the First World War worth winning?
PAGES 66–67

Over To You

1a A strike of workers in all or most industries.

1b In support of coal miners who were about to have their pay reduced and their hours of work increased.

1c In 1927, the government introduced a new law making general strikes illegal – a similar law is in force today.

2a He couldn't get a job, and felt unfairly treated.

2b Answers will vary but should mention how interpretations like this demonstrate the strike's impact on a person, and show reasons for other things – such as emigration.

3a • Property-owning woman in 1918: answers may vary but may say that they would be happier as a result of electoral reform, although their role in the job market was quite similar, based on the chart.
• Unemployed worker in 1922: answers may vary but may say that they would be unhappy as a result of high unemployment, but hopeful of change.
• Someone living in a newly built council house: answers may vary but may say that they would be happy with the social reforms but concerned about unemployment.

3b Students may say that people's lives are different, and have different experiences, even if they live in the same country in the same period of history.

1 It shows that women's roles changed little between 1914 and 1931.

2 There were positive and negative changes. In 1918 women aged over 30 who owned property were given the right to vote (this totalled around 8.5 million women). Also, a new law made it illegal to exclude women from jobs because of their gender. As a result, more jobs became open to women and they became lawyers and politicians, for example. And in 1928 all women over 21 were given the vote. Now women had the same voting rights as men. However, on the negative side, when the men returned home from battle, they simply went back to the jobs they had been doing before, and most of the women who had replaced the men during wartime went back to looking after the home and children. By the 1930s, women were doing much the same work as they had done before the First World War.

3.2 The 'Roaring Twenties'
PAGES 68–69

Over to You

1a 1922
1b lidos
1c Charleston
1d *The Jazz Singer*
2 A woman who cut her hair short and wore shorter dresses. Some flappers smoked and drank openly, drove motorbikes and wore heavy make-up.
3 British people began to copy American entertainment and fashions. For example, the style of 'flappers' became common, and US jazz music could be heard in British nightclubs as people danced the 'Charleston'

and 'One Step'. US films and movie stars became popular and they even influenced how people spoke.

1 It is photograph from 1900 of Blackpool seafront, a popular seaside resort at this time. There were many key attractions that drew holidaymakers there. For example, there was a pier to walk along, Blackpool Tower, and amusements such as a 'big wheel'. The beach was also an attraction – it is very crowded, with people paddling. There are also bathing huts near the sea where people got changed (67 words).

2 Student answers will reflect how the photograph is useful because the crowds clearly indicate the popularity of Blackpool, and the amount of attractions built reflect the fact that people must have come to use them. However, they may say that this only shows Blackpool on one day – we do not know whether this was a particular event – so what about other days? And we do not know about the popularity of other resorts.

3.3 Independence in Ireland
PAGES 70–71

Over to You

1a The Union flag is a combination of the individual flags of England, Scotland and Ireland. If students draw diagrams they will show the various elements to the Union Flag.

1b Answers will vary but may focus on the fact that the England flag is on top/ dominates the flag, while the other nations are underneath, as if England has them under control.

2a Nationalists wanted Ireland to have its own Parliament and run itself, while unionists, who lived mainly in the north, supported the 'union' between Ireland and Britain.

2b In April 1916, a group of nationalists took control of Dublin and declared independence. The British sent in troops to deal with the situation and after five days the Easter Rising had been stopped.

2c Nationalists, because they wanted an independent Ireland, and this was an attempt to achieve this.

3 In 1921, the northern part of Ireland (where the majority of people were unionists) remained part of Britain (Northern Ireland), while southern Ireland (mainly nationalists) became the Irish Free State and ran its own affairs (but remained part of the British Empire).

3.4A The 'Hungry Thirties'
PAGES 72–73

Over to You

1a Students may write that the worst hit areas are shaded red and orange, but should also explain where these places are – Northern England, Scotland, Wales (especially south), Northern Ireland.

1b Coal, iron, steel and cloth were produced in these areas, and there was less demand for these materials, so fewer workers were needed.

2a Husband's physical appearance has changed, and they cannot buy or enjoy the things they used to do.

2b Word choices will vary, but may include 'upset', 'frustrated', 'depressed', 'worried', 'determined' etc.

3a To draw attention to the plight of the unemployed in the north-east town of Jarrow.

3b Capital city, a long way from Jarrow so it was a chance to drum up support/sympathy.

1 Jarrow's local MP.

2 Little impact overall, failed to win special attention for their cause, but the marchers themselves were generally well received.

3 Answers will vary, but they might look at the lives of some of the individuals on the march and see' what happened next' or perhaps at the MP Ellen Wilkinson herself. They might choose to research the government response to the crisis.

3.4B The 'Hungry Thirties'
PAGES 74–75

Over to You

1 Some industries, such as car making and radio manufacturing, were doing better because they were becoming very popular and more affordable. Some areas (like the northeast of England and parts of Wales) were struggling because some of the more traditional industries – coal, iron, steel and cloth – were located there and were finding it difficult to compete with foreign competition.

2 Midlands and south.

3a A political party with ideas similar to the Nazi Party in Germany – they wanted a strong government that could deal with Britain's problems and reclaim its position as one of the most powerful nations in the world.

3b In times of crisis, where they think the current government cannot deal with issues, some people listen to extreme ideas and radical solutions.

3c Labour Party supported social justice/fairness for all and working-class people were particularly attracted to this in the 1930s because of the Depression.

Interpretation Analysis

1   The writer describes that some industries were doing

well (e.g. plastics and artificial fabrics), but these were based in southern England, rather than the north – and people in the south had no idea of how bad the depression was in other parts of the country.

2   Most students will probably agree that there were regional, economic divisions in the country at this time.

Chapter 3 Have you been learning?

Answers guidance

Chapter 3 Have you been learning?

Quick Knowledge Quiz

PAGE 76

1   **a**   David Lloyd George
2   **c**   8.5 million
3   **b**   flappers
4   **b**   1926
5   **a**   unionists
6   **a**   Dublin
7   **c**   Anglo-Irish Treaty

8   **b**   the Great Depression
9   **c**   Ellen Wilkinson
10 **a**   Labour Party

Literacy Focus

PAGE 77

Note-taking

Student answers will vary, but notes may look like this:

1a 1920s; govt improves lives e.g. Education Act 1918–14 leaving, SEN recognised (39 words down to 12).

1b OAP +; ex-soldiers work, injured & disabled; more people claim benefits if lost job; tenants' rent stays low (47 words down to 18).

1c 1919 Ministry of Health better healthcare; 200,000 new homes – council houses; target 500,000 missed; rent too high for some (65 words down to 19).

Assessment summary

The assessments in this textbook have been carefully designed and tested with History teachers to support student progression throughout the course. This specific assessment is written to support Year 8 or Year 9 students in tackling questions relating to historical interpretations.

 How far do you agree with **Interpretation A** about the impact of the Depression on ordinary people in Britain? (20)

▼ **INTERPRETATION A** Josh Brooman, a historian, writing in a GCSE school history textbook, *People in Change*, published in 1994.

'The 1930s is often remembered as a period of depression but it was also a period when people in Britain were able to expand their experiences and improve their lives. The BBC gave people radio and then television, and by 1939 there were 80,000 television sets in London alone. The number of people going on holiday increased immensely. Hotels and boarding houses, fish and chip shops, ice-cream stands, fairgrounds and dancehalls all expanded. The holiday camps flourished, the most famous being Butlins in Skegness.'

Students will start by thinking about the content of the interpretation and summarising what the author is saying about the topic (Question 1). They will then consider what they know about the topic, and write a short summary of this. Students must then make a judgement about how far their own knowledge of the topic matches with the content of the interpretation (Question 3), leading them to conclude by stating the extent to which they agree with it.

Students are provided with sentence starters and tips to help them structure their answers.

For the mark scheme, see page 87

A note about the end-of-chapter assessments

There is an assessment for each Student Book chapter. Each is structured like a GCSE exam-style question, with scaffolding steps to support KS3 students. Each assessment has a total of 20 marks, and is designed to be completed in a typical lesson – each has been written with a time allowance of about 30 minutes.

There is a mark scheme for each assessment. You can choose how to give student outcomes: a mark out of 20; a percentage; a performance indicator (we use a three-stage indicator – 'Developing', 'Secure', 'Extending' – but you could adapt to match any performance indicators used in your school); or a GCSE grade indicator. To convert raw marks to a performance or GCSE grade indicator, use this table:

Raw marks			
0	1–6	7–13	14–20
GCSE grade (9–1) indicators*			
U	1–3	4–6	7–9
Performance indicator			
Ungraded	Developing	Secure	Extending

* Please appreciate that these are approximate grades based on grade boundaries from recent GCSE exam papers. If a student achieves a Grade 7 in one of these assessments, it is not the equivalent of a Grade 7 at GCSE. Instead it is an indicator of the grade the student could expect to get if they continue on their flight path through KS3 and GCSE. Please note:
  • the raw-mark boundaries are based on but do not match precisely those for recent GCSE exam papers: this is because our assessments are focused around one exam-style question, likely to be done at the end of a chapter (topic) rather than at the end of the course. Secondly, we provide carefully considered scaffolded steps to allow KS3 students to tackle high level questions and gain confidence through the deliberate practice of building up detailed answers.
  • the assessments for Student Book 3 are progressively more demanding in that they use higher-order command words and provide less scaffolded support – if you set one of them for Year 8 students, please take that into account when awarding GCSE grade indicators.

Entering student outcomes into the Kerboodle Markbook

The Kerboodle Markbook records scores and percentages to allow for quick comparison of performance. If you want to use the Markbook to record student outcomes, you will need to enter the appropriate values given in the raw marks row of the table above.

Links to GCSE

By the end of KS3, students should be familiar with the History skill of analysing interpretations. At GCSE, most exam boards specifically ask students to analyse interpretations. For example:

AQA:

- How convincing is **Interpretation C** about... ? Explain your answer using **Interpretation C** and your contextual knowledge. (8)

Edexcel:

- How for do you agree with **Interpretation 2** about...? (20)

OCR A:

- Study **Interpretation A**. Do you think this interpretation is a fair comment on... ? (25)

Eduqas:

- Read **Interpretation D**. How far do you agree with this interpretation of... ? (16)

WJEC:

- Read **Interpretation D**. How far do you agree with this interpretation of... ? (16) (SPaG 3)

Links to KS3 History resources

Student Book

This assessment question links to these lessons:

3.3A/B The 'Hungry Thirties'

Kerboodle

Support for this assessment question on Kerboodle:

TWI 3 Assessment presentation: Interpretation analysis
TWI 3 Assessment worksheet (Core): Interpretation analysis
TWI 3 Assessment worksheet (Foundation): Interpretation analysis

Curriculum and Assessment Planning Guide

Support for this assessment question in this guide:

3 Assessment mark scheme – page 87
3 Assessment sample student answers – pages 88–89

Student name: _____   Date: _____

Mark scheme

Assessment bands	Marks	GCSE grade indicators*	I have...
	0	Ungraded	
Developing	1–6	1–3	☐ shown a basic understanding of the content of the interpretation. ☐ included a limited summary of supporting knowledge. ☐ reached a basic judgement on whether I agree or disagree with interpretation, without any reference to supporting knowledge. Key words are not always used correctly.
Secure	7–13	4–6	☐ shown good understanding of the content of the interpretation. ☐ included a detailed summary of relevant supporting knowledge. ☐ written a well-supported judgement on how far I agree with the interpretation, with reference to some relevant supporting knowledge. Some key words are used correctly.
Extending	14–20	7–9	☐ shown a developed understanding of the content of the interpretation. ☐ included a detailed summary of relevant supporting knowledge that supports and/or contradicts the content of the interpretation. ☐ written a well-organised, well-supported judgement on how far I agree with the interpretation, with reference to detailed, relevant supporting knowledge. All key words are used correctly.

* IMPORTANT: These are approximate indicators devised using publicly available information on the new GCSE grades. They are designed to assist in the process of tracking and monitoring. They cannot and should not be used to replace teachers' professional judgement. Teachers should use their own discretion in applying them, taking into account the cumulative test scores of an individual student (rather than just one assessment point), and should refer to their institution's assessment policy.

Mark: _____

Comment:

Sample student answers

Assessment: Interpretation analysis

STUDENT BOOK PAGE 79

How far do you agree with **Interpretation A** about the impact of the Depression on ordinary people in Britain? (20)

Sample Developing band answer

In Interpretation A the author writes about how life improved for ordinary people by saying that more people went on holiday and new technology was making life better for people. It is true that life did start to improve for some people in Britain during the 1930s, but this depended on the area of the country you lived in. People who worked in car manufacturing in the Midlands had regular work and money to enjoy their leisure time, but this was not the case everywhere. People in other areas had lost their jobs in shipbuilding and coal mining because of the Depression.

Sample Secure band answer

In Interpretation A, the author writes that the ordinary people of Britain were able to expand their experiences during the 1930s despite the period being seen as a time of depression. The interpretation says that people could go on holidays, enjoy new technology, and spend their leisure time being entertained.

I know that Britain in the 1930s was a time when many people suffered great hardship because of the Depression, which hit those who worked in industries such as shipbuilding and coal mining. In certain areas of Britain unemployment rose and many families found themselves with very little money. However, there were some areas of the country, such as the Midlands and the south of England, which enjoyed a boom in the new industries such as car manufacturing and radio production. Life for these people did improve.

To conclude, Interpretation A says that life improved for all with holidays, entertainment and new technology such as radios. My overall impression of the 1930s is that life was difficult for many people and families found it hard to survive. This does not fit with the interpretation as it implies that the Depression had no impact on ordinary people. Therefore, I disagree with the interpretation as although some people in some areas experienced an improved standard of living, this was not the case for many people who were badly affected by the Depression.

Sample Extending band answer

In Interpretation A, the author writes that although we remember the 1930s as a period of depression we should also recognise it as a period when life improved for many people and new experiences were available for ordinary people. The author goes on to say that radios and TVs were more widely available, more people could go on holiday – including to the new holiday camps, and entertainment was available for people's leisure time.

The interpretation encourages us to view the decade in a different way from how it has often been remembered. Britain in the 1930s was a time when many people were unemployed, and the period became known as the 'Hungry Thirties'. This was especially the case in places like the north of England, Scotland and Wales where many people had been employed in coal mining, shipbuilding, steel production and textiles – industries that were going into decline. There was less money available for unemployment benefit so the government introduced a Means Test, cutting the amount that some families received.

However, certain groups did start to see life improving, such as those who worked in car manufacturing in the Midlands and those in areas such as the south of England who made new electrical goods. In addition, there was some progress in the area of women's rights and access to education and employment. The government did start to invest more money into the areas that had been hit the hardest by unemployment, but this was at the end of the decade.

To conclude, Interpretation A says that we should remember the 1930s as a time when life improved for many people – and therefore implies that the Depression had minimal impact on ordinary people. The author wants us to see the decade as a positive one that offered new opportunities to all. However, my overall impression of the 1930s is that many people were unemployed and unable to find new work, and so were not able to enjoy the new technology or go on holiday, and so could not 'expand their experiences' or 'improve their lives'. This does not fit with what the author of Interpretation A writes. Therefore, I disagree with Interpretation A as I feel it presents the 1930s as a time when lots of progress was made without highlighting the regional differences and diverse experiences of ordinary people in Britain. I think that the Depression had a huge impact on the lives of many ordinary people in certain parts of the country and this is not what is said in Interpretation A.

Links to KS3 History National Curriculum

Note: **4.3A/B** *What was Germany like in the 1920s?* and **4.5A/B/C** *What was life like in Nazi Germany?* have been reviewed by the Holocaust Educational Trust.

The latest KS3 History National Curriculum states that students should 'gain historical perspective by placing their growing knowledge into different contexts, understanding the connections between local, regional, national and international history', and that is what Chapter 4 allows them to do. Students will build on their knowledge of the 1920s and 1930s to explain the rise of the Nazi Party. Furthermore, 'the inter-war years: the Great Depression and the rise of dictators' is an example area suggested in the National Curriculum. The lessons cover this area of history in detail, moving from the idea of democracy and dictatorship to communism and fascism.

Throughout the lessons, students will offer opinions, make comparisons, work as part of a team and sort through a variety of sources. They will be given the opportunity to make links between different ideas – and events – and show how one can lead to (or influence) another. They will think about the significance of events and individuals and use writing to develop their ideas.

Skills and processes covered in this chapter

		Lesson/activity in the Student Book
History Skills	Knowledge and understanding	4.1 Over to You: 1a, 1b, 3a, 3b; Knowledge and Understanding: 1
		4.2A Over to You: 2a, 2b, 2c, 3, 4
		4.2B Over to You: 1, 2; Causation: 1
		4.3A Over to You: 1a, 1b, 1c, 2; Knowledge and Understanding: 1, 2
		4.3B Over to You: 1a, 1b, 1c, 2
		4.5A Over to You: 2
		4.5B Over to You: 1, 4a, Source Analysis: 2, 3, 4
		4.6A Over to You: 1, 2a, 2b
		4.6B Over to You: 2a, 2b, 4a
		Have you been learning? Quick Knowledge Quiz: 1, 2, 3, 4, 5, 6, 7, 8, 9, 10
	Interpretation analysis	4.3A Over to You: 3
		4.5C Over to You: 5; Interpretation Analysis: 1, 2
		4.6B Interpretation Analysis: 1, 2
	Source analysis	4.3A Over to You: 4a, 4b
		4.3B Over to You: 3a, 3b
		4.4 Over to You: 1a, 1b, 3a, 3b
		4.5A Over to You: 1
		4.5B Over to You: 3, 4b, Source Analysis: 1, 2, 3, 4, 5
		4.5C Over to You: 2a, 2b, 3, 4
		4.6A Over to You: 3; Source Analysis: 1, 2, 3
		4.6B Over to You: 3a, 3b
	Significance	
	Cause and consequence	4.2A Over to You: 1
		4.2B Causation: 2
		4.3B Over to You: 4

		Lesson/activity in the Student Book
		4.4 Over to You: 2; Causation: 1a, 1b, 1c, 1d, 1e, 2
		4.5A Over to You: 3, 4a, 4b
		4.5B Over to You: 2a, 2b, 3
		4.5C Over to You: 1
		4.6A Over to You: 3
		4.6B Over to You: 1, 2c, 4b
		4 Assessment: Causation: 1, 2, 3, 4
	Diversity/Similarity and difference	**4.1** Over to You: 2
		4.2B Over to You: 3a, 3b
	Change and continuity	**4.3B** Change: 1
		4.5A Change: 1
Literacy and Numeracy	Literacy	**Have you been learning?** Literacy Focus: 1, 2, 3, 4
	Numeracy	**4.4** Over to You: 2

Lesson sequence

Lesson title	Student Book pages	Objectives
4.1 Democracy and dictatorship	pp 80–81	• Describe the differences between a democracy and a dictatorship. • Identify the main features of each type of government.
4.2A Two types of dictatorship	pp 82–83	• Define both 'fascism' and 'communism'. • Explain where and how these two extreme political beliefs took hold.
4.2B Two types of dictatorship	pp 84–85	
4.3A What was Germany like in the 1920s?	pp 86–87	• Describe the changes taking place in Germany in the 1920s. • Examine Hitler's attempted takeover of Germany.
4.3B What was Germany like in the 1920s?	pp 88–89	
4.4 Why did Hitler become so popular?	pp 90–91	• Explain the growth of the Nazi Party in the late 1920s and early 1930s. • Examine key factors in Hitler's rise in popularity.
4.5A What was life like in Nazi Germany?	pp 92–93	• Assess how life changed for Germans under Nazi rule. • Explain how the Nazis justified the way they ruled.
4.5B What was life like in Nazi Germany?	pp 94–95	
4.5C What was life like in Nazi Germany?	pp 96–97	
4.6A Why was there another world war?	pp 98–99	• Examine the build up to the outbreak of war in 1939. • Assess the views of modern historians relating to the outbreak of war.
4.6B Why was there another world war?	pp 100–101	
Chapter 4 Have you been learning?	pp 102–103	• Choose the correct answer from the given options for a quick recap. • Assess an interpretation of Hitler's role in the outbreak of war.

Lesson title	Student Book pages	Objectives
Chapter 4 History skill: Causation	p 104	• Examine how to respond to a question on the causes of an event.
Chapter 4 Assessment: Causation	p 105	• Compare different causes relating to Hitler's rise to power. • Construct an answer that identifies specific reasons for Hitler's rise to power.

Links to the GCSE curriculum

This chapter provides some historical context to the following:

AQA: Germany 1890–1945: Democracy and Dictatorship

AQA: Russia 1894–1945: Tsardom and Communism

AQA: The Inter-War Years 1918–1939

Edexcel: Weimar and Nazi Germany 1918–1939

Edexcel: Russia and the Soviet Union 1917–1941

OCR A: The Changing International Order 1918–2001

OCR A: Germany 1925–1955: The People and the State

OCR B: Living under Nazi Rule 1933–1945

Eduqas: Germany in Transition 1919–1939

Eduqas: The Development of Germany 1919–1991

Eduqas: The Development of Warfare in Britain c500–Present

WJEC: Germany in Transition 1919–1939

WJEC: The Development of Warfare c1250–Present

WJEC: Depression, War and Recovery 1930–1951

Exam-style questions covered in this chapter

Exam board	Lesson/activity question location	Command words	History skills/concepts
AQA	4.1 Over to You: 2	Explain two ways... different	Similarity and difference
	4.1 Knowledge and Understanding: 1	Describe...	Knowledge and understanding
	4.2B Over to You: 3a, 3b	Explain two ways... similar/different	Change and continuity
	4.3A Over to You: 4b	How useful...	Source analysis
	4.3A Knowledge and Understanding: 1, 2	Describe...	Knowledge and understanding
	4.3B Change: 1	In what ways...	Change and continuity
	4.4 Causation: 2	How far do you agree?	Cause and consequence
	4.5A Change: 1	In what ways...	Change and continuity
	4.5B Source Analysis: 5	How useful...	Source analysis
	4.6A Over to You: 2b	Write an account...	Knowledge and understanding
	4.6A Source Analysis: 3	How useful...	Source analysis
	4.6B Interpretation Analysis: 1	How does... differ...	Interpretation analysis
	4.6B Interpretation Analysis: 2	Which interpretation... more convincing	Interpretation analysis

Exam board	Lesson/activity question location	Command words	History skills/concepts
Edexcel	4.1 Knowledge and Understanding: 1	Describe…	Knowledge and understanding
	4.3A Over to You: 4b	How useful…	Source analysis
	4.3A Knowledge and Understanding: 1, 2	Describe…	Knowledge and understanding
	4.4 Causation: 2	How far do you agree?	Cause and consequence
	4.5B Source Analysis: 5	How useful…	Source analysis
	4.6A Over to You: 2b	Write a narrative account…	Knowledge and understanding
	4.6A Source Analysis: 3	How useful…	Source analysis
	4.6B Interpretation Analysis: 1	What is the main difference…	Interpretation analysis
OCR A	4.1 Knowledge and Understanding: 1	Describe…	Knowledge and understanding
	4.2B Causation: 2	Explain why…	Cause and consequence
	4.3A Over to You: 4b	How useful…	Source analysis
	4.3A Knowledge and Understanding: 1, 2	Describe…	Knowledge and understanding
	4.4 Causation: 2	How far do you agree?	Cause and consequence
	4.5B Source Analysis: 5	How useful…	Source analysis
	4.5C Interpretation Analysis: 2	Do you think this interpretation…	Interpretation analysis
	4.6A Source Analysis: 3	How useful…	Source analysis
OCR B	4.3A Over to You: 4b	How useful…	Source analysis
	4.4 Causation: 2	How far do you agree?	Cause and consequence
	4.5B Source Analysis: 5	How useful…	Source analysis
	4.6A Source Analysis: 3	How useful…	Source analysis
	4.6B Interpretation Analysis: 1	How far do they differ…	Interpretation analysis
Eduqas	4.1 Knowledge and Understanding: 1	Describe…	Knowledge and understanding
	4.2B Causation: 2	Explain why…	Cause and consequence
	4.3A Knowledge and Understanding: 1, 2	Describe…	Knowledge and understanding
WJEC	4.1 Knowledge and Understanding: 1	Describe…	Knowledge and understanding
	4.3B Over to You: 1a, 1b, 1c	Complete the sentences…	Knowledge and understanding
	4.2B Causation: 2	Explain why…	Cause and consequence
	4.3A Knowledge and Understanding: 1, 2	Describe…	Knowledge and understanding

A brief history

4.1 Democracy and dictatorship

This chapter starts with defining different types of government with the first order concepts of: democracy and dictatorship. Links are made with Chapter 3 and showing how war led to some countries becoming dictatorships. The key features of each ideology are then broken down in a way that students will be able to access. They will then apply this knowledge with an activity comparing a democracy and a dictatorship. Students are then asked to consider the political system we have in Britain and compare that to others around the world; this could be a good way to extend cultural capital by looking at current affairs.

4.2A/B Two types of dictatorship

Students are often fascinated to learn about Marx and Engels, and how their writing influenced Europe. There is an opportunity here to link back to Book 2: *Revolution, Industry and Empire 1558–1901 Student Book* to ensure the students make the connection between what they learned about the Industrial Revolution and the work of these two political philosophers. Students then look at case studies of Russia and Italy, building on their idea of a dictatorship by focusing on communism and fascism. The common theme to come out of both case studies is control. Students get a chance to see the difference by comparing the dictatorships in Russia and Italy and considering why these forms of controlling governments were attractive to the people.

4.3A/B What was Germany like in the 1920s?

This spotlight on Germany will allow students to reflect on what they already know about Britain in the 1920s and compare it to Weimar Germany and the many groups assimilated in it. Students can see the various problems facing the Weimar Republic economically, politically and socially, building towards the Spartacist Uprising and the Kapp Putsch. Students are then asked to evaluate the usefulness of a source as evidence of the impacts of hyperinflation, which then builds effectively to Hitler and the Munich Putsch. Recovery in 1920s Germany marks an end to Hitler's dominance, something students will be expected to suggest reasons for. This lesson ends with students evaluating how Germany changed in the 1920s.

4.4 Why did Hitler become so popular?

The rise of the Nazis is a topic students are always interested to know about – it is a great way to show them how several factors can contribute to an event. The lesson starts with looking at Hitler as a skilled

Timeline

1840s
Karl Marx and Friedrich Engels are writing and spreading ideas about communism.

1917
The Russian Revolution takes place.

January 1919
Spartacist Uprising in Berlin.

1919–1933
The period known as Weimar Germany.

1919
Mussolini forms the Fascist Party in Italy.

1920
The Kapp Putsch takes place.

1922
Mussolini and his supporters march on Rome.

1923
The financial crisis in Germany leads to hyperinflation.

1923
Hitler launches the Munich Putsch.

1932
The Nazis are the most popular political party in Germany.

1933
Hitler becomes Chancellor.

1934
After the death of Hindenburg Hitler becomes the Führer.

1934
Hitler introduces rearmament in secret, going against the terms of the Treaty of Versailles.

1935
The Nazis introduce the National Labour Service.

1936
Hitler remilitarises the Rhineland.

1938
The Nazis invade Austria (this is also known as the Anschluss).

1939
After the invasion of Czechoslovakia and Poland the Second World War starts.

orator and then moves on to the Great Depression; using students' prior knowledge to understand Germany in the 1920s will unequivocally aid their retention. The new tactics and organised approach of the Nazi Party and the discontent with the Weimar Government paints the picture of Hitler securing power. Students will then be expected to apply what they have learned by answering a 'how far do you agree?' style question, explaining the main reason for the popularity of the Nazis. This builds to every GCSE specification in terms of both content and skill.

4.5A/B/C What was life like in Nazi Germany?

Life in Germany during the Nazi regime is definitely a topic that falls under the category of 'uncomfortable history' as students need to evaluate the Nazi regime and its control over different groups. Students will learn to think like historians by analysing the impact of Nazi rule on the lives of women, the young, workers and minorities, with a focus on the forced removal of the German Jewish identity. The role of censorship will show how this control was consolidated by the Nazis. Students will apply the content by analysing sources and then by analysing Hitler's success; they should be encouraged to use as many laws, people and events as possible to support their judgement.

4.6A/B Why was there another world war?

This lesson details the road to war taking students back to the Treaty of Versailles and why the terms made Hitler, and the people of Germany, so angry. Hitler's three main aims are outlined and then students can see the chronology of how he tries to achieve those aims. They will then need to evaluate the responsibility of other actors such as Britain and the USSR. This lesson is full of key people and dates so it would be wise to add to the lesson by creating a concept timeline to ensure the students have retained the steps to war. This will be useful when they go on to analyse both the content and provenance of sources and interpretations.

Further reading and links

For teachers:

* *Travellers in the Third Reich* by Julia Boyd (Elliot & Thompson, 2018) is a fascinating journey through 1920s and 1930s Germany. Boyd uses diaries and letters from some well-known writers, aristocrats and politicians to give a compelling insight into the time.

* Revolutions can be seen as quite male dominated, but women have played an important role in many revolutions. Enrich your teaching by reading an article

from the British Library: 'Women and the Russian Revolution' by Katie McElvanney. The article includes images of items from the collection that can be enlarged and explored in further detail. Go to bl.uk/ and search for 'Women and the Russian Revolution', then click on 'Women and the Russian Revolution – British Library' for the McElvanney article.

For students:

* BBC Bitesize has a collection of 16 clips that will help students consolidate their learning of the rise of the Nazis and the road to war. Encourage students to watch the clips on the Spanish Civil War to add context to their understanding of fascism. Go to bbc.co.uk/bitesize/subjects/and click History > Higher History > Europe and World > Appeasement and the Road to War to find useful clips.

* Get the students to read *Once* by Morris Gleitzman (Puffin, 2006), a story of a Jewish boy in Nazi occupied Europe. This will enrich their understanding of how minorities were treated by the Nazis.

Beyond the classroom

* Berlin has many sites to explore that are linked to the rise of the Nazis and their various methods of control. A trip to the city would be an excellent opportunity for enrichment and would allow the students to see and understand the legacy of the Second World War.

* Every year Amnesty International runs its Write for Rights Campaign, through which students can write messages of support for people living in dictatorships or under other restrictive regimes. Get students to run this campaign in the school and have them explain the differences between democracies and dictatorships to their fellow students.

* The Holocaust Educational Trust organises a fantastic project called Lessons from Auschwitz that runs trips for students to Poland to visit Auschwitz and meet Jewish leaders and sometimes Holocaust survivors. After the trip, students are expected to share their experience with their peers – this could be done in an all-school assembly.

* Examining the way different countries are run or controlled is as valid today as ever. Exploring which countries are democracies, dictatorships and nominally communist – and what this means in terms of international relationships – is an ideal topic to be studied in conjunction with Citizenship.

Answers guidance

The answers provided here are examples, based on the information provided in the Student Book. There may be other factors which are relevant to each question, and students may draw on as much of their own knowledge as possible to give detailed and precise answers. There are also many ways of answering questions, including exam-style questions (for example, of structuring an essay). However, these exemplar answers should provide a good starting point.

4.1 Democracy and dictatorship
PAGES 80–81

Over to You

1a Student presentations will vary.

1b Answers will vary but an example is: Dictatorship: type of government where one person or group makes all the rules and decisions without input from others. (18 words) Democracy: type of government where people vote in elections for the people who represent them in parliament. (17 words)

2 In a dictatorship, ordinary people have no say in how their country is run. There are no regular elections because the country is run by one political party or one person – the dictator. In a democracy, people have a say in how their country is governed. They vote in regular elections in which there are several political parties to choose from. The people are represented by the organisations they elect – e.g. parliament or councils.

3a Students should choose democracy because of the electoral system, various freedoms they enjoy etc.

3b Students may suggest North Korea or another dictatorship.

Knowledge and Understanding

1 Students may mention regular elections in which there are several political parties to choose from; people represented by the organisations

they elect – e.g. parliament or councils; people usually have a number of 'freedoms' or rights – e.g. freedom of speech and freedom of information etc.

4.2A Two types of dictatorship
PAGES 82–83

Over to You

1 Huge numbers of casualties and food shortages during the First World War led to a year of revolution in 1917, in which Tsar Nicholas II abdicated. Russia became a communist country on 1 September 1917, and the Tsar and his family were executed in 1918.

2a A theory about how to run a country in which there would be no different classes. Money and goods are shared out equally and the country is run so that everyone is equal. No need for money, or even laws, because everyone lives a simple life, sharing all they have with each other. (50 words)

2b Type of government where one person or group makes all the rules and decisions without input from others.

2c There were no other political parties except the Communist Party and there were very strict rules and limited freedoms.

3 Answers may or may not include an annotated flag, but will explain that the red background represents the revolution and the golden star represents power. This power is now controlled by the factory workers (represented by the hammer) and the farm workers (represented by the sickle).

4 Answers will vary, but may say that communism promotes a more equal society with no great differences between rich and poor, so the rich might fear that their lives would change as their wealth disappeared.

4.2B Two types of dictatorship
PAGES 84–85

Over to You

1 Answers may or may not include an annotated flag, but will explain that the eagle is a traditional symbol of power and alertness, while the bundle the eagle is clutching is called a 'fascio'. It represents strength in numbers, unity and law, and the axe symbolises power.

2 • fascism – a political system where the government controls all aspects of people's lives in an attempt to make the nation stronger than others.
   • communism – a political system where all people are equal and all property and business is owned by the state and run for the benefit of all.
   • Mussolini – the fascist leader of Italy who took control in 1922.
   • USSR – from 1922, this was the new name for Russia and the areas it controlled.
   • Karl Marx – writing partner of Friedrich Engels.
   • fascio – one of the symbols of Italy's Fascist Party.

3a Answers might include: they were different types of dictatorship – one communist, one fascist; different countries; different origins; different ideas about equality.

3b Answers might include that both began as a result of problems associated with the First World War; both involve high levels of government control (of press, electoral systems, etc.).

Causation

1 Winning side, the side of Britain, France and USA.

2 Answers will vary, but may explain that Italy suffered with high unemployment and rising food prices after the war. A series of different governments seemed unable to do anything about this, and groups of armed bandits roamed the countryside stealing and murdering. Some Italians were terrified that communists might take over, so increasingly Italians turned to Mussolini who promised to bring discipline, glory and pride back to Italy.

4.3A What was Germany like in the 1920s?

PAGES 86–87

Over to You

1a Free Corps: Ex-soldiers who joined the government to end the Spartacist Uprising. They also formed part of the Kapp Putsch in 1920.

1b Spartacists: communists who wanted a revolution similar to the one in Russia. They revolted against the German government in 1919.

1c putsch: German word for revolution or rebellion.

2 A sudden, dramatic rise in prices.

3 They could not afford much at all (only one loaf of bread and a small piece of cheese or some oatmeal) and the friend, despite wanting to buy shoes, could only afford a cup of coffee.

4a The money has such little value that it is being used to play with rather than buy goods.

4b It shows how money was worthless and had more value as a toy than as currency. It shows the inability of the government to deal with the financial crisis.

Knowledge and Understanding

1 Answers might include a series of attempted takeovers/ rebellions (Spartacists/Kapp), or hyperinflation meant money became practically worthless. Also, the country's factories, farms and mines had been exhausted by the war and a series of bad harvests meant that there was little food.

And the government was also criticised for agreeing to the Treaty of Versailles.

2 Answers might include the country's factories, farms and mines had been exhausted by the war and a series of bad harvests meant that there was little food. The Treaty of Versailles meant that land was taken so many Germans found themselves ruled by another country. Also, hyperinflation meant money became practically worthless.

4.3B What was Germany like in the 1920s?

PAGES 88–89

Over to You

1a Austria

1b Munich, Germany

1c the German Workers' Party

2 The Nazis' own private army that beat up people who criticised Hitler or the party.

3a Answers might include upset, angry, disappointed, vengeful.

3b Answers might suggest he called them 'criminals' because he thinks they have done something wrong – and 'November' relates to the month the war ended.

4 It found it increasingly difficult to persuade Germans they needed the Nazis when the country was doing so well.

Change

1 Answers might include: fewer threats from extreme groups, economy under control, cultural advances of later Weimar period.

4.4 Why did Hitler become so popular?

PAGES 90–91

Over to You

1a He is practising speeches, without an audience.

1b He wanted to have maximum

impact when he talked, so would rehearse what he looked like to an audience to make sure he made the most of what the audience saw.

2 Answers should reflect that, as unemployment increased, so did the number of votes for the Nazis.

3a The people in the poster: unemployed people; older voters; women with children; anyone affected by the Depression.

3b Answers might include that the Nazis used the Depression to get votes, tried to appeal to a large number of people, were well organised and had a clear election plan.

Causation

1a–e Student notes will reflect the information in the spread.

2 Answers will focus on the reason in the question (Hitler's talents as a public speaker) but will also mention other factors, before arriving at a conclusion.

4.5A What was life like in Nazi Germany?

PAGES 92–93

Over to You

1 Because the way the woman is portrayed fits into the role that the Nazis had planned for women to have babies, be a partner for her husband and go to church (Kinder, Kirche and Küche – children, church and cooking).

2 The Nazis set up a number of schemes, programmes and organisations to get people back to work – e.g. the National Labour Service.

3 Improved popularity because he was delivering on an election promise.

4a Because he was determined to control the way people thought – he wanted people to conform and knew that he needed someone to be responsible for it because it was so important.

4b Important to get his exact message across, so he needed someone he could rely on to do what he wished.

Change

1 Before the Nazis came to power, over six million Germans were out of work – but the Nazis set up schemes, programmes and organisations to create jobs. They set up the National Labour Service, which gave men aged between 18 and 25 jobs in the countryside such as digging ditches and planting trees. They wore uniforms and lived in camps, and were given free meals and a small wage. The Nazis also provided work building roads, schools, hospitals and railways, and in making the army bigger and building tanks, fighter planes and battleships. Many jobs were also created by firing people, such as Jewish workers.

4.5B What was life like in Nazi Germany?
PAGES 94–95

Over to You

1 • hereditary: passed on from parents to their children
  • sterilise: to deprive someone of the ability to produce children, usually by removing or blocking the sex organs

2a Great propaganda victory; medal table showed how talented and strong the German race was and how it was superior to other 'inferior' races; chance to show off German technology.

2b Getting them to give the Nazi salute might have shown some support for the regime.

3 Student answers will vary, but should focus on how the Nazis were trying to show people

that killing/sterilizing those with hereditary diseases was a 'good thing' because it saved money – *their* money. Also they were attempting to make it more acceptable/palatable – it was saving money, so was 'justified'.

4a The secret police in Nazi Germany.

4b Student answers may include that that they would listen out for negative comments, help the Gestapo and tell on their neighbours.

Source Analysis

1 Student answers will focus on the mainly positive feelings – admiration, respect, etc.

2 Student answers will focus on the positive aspects of the regime – high employment, work programmes, new roads, schools, hospitals and railways.

3 People being persecuted, acts of antisemitism, arrest of political prisoners, etc.

4 He was referring to the fact that he had managed to get the Reichstag to give Hitler the power to make his own laws, and that he had banned all other political parties, and trade unions.

5 Students answers will mostly emphasise the usefulness in that it shows the power of the Nazis' ability to put on a show/persuade people about their cause; shows that some people supported what Hitler was doing; might be a link to the fact that the UK was suffering at this time under the Great Depression and Hitler seemed to be performing an economic miracle.

4.5C What was life like in Nazi Germany?
PAGES 96–97

Over to You

1 Hitler wanted young people to be loyal to him and the Nazi

Party because he realised that in future he may have to call on them to fight and perhaps die for him. He also wanted young people to be fully occupied and totally filled with Nazi beliefs and ideals.

2a To prepare them for the different lives the Nazis planned for them.

2b The study of how to 'improve' the mental and physical characteristics of the human race. Taught to students so they might think eugenics was OK/Nazi treatment of persecuted groups was justified.

3 To get students used to the ideas contained in the question. If it was taught in school, children might think that it was OK.

4 Because the Nazis had a racist, stereotypical view of Jewish people – and they wanted German schoolchildren to think that Jews were nasty.

5 Students will write that changes were subtle at the beginning, starting with changes in attitude from teachers and neighbours. Also there were changes at school (for example, saying 'Heil Hitler' instead of 'good morning').

Interpretation Analysis

1 Uniforms, holidays, rallies – before the Hitler Youth, he had not done anything like this.

2 It might explain their popularity among some young people who had not experienced the sort of things the Nazis were offering.

4.6A Why was there another world war?
PAGES 98–99

Over to You

1 Answers will vary, but may include: getting back German land, building up his army, navy and air force, creating living space, uniting all German speakers.

2a Agreement Germany had to sign at the end of the First World War, mainly consisting of punishments.

2b Answers will include the building up of armed forces (e.g. by 1935, Hitler had thousands of planes, dozens more battleships than he was allowed, and around 500,000 soldiers), and in 1936 he re-entered the Rhineland.

3 Fear of starting another war. Some felt that the Germans should be allowed to build up their armed forces if they wanted to. Lord Lothian (Source D) didn't see German troops entering the Rhineland as a threat as they were entering land that was already theirs.

Source Analysis

1 Weaker than the other nations in terms of its military.

2 It might explain why Hitler felt it important to put his military in the Rhineland as he felt he needed to defend Germany's border.

3 Answers should reflect that the postcard shows how Germans felt weak in comparison to other nations so explains to some extent

why Hitler began to build up armed forces, but there were other reasons too, relating to his aims.

4.6B Why was there another world war?

PAGES 100–101

Over to You

1 He marched troops into Austria and united Germany with Austria, which was forbidden under the Treaty of Versailles.

2a Policy of giving someone what they want in the hope that they will stop their demands.

2b Failed to stand up to Hitler and prevent him from breaking the Treaty of Versailles, then allowed him to take the Sudetenland in 1938 after the Munich Conference.

2c Fear of war, memories of First World War still fresh.

3a Neville Chamberlain, British Prime Minister. Going to Munich to meet Hitler.

3b There is 'still hope' that there will be a peaceful solution to the crisis, rather than war.

4a Deal between Germany and Russia to agree not go to war over Poland. A secret part of the deal agreed that Russia

could have part of Poland if it let the Germans invade Poland.

4b Russia might feel threatened if the Germans continued to push soldiers in Russia's direction, so he made the Nazi-Soviet Pact, which enabled him to concentrate forces on Poland without interference from the Russians.

Interpretation Analysis

1 Interpretation F says that Hitler's long-term plan was to carry out plans he set out many years before by invading Poland and Russia. Interpretation G claims that Hitler had no plan, but took advantage of opportunities presented to him by politicians from other European countries.

2 Answers should reference both interpretations and explain which one students think supports their view about the outbreak of war – do they think it was part of a long-term plan, or do they believe Hitler took advantage of opportunities presented to him?

Chapter 4 Have you been learning?

Answers guidance

Chapter 4 Have you been learning?

Quick Knowledge Quiz

PAGE 102

1 **b** democracy
2 **c** Marx and Engels
3 **c** Russia/USSR
4 **a** the Spartacists
5 **c** Mussolini
6 **b** hyperinflation
7 **a** Austria in 1889

8 **b** Gestapo
9 **a** rearmament
10 **b** 3 September 1939

Literacy Focus

PAGE 103

Understanding interpretations

1 Lebensraum was Hitler's policy of expansion.

2 The two main views concern Hitler's expansion across Europe. One argument claims that he had a master plan for

expansion. The other states that he simply took advantage of opportunities and other people's mistakes.

3 First view – Hugh Trevor-Roper. Second view – A.J.P. Taylor.

4 Answers may vary, but an example might be: I agree with the argument put forward by Hugh Trevor-Roper. Hitler's plans for Lebensraum were laid out in his book, *Mein Kampf,* which showed he had clear aims.

Chapter 4 Assessment: Causation

Assessment summary

The assessments in this textbook have been carefully designed and tested with History teachers to support student progression throughout the course. This specific assessment is written to support Year 8 or Year 9 students in tackling questions relating to causation.

> Explain why Hitler emerged as Chancellor of Germany by 1933.
>
> You may use the following in your answer:
> - strengths of Hitler
> - the Great Depression.
>
> You must also use information of your own. (20)

The first stage is for students to plan their answers by considering the two given reasons why Hitler emerged as Chancellor of Germany by 1933 (Question 1). Students must also mention other reasons in addition to the two given one. Then students must consider what they know about the topic, and use this knowledge to add as much detail as possible and 'set up' their answer (Question 2). They should write their answers, following the order as set out in the question (Question 3). While writing their answers, students should try to make links between the different reasons and highlight any causes and/or consequences (Question 4).

Starter sentences are provided to support students in this assessment.

For the mark scheme, see page 102.

A note about the end-of-chapter assessments

There is an assessment for each Student Book chapter. Each is structured like a GCSE exam-style question, with scaffolding steps to support KS3 students. Each assessment has a total of 20 marks, and is designed to be completed in a typical lesson – each has been written with a time allowance of about 30 minutes.

There is a mark scheme for each assessment. You can choose how to give student outcomes: a mark out of 20; a percentage; a performance indicator (we use a three-stage indicator – 'Developing', 'Secure', 'Extending' – but you could adapt to match any performance indicators used in your school); or a GCSE grade indicator. To convert raw marks to a performance or GCSE grade indicator, use this table:

Raw marks			
0	1–6	7–13	14–20
GCSE grade (9–1) indicators*			
U	1–3	4–6	7–9
Performance indicator			
Ungraded	Developing	Secure	Extending

* Please appreciate that these are approximate grades based on grade boundaries from recent GCSE exam papers. If a student achieves a Grade 7 in one of these assessments, it is not the equivalent of a Grade 7 at GCSE. Instead it is an indicator of the grade the student could expect to get if they continue on their flight path through KS3 and GCSE. Please note:
- the raw-mark boundaries are based on but do not match precisely those for recent GCSE exam papers: this is because our assessments are focused around one exam-style question, likely to be done at the end of a chapter (topic) rather than at the end of the course. Secondly, we provide carefully considered scaffolded steps to allow KS3 students to tackle high level questions and gain confidence through the deliberate practice of building up detailed answers.
- the assessments for Student Book 3 are progressively more demanding in that they use higher-order command words and provide less scaffolded support – if you set one of them for Year 8 students, please take that into account when awarding GCSE grade indicators.

Entering student outcomes into the Kerboodle Markbook

The Kerboodle Markbook records scores and percentages to allow for quick comparison of performance. If you want to use the Markbook to record student outcomes, you will need to enter the appropriate values given in the raw marks row of the table above.

Links to GCSE

By the end of KS3, students should be familiar with the History skill of causation. At GCSE, most exam boards specifically ask students to make judgements on the causes of events. For example:

AQA:

- Has... been the main factor/main way in...? Explain your answer with reference to... and other factors/ways. (16) (SPaG 4)

- Which of the following was the more important reason...
  - ...
  - ...?
- Explain your answer with reference to both reasons. (12)

- '...' How far do you agree with this statement? Explain your answer. (16) (SPaG 4)

Edexcel:

- Explain why.../what was important about... (12)

- 'The most significant reason/consequence/ cause... was...' How far do you agree? Explain your answer. (16)

OCR A:

- Explain why... (10)

- '...' How far do you agree? (24)

OCR B:

- How far do you agree that...? Give reasons for your answer. (18)

- '...' How far do you agree with this view? (18)

Eduqas:

- Why was...? (12)

- Explain why... (9)

- Outline how... changed... In your answer you should provide a written narrative discussing the main causes... across three historical eras. (16) (SPaG 4)

WJEC:

- Explain why... (12)

- This question is about the causes of... To what extent has... been the main/most effective... over time? (16) (SPaG 4)

- How far did/Was... the main cause/reason...? Use your own knowledge and understanding of the issue to support your answer. (16) (SPaG 3)

Links to KS3 History resources

Student Book

This assessment question links to these lessons:

4.3A/B What was Germany like in the 1920s?
4.4 Why did Hitler become so popular?

Kerboodle

Support for this assessment question on Kerboodle:

TWI 4 Assessment presentation: Causation
TWI 4 Assessment worksheet (Core): Causation
TWI 4 Assessment worksheet (Foundation): Causation

Curriculum and Assessment Planning Guide

Support for this assessment question in this guide:

4 Assessment mark scheme – page 102
4 Assessment sample student answers – pages 103–104

Student name: _____ Date: _____

Mark scheme

Assessment bands	Marks	GCSE grade indicators*	I have...
	0	Ungraded	
Developing	1–6	1–3	☐ given a very general explanation of one or two of the causes/reasons/factors of Hitler's appointment as Chancellor, which shows limited organisation. ☐ written an answer that shows limited knowledge and understanding of the period and the events relating to Hitler's appointment as Chancellor.
Secure	7–13	4–6	☐ written a detailed explanation of several causes/reasons/factors relating to Hitler's appointment as Chancellor. I have shown some links between the causes/ reasons/factors but my answer lacks a clear structure. ☐ written an answer that shows a range of accurate knowledge and understanding of the period and the events in the question. Some key words are used correctly. NOTE: Marks should only go above 10 if you have added extra detail that goes beyond the bullet points in the question.
Extending	14–20	7–9	☐ written a well-developed explanation of several causes/reasons/factors relating to Hitler's appointment as Chancellor. I have made good links between the causes/ reasons/factors and their consequences, and my answer is clearly and logically structured. ☐ included a wide range of accurate and detailed knowledge and understanding of the period and the events in the question. All key words are used correctly. NOTE: You cannot get to this level if you have not included extra detail in addition to the two bullet points in the question.

* IMPORTANT: These are approximate indicators devised using publicly available information on the new GCSE grades. They are designed to assist in the process of tracking and monitoring. They cannot and should not be used to replace teachers' professional judgement. Teachers should use their own discretion in applying them, taking into account the cumulative test scores of an individual student (rather than just one assessment point), and should refer to their institution's assessment policy.

Mark: _____

Comment:

Sample student answers

Assessment: Causation

STUDENT BOOK PAGE 105

Explain why Hitler emerged as Chancellor of Germany by 1933.
You may use the following in your answer:
- strengths of Hitler
- the Great Depression.
You must also use information of your own. (20)

 Sample Developing band answer

There were many reasons that Hitler emerged as Chancellor in 1933. One of the reasons was that he was a brilliant speaker. Hitler used a loud voice and body language to persuade people of his ideas.

The Great Depression was another reason for Hitler becoming Chancellor as he promised to make life better again.

 Sample Secure band answer

In January 1933 Hitler became Chancellor due to many factors. One of the reasons that Hitler emerged as leader was the Great Depression. The Great Depression meant that countries stopped buying and selling from each other – this meant lots of German factories closed and millions of people lost their jobs. Families were starving and many lost their homes. At this time Hitler started to speak about how he would help the country and he promised jobs for everyone who voted for him. Many German people were also worried about communism which meant that they would vote for the Nazis in an attempt to stop the spread of communism after the Great Depression.

Another reason for Hitler's emergence as Chancellor was his strengths as a leader, for example. Hitler was a powerful public speaker and he used this skill to persuade people to vote for him. The Nazi Party would hold big meetings, sometimes called rallies, where Hitler would give speeches. He would talk about the Great Depression and the Treaty of Versailles and how he could make Germany powerful again. This worked as people were so desperate because of the effects of the Great Depression. Also, Hitler changed the Nazi Party to make it a proper political party. He used media to spread the beliefs of the Nazis in newspapers and on the radio. He created youth groups so young people grew up believing that the Nazis were the right party to vote for. This increased Hitler's popularity and led to him becoming Chancellor in 1933. In conclusion, there were a number of reasons why Hitler emerged as Chancellor of Germany including the Great Depression and his strength as a public speaker.

Sample Extending band answer

There are a number of different factors that combined to make the Nazi Party popular and allow Hitler to become Chancellor in 1933. I will begin with what I think is the most important cause – the strength of Hitler, convincing the people that he and his party were the best people to make Germany a strong and powerful country again – before looking at other factors that enabled Hitler to become Chancellor.

In the July 1932 election the Nazis got nearly 14 million votes and became the biggest party in Germany. This was a dramatic increase from 1928 when Hitler and the Nazis were the eighth most popular political party in Germany and got only 800,000 votes in elections. Hitler was a passionate and powerful public speaker and he used this skill to convince people to support him, including at the large public rallies he held. The chancellors during 1932 had been weak and unable to do anything to improve the state of Germany, and people were unhappy with the job they had done. With Hitler's public support the President, Hindenburg, had no option but to appoint Hitler as Chancellor.

The Great Depression was another factor that led to Hitler becoming Chancellor. In 1929 trade slowed down. Countries stopped trading with each other which led to factories closing and mass unemployment. By 1933 in Germany six million people were unemployed. Though the Great Depression made people want to change the government, it was Hitler's speeches and promises – including jobs for those who voted for him – that led to people voting for him, which in turn put him in a position to be Chancellor.

The Great Depression also made people worried that communism would spread to Germany. This was a concern of the upper and middle classes who would lose money and land. Hitler therefore gained more support by sending his stormtroopers to fight communist gangs.

Another factor that helped Hitler become Chancellor was how well organised the party was. Hitler knew that if he was to become Chancellor he would need to be part of a serious political party rather than try to take power in the same way he had in the Munich Putsch of November 1923. The Nazi Party had offices all over Germany to recruit people, and they used new media such as radio broadcasts and cinema news reports, as well as buying newspapers and printing millions of leaflets and posters, to deliver their message. They also targeted the young in youth groups such as the Hitler Youth Organisation. Although all of these helped Hitler become more popular, it is fair to argue that without Hitler's strength as a public speaker, as someone who delivered a strong message, and who was not afraid to use force on his opponents, he would not have been in a strong enough position to become Chancellor in 1933.

In conclusion, there were a number of factors that led to Hitler becoming Chancellor in 1933. He took advantage of the Great Depression, people's fears of communism and their anger at previous chancellors, and showed his strength as the person to lead Germany. In addition, without his powerful speeches, use of the media and intimidation, the Nazi Party would not have got as much support as it did in 1932 and Hitler would not have been in a position to become Chancellor.

Chapter 5 The Second World War

Links to KS3 History National Curriculum

Note: *5.11A/B The journey to the 'Final Solution'* has been reviewed by the Holocaust Educational Trust.

There are many events and people in Chapter 5 that students will already know about. However, this chapter really does add 'meat on the bones' of familiar topics, which will be fascinating for students to explore further. The various enquiries require the students to take the content and investigate, analyse and make judgements; all key aims of the latest KS3 History National Curriculum.

Students will gain a much-needed understanding of chronology while studying key events and people. For example: 'The Second World War and the wartime leadership of Winston Churchill' are given as examples of topics in the latest KS3 History National Curriculum. This element will give more context to key battles and events of the war and what happened after the war, and will give students the opportunity to make a judgement on Churchill's leadership. Furthermore, the Holocaust, which must be studied, is delivered in an engaging way looking at change and continuity regarding Nazi policies.

The sections in this chapter challenge students to use a wide range of historical skills. They will make links between different events and changes and will use writing to explore and develop ideas. This chapter will allow students to place the history of Britain within the context of the wider world – another key aim of the National Curriculum.

Skills and processes covered in this chapter

		Lesson/activity in the Student Book
History Skills	Knowledge and understanding	**5.1A** Over to You: 1a, 2a, 2b
		5.1B Over to You: 1, 2, 3a
		5.1C Over to You: 1, 2a, 3
		5.2A Over to You: 1a
		5.3A Over to You: 1, 2a
		5.3B Over to You: 3a, 3b, 4
		5.4 Over to You: 1a, 1b, 1c, 3
		5.5A Over to You: 1a, 3
		5.5B Over to You: 3
		5.6 Over to You: 1, 2
		5.8 Over to You: 1, 2, 4
		5.9A Over to You: 1
		5.9B Over to You: 1
		5.10A Over to You: 1; Knowledge and Understanding: 1, 2
		5.10B Over to You: 1b
		5.11A Over to You: 1, 2a, 2b, 2c
		5.11B Over to You: 1a, 1b, 2
		5.12 Over to You: 1, 2a, 3a
		5.13 Over to You: 1; Knowledge and Understanding: 1
		Have you been learning? Quick Knowledge Quiz: 1, 2, 3, 4, 5, 6, 7, 8, 9, 10
	Interpretation analysis	**5.2B** Over to You: 2a, 2b; Interpretation analysis: 1, 2
		5.4 Interpretation Analysis: 1
		5.5A Interpretation Analysis: 1, 2

		Lesson/activity in the Student Book
		5.5B Over to You: 1a, 1b, 2a, **2b**
		5.10B Over to You: 1a
		5.12 Over to You: 2c
		5 Assessment: Interpretation analysis: 1, 2, 3
	Source Analysis	**5.1A** Source Analysis: 1, 2
		5.1B Source Analysis: 1, 2, 3
		5.2A Over to You: 2, 3 Source Analysis: 1, 2
		5.2B Over to You: 1a, 1b, 2a, 2b
		5.3B Over to You: 2
		5.4 Over to You: 2a, 2b, 2c
		5.5A Over to You: 2a, 2b, 2c, 2d, 2e
		5.5B Over to You: 2a, 2b; Source Analysis: 1, 2, 3, 4
		5.9A Source Analysis: 1, 2
		5.10A Over to You: 2, 3, 4
		5.10B Over to You: 1a; Source Analysis: 1, 2
		5.11A Over to You: 4a, 4b
	Significance	**5.8** Significance: 1, 2
	Cause and consequence	**5.1A** Over to You: 1b
		5.1B Over to You: 2, 3b
		5.1C Over to You: 2b; Causation: 1
		5.2A Over to You: 1b
		5.2B Over to You: 3a, 3b, 3c
		5.3A Over to You: 2b
		5.3B Over to You: 1b, 1c; Causation: 1
		5.5A Over to You: 1b, 3
		5.7 Over to You: 1, 2a, 2b
		5.8 Over to You: 3
		5.9A Over to You: 2, 3
		5.10A Over to You: 4
		5.10B Over to You: 2
		5.11B Over to You: 3a, 3b
		5.12 Over to You: 1, 2b, 3b
		5.13 Over to You: 2, 3
	Diversity/Similarity and difference	**5.2A** Over to You: 3
		5.2B Over to You: 2a, 2b

		Lesson/activity in the Student Book
	Change and continuity	**5.5B** Over to You: 1b
		5.6 Over to You: 3; Change: 1, 2
		5.10B Over to You: 3
		5.11A Over to You: 3
		5.11B Change: 1
Literacy and Numeracy	Literacy	**5.3B** Over to You: 3b
		5.6 Over to You: 2
		Have you been learning? Literacy Focus: 1
	Numeracy	**5.3B** Over to You: 1a

Lesson sequence

Lesson title	Student Book pages	Objectives
5.1A The Second World War: an overview	pp 106–107	• Recall key terms such as 'Blitzkrieg' and 'Blitz'.
5.1B The Second World War: an overview	pp 108–109	• Identify key turning points of the war.
5.1C The Second World War: an overview	pp 110–111	• Outline the sequence of the main events of the Second World War.
5.2A How should we remember Dunkirk?	pp 112–113	• Identify reasons why the Dunkirk evacuations could be considered both a success and a failure.
5.2B How should we remember Dunkirk?	pp 114–115	• Examine different opinions about the Dunkirk evacuation.
5.3A Who were 'the Few'?	pp 116–117	• Examine Operation Sealion.
5.3B Who were 'the Few'?	pp 118–119	• Assess why Hitler wasn't able to invade Britain in September 1940.
5.4 Soldiers of Empire	pp 120–121	• Examine which countries helped Britain fight during the Second World War. • Identify the contribution of these 'soldiers of Empire', and the countries that sent them.
5.5A Evacuation	pp 122–123	• Define the word 'evacuation' and explain why it took place.
5.5B Evacuation	pp 124 125	• Assess the experiences of evacuees and their hosts.
5.6 The home front	pp 126–127	• Recall key terms and concepts such as rationing, Home Guard and total war. • Identify ways in which the Second World War affected ordinary citizens.
5.7 How did the Second World War change health and medicine?	pp 128–129	• Recall key developments in health and medicine during and after the Second World War. • Assess the impact of the war on surgery, health and medicine.
5.8 Penicillin and the war	pp 130–131	• Examine the development of penicillin. • Assess the impact of penicillin.
5.9A Why is Sir Arthur Harris such a controversial figure?	pp 132–133	• Explain the difference between precision bombing and area bombing.
5.9B Why is Sir Arthur Harris such a controversial figure?	pp 134–135	• Formulate an opinion on why you think Dresden was bombed.

Lesson title	Student Book pages	Objectives
5.10A Why is Winston Churchill on a £5 note?	pp 136–137	• Outline why Winston Churchill appears on a £5 note.
5.10B Why is Winston Churchill on a £5 note?	pp 138–139	• Assess whether you think he was a 'truly great leader' or not.
5.11A The journey to the 'Final Solution'	pp 140–141	• Identify why Hitler and the Nazis persecuted Jewish people.
5.11B The journey to the 'Final Solution'	pp 142–143	• Examine how the 'Final Solution' was organised.
5.12 The war goes nuclear	pp 144–145	• Explain how and why the USA joined the Second World War. • Assess the immediate impact of the nuclear attack in 1945.
5.13 A United Nations	pp 146–147	• Explain what the United Nations is and what it does. • Examine how the UN is organised.
Chapter 5 Have you been learning?	pp 148–149	• Choose the correct answer from the given options for a quick recap. • Use connectives to improve a historical narrative.
Chapter 5 History skill: Interpretation analysis	p 150	• Explore how to compare interpretations.
Chapter 5 Assessment: Interpretation analysis	p 151	• Consider why two interpretations of Winston Churchill differ and explain whether you agree with either of them.

Links to the GCSE curriculum

This chapter provides some historical context to the following:

AQA: Germany 1890–1945: Democracy and Dictatorship

AQA: Conflict and Tension between East and West 1945–1972

AQA: Russia 1894–1945: Tsardom and Communism

Edexcel: London and the Second World War 1939–1945

Edexcel: Weimar and Nazi Germany 1918–1939

Edexcel: Russia and the Soviet Union 1917–1941

OCR A: Germany 1925–1955: The People and the State

OCR A: War and British Society c790–c2010

Eduqas: Changes in Health and Medicine in Britain c500–Present

Eduqas: The Development of Germany 1919–1991

Eduqas: The Development of the UK 1919–1990

Eduqas: The Development of Warfare in Britain c500–Present

WJEC: Changes in Health and Medicine c1340–Present

Exam-style questions covered in this chapter

Exam board	Lesson/activity question location	Command words	History skills/concepts
AQA	**5.1A** Source Analysis: 2	How useful…	Source analysis
	5.1B Source Analysis: 3	How useful…	Source analysis
	5.2A Source Analysis: 2	How useful…	Source analysis
	5.2B Interpretation Analysis: 2	How convincing…	Interpretation analysis
	5.3B Causation: 1	…more important reason…	Cause and consequence
	5.4 Interpretation Analysis: 1	How convincing…	Interpretation analysis
	5.5B Source Analysis: 4	How useful…	Source analysis

Exam board	Lesson/activity question location	Command words	History skills/concepts
AQA	5.6 Change: 1,2	Explain two ways... similar/different	Change and continuity
	5.8 Significance: 2	Explain the significance...	Significance
	5.9A Source Analysis: 2	How do you know?	Source analysis
	5.10A Knowledge and Understanding: 2	Describe...	Knowledge and understanding
	5.10B Source Analysis: 2	Critical...how do you know...	Source analysis
	5.11B Over to You: 2	Describe...	Knowledge and understanding
	5.11B Change: 1	Explain two ways... different	Change and continuity
	5.13 Knowledge and Understanding: 1	Describe...	Knowledge and understanding
Edexcel	5.1A Source Analysis: 2	How useful...	Source analysis
	5.1B Source Analysis: 3	How useful...	Source analysis
	5.1C Causation: 1	Explain two of the following...	Cause and consequence
	5.2A Source Analysis: 2	How useful...	Source analysis
	5.5A Interpretation Analysis: 2	What is the main difference...	Interpretation analysis
	5.5B Source Analysis: 4	How useful...	Source analysis
	5.10A Knowledge and Understanding: 2	Describe...	Knowledge and understanding
	5.11B Over to You: 2	Describe...	Knowledge and understanding
	5.13 Knowledge and Understanding: 1	Describe...	Knowledge and understanding
OCR A	5.1A Source Analysis: 2	How useful...	Source analysis
	5.1B Source Analysis: 3	How useful...	Source analysis
	5.2A Source Analysis: 2	How useful...	Source analysis
	5.5B Source Analysis: 4	How useful...	Source analysis
	5.10A Knowledge and Understanding: 2	Describe...	Knowledge and understanding
	5.11B Over to You: 2	Describe...	Knowledge and understanding
	5.13 Knowledge and Understanding: 1	Describe...	Knowledge and understanding
OCR B	5.1A Source Analysis: 2	How useful...	Source analysis
	5.1B Source Analysis: 3	How useful...	Source analysis
	5.2A Source Analysis: 2	How useful...	Source analysis
	5.5B Source Analysis: 4	How useful...	Source analysis
Eduqas	5.9A Source Analysis: 2	What was the purpose...	Source analysis
	5.10A Knowledge and Understanding: 2	Describe...	Knowledge and understanding
	5.11B Over to You: 2	Describe...	Knowledge and understanding
	5.13 Knowledge and Understanding: 1	Describe...	Knowledge and understanding
WJEC	5.4 Over to You: 1a, 1b, 1c	Complete the sentences...	Knowledge and understanding
	5.9A Source Analysis	What was the purpose...	Source analysis
	5.10A Over to You: 1	Complete the sentences	Seconded and understanding
	5.10A Knowledge and Understanding: 2	Describe...	Knowledge and understanding
	5.11B Over to You: 2	Describe...	Knowledge and understanding
	5.13 Knowledge and Understanding: 1	Describe...	Knowledge and understanding

A brief history

5.1A/B/C The Second World War: an overview

The chapter starts with a focus on the key term 'Blitzkrieg'. Students will explore the different stages of Blitzkrieg and how the Nazis used this method of warfare to sweep across Europe. Students are often very engaged by the events of Operation Sealion and the Battle of Britain. The series of overviews provided in this lesson allow the students to make judgements on the war while linking back to previous learning on Hitler's aims. They will grasp the 'global' nature of the war, then move on to look at turning points such as the battles of Midway, Stalingrad and El Alamein. Students will consolidate their knowledge using the different source utility activities. They will have to use their inference and analysing skills to describe sources and then explain how useful they are. Students are also encouraged to consider the turning points of the war, drawing on their cause and consequence skills.

5.2A/B How should we remember Dunkirk?

Students will draw on their knowledge of Blitzkrieg to help them understand the Allied forces being pushed to the coast. They will then explore Operation Dynamo; the numbers could seem quite abstract so show the students as many pictures and film clips as you can to allow them to see the scale of Dunkirk. Students will use sources to determine whether Dunkirk is being portrayed as a success or failure for the British; they will also compare the viewpoints. This will then be taken a step further by analysing the German reaction to Dunkirk and why it was viewed as a German victory.

5.3A/B Who were 'the Few'?

Operation Sealion and the Battle of Britain are undeniably exciting, so this lesson will get the students engaged. A comparison of the two air forces shows that the Luftwaffe was in better shape than the RAF; however, as with Dunkirk, chance is explored as a factor for the British victory. Once an overview of the main planes used in the Battle of Britain has been explored the students will complete a numeracy activity to help them compare the aircraft. They will then apply the content by analysing Churchill's words about 'the Few'. This will culminate in students making a judgement on the most important reason for British victory. Their answers should be fully explained.

5.4 Soldiers of Empire

The theme of empire troops was also explored in Chapter 2 when looking at the First World War (2.7A/B Soldiers of Empire). Students will explore

Timeline

November 1938
Nazis target Jewish shops and synagogues in an attack known as Kristallnacht.

1 September 1939
Germany invades Poland using Blitzkrieg, starting the Second World War.

Spring 1940
Germany attacks France, Denmark, Norway, the Netherlands and Belgium.

May 1940
Winston Churchill becomes Prime Minister.

May 1940
The Battle of Dunkirk.

July 1940
Hitler launches Operation Sealion, which leads to the Battle of Britain.

27 September 1940
The Tripartite Pact is signed between Germany, Japan and Italy creating the Axis powers.

June 1941
Florey and Chain get money from the US government to develop penicillin.

June 1941
Operation Barbarossa is put into action for Hitler's goal of taking over the Soviet Union.

7 December 1941
Japan attacks Pearl Harbor.

January 1942
Nazi Leaders are informed of the 'Final Solution' at the Wannsee Conference.

6 June 1944
D-Day.

January 1945
The RAF bombs the German city of Dresden.

6 August 1945
A nuclear bomb is dropped on Hiroshima, Japan.

9 August 1945
A second nuclear bomb is dropped on the Japanese port of Nagasaki, ending the war.

1945
The United Nations is created.

1946
The National Blood Transfusion Service is set up.

the various countries of the British Empire and Commonwealth that fought for Britain. Students will also explore the resources offered by these countries that were vital in Britain's eventual victory. A source analysis activity looking at a propaganda poster will give students a chance to combine their previous learning on propaganda analysis with this new content. They will then use this sequence of learning to answer a GCSE style 'how convincing' question.

5.5A/B Evacuation

Linking to the Battle of Britain and the Blitz students will now look at the social history of the Second World War. They will get a sense of what it was like for evacuees as they see the two ways that children found homes once they made it to the countryside, and how they were treated by their hosts. Students will get a sense of the class differences between the evacuees and their country hosts. This lesson could be taken a step further by getting students to consider how much has changed in cities since the Industrial Revolution.

5.6 The home front

Now that students have built on their overview of the various battles of the Second World War they will evaluate the impact on civilians in towns and cities across Britain. The term 'total war' is explored to explain the resources that were pulled from all areas of life. Students will make a judgement on the three biggest changes to civilian life. Students are also asked to demonstrate change by comparing the home fronts of the First and Second World Wars showing change. More able students should try to categorise the similarities and differences for a more sophisticated response.

5.7 How did the Second World War change health and medicine?

Building on advances in medicine throughout the First World War students will see how these advances were developed in the Second World War. Examples include: the development of blood transfusions, plastic surgery and heart surgery, as well as antibiotics, which were new to the era. The focus on both medical and public health develops the concept of 'total war' – the government had no option but to help everyone. Students then evaluate medical advances linked to war, explaining how the war impacted their development.

5.8 Penicillin and the war

Students will now have a good understanding of how medicine developed throughout the two world wars, but they must now focus on the impact of penicillin.

The cartoon story will help them understand the development of penicillin and how luck and chance can be important factors in history. Students will then evaluate the role of the individual using interpretations. Finally, they will explain the significance of Fleming's discovery. Answers should consider the immediate importance, and then the short- and long-term significance. More able students should be able to explain why it is significant today.

5.9A/B Why is Sir Arthur Harris such a controversial figure?

This enquiry-focused lesson will undoubtedly result in some healthy debate. The students are given questions to consider as they progress through the lesson; it would be a great idea to get them to record their opinions at different stages of the enquiry – consider using a whole class opinion line with sticky notes, which students place somewhere along the line depending on how strongly they agree or disagree with a statement. Students are required to use specific knowledge when discussing precision and area bombing. The different opinions about the bombing of Dresden will be explored; it is up to the students to use the data provided to write a speech giving their opinion on the civilian attack. This would be a great opportunity to develop oracy.

5.10A/B Why is Winston Churchill on a £5 note?

Churchill is one of those figures from history whom students always know. This lesson not only gives them a more well-rounded idea of Churchill, but it also allows them to form an opinion on his significance. They will build their opinions using sources and interpretations that offer insight and judgement on Churchill's leadership. Students will consider Churchill as a war leader and whether he did a good job or not – they should refer back to the questions at the start of the lesson to support their judgements. A good way to take this lesson further is to get students to consider why the different opinions/interpretations of Churchill exist, using the provenance of the sources and interpretations.

5.11A/B The journey to the 'Final Solution'

This lesson starts with much-needed context of antisemitism in Europe and then progresses to a timeline of anti-Jewish laws in Germany under the Nazis. Students will gather content that shows how Jewish persecution grew in Germany and Nazi-occupied Europe over the years – they will also have to deal with the realisation that normal citizens were responsible for helping enforce Nazi laws. The lesson then progresses to explain the 'Final Solution' and the Holocaust – it is important that you create a space where students can ask questions and express their feelings on the content being delivered. This is essential as students are asked to consider the use of language and labels in history with the key term *Holocaust* and then consider whether Auschwitz-Birkenau should be a museum. Students will then apply what they have learned to a question about change, comparing Nazi persecution of Jewish people before the war with persecution during the war.

5.12 The war goes nuclear

Students will gain more context of the global war through this lesson focusing on Japan. Students should go back and look at their timeline from the first lesson of this chapter to see where they placed Pearl Harbor as an important event. They will learn about the bombs in Hiroshima and Nagasaki and then President Truman's justifications. The 'Later on' feature shows the lasting legacy of the bombs on the Japanese people – this adds a more human aspect to the history. Students will consolidate this by using interpretations to identify justifications and explain why America denied the legacy of the bombs.

5.13 A United Nations

The aftermath of war can be quite a difficult concept for students to grasp so it would be advisable to make comparisons to the First World War and the League of Nations. Students will explore the different branches of the United Nations while looking at the positive and negative aspects of the organisation. A way to take this lesson further would be to look at current cases for the UN, partnering up with your RE, Citizenship and/or Politics departments. Students will analyse the effectiveness of the UN and then describe its role in improving the world.

Further reading and links

For teachers:

- *The Phoney Victory: The World War II Illusion* by Peter Hitchens (I B Tauris, 2018) offers a new take on the part Britain and Churchill played in the war. It also explores the motives for tackling Nazism. This would help add further depth to the lesson on Churchill.

- The final episode of Andrew Marr's *History of the World* TV series (BBC, 2012) explores the Manhattan Project (the research project that produced the first nuclear weapons) and the impact

the bombs created on Japan. This will help you answer the questions the students will undoubtedly have about nuclear weapons during the war.

For students:

- Get students to read *Goodnight Mister Tom* by Michelle Magorian. This novel gives an insight into the Blitz and evacuation. However, it also deals with the issues of poverty and abuse. This is a great story to help your students consolidate their learning.

- The BBC has a collection of very powerful videos, part documentary part dramatisation, that show the changing policies towards the Jews in Nazi Germany. From your search engine, search 'BBC Two Nazi Germany' to find the clips.

Beyond the classroom

- Visits to some of the superb sights and places of interest around the country are obvious enrichment opportunities – for example, the Imperial War Museums (in London, Manchester and Cambridgeshire), Churchill's War Rooms, HMS *Belfast* and Bletchley Park.

- Set up a school United Nations for the students to run. They should use this enrichment opportunity to discuss issues facing the UN today.

- Get some students to work with the Geography and Science departments to make a display on the use of nuclear weapons during the Second World War.

- There are not many living survivors of the Holocaust who are still able to travel to school but there are organisations that can arrange a visit to your school, such as the Holocaust Educational Trust. This would give students more information about the persecution of Jews in Nazi-controlled Europe.

- Antibiotics were developed during the Second World War with penicillin being used widely from the 1940s. However, some bacteria have 'learned' how to resist the drugs, which mean certain antibiotics no longer work against these bacteria. Today, medical experts warn of the dangers of overuse of antibiotics, and scientists are working hard to develop new ones that can tackle the resistant bacteria. Get your class to work with the Science department to create an assembly on the history of antibiotics and the current concerns of medical professionals about their effectiveness.

Answers guidance

The answers provided here are examples, based on the information provided in the Student Book. There may be other factors which are relevant to each question, and students may draw on as much of their own knowledge as possible to give detailed and precise answers. There are also many ways of answering questions, including exam-style questions (for example, of structuring an essay). However, these exemplar answers should provide a good starting point.

5.1A The Second World War: an overview
PAGES 106–107

Over to You

1a The Blitz was the name given to the German air raids on major British cities from 1940–1941, whereas Blitzkrieg was the intense German military campaign using tanks, aircraft and troops to try to bring about a swift victory.

1b Answers may include: surprise attack meant the enemy wasn't prepared; lots of the latest weaponry attacking in the same place meant they could break through; speed was a factor too, with no time for the enemy to bring in reinforcements.

2a Going well for the Germans – e.g. Hitler's armies occupied much of central Europe, and there was little the defending armies could do. However, the invasion of Britain was stopped.

2b Not so well – e.g. British cities under attack, few allies in Europe, British, French and Belgian troops escaped from Dunkirk to England – so in retreat too. However, Britain won the Battle of Britain.

Source Analysis

1 In the spring of 1940, Germany attacked France, Denmark, Norway, the Netherlands and Belgium. Thousands of British, French and Belgian troops escaped from Dunkirk to Britain in a fleet of yachts, paddle steamers, warships, and even rowing boats.

2 Answers will vary but will perhaps focus on the negative (because Cundall wasn't there). However, the fact that he used published accounts, photographs and eye-witness reports means that many of the details may be accurate. It shows that the government thought the event was worth officially recording, so it is useful for the historian to know that the government thought this was an important event. Also it gives the historian some idea of the scale of the event, the danger etc.

5.1B The Second World War: an overview
PAGES 108–109

Over to You

1 Answers will reflect the dominance Hitler had over major European countries; however, reference might be made to Britain and the USSR not totally under Hitler's control.

2 In December 1941, after Japan had launched a surprise attack on the US naval base of Pearl Harbor in Hawaii. This was an attempt to knock out America's navy in one go (and give it control of the rich lands in the Far East).

3a Answers should reflect that it is the time at which a situation starts to change in an important way.

3b Because as a result of what happened there, the direction of the war began to change towards an Allied victory and against Italy, Germany and Japan. For example, the Battle of Midway (June 1942) was a turning point because the Japanese advance was stopped and gradually the Americans began to drive them back, island by island.

Source Analysis

1 Adolf Hitler and Hermann Goering (another leading Nazi).

2 It was very cold in the USSR, which meant they had to stop and go home, and the way back will be tough on the German army.

3 Answers should focus on how it gives us some idea of why the campaign failed (cold) and the impact on the German army (dead bodies), as well as the fact that this was a failure/mistake and led to a change in the direction of the war – retreat rather than expansion.

5.1C The Second World War: an overview
PAGES 110–111

Over to You

1 Answers will reflect the key events and dates.

2a Answers may vary, but 'Bad times for Britain' could go around the time of Dunkirk or the Blitz, 'Things are changing' might go near one of the turning points identified (Battle of Stalingrad) and 'Victory' may go near the end, with victory over Germany and/or Japan.

2b Students will justify why they have chosen where they have put the headings.

3 Answers will vary, but students should justify why they think the image(s) should be used.

Causation

1 • America joined the war in 1941 after the Japanese attack on Pearl Harbor and immediately brought its vast resources to bear on Japan and its allies – this was important on D-Day, for example, when British, US and other Allied troops landed on beaches in Normandy, north-west France. Despite brutal fighting on the beaches and in the French countryside, the Allies were able to advance and the Germans were gradually pushed back.

- In Egypt, at El Alamein, British troops defeated the Germans. With help from the Americans, the British drove the Germans out of North Africa and invaded Italy. Eventually, one of Germany's key allies was defeated, and another front opened up as the Germans pushed back.
- Blitzkrieg involved fast-moving columns of tanks supported by infantry soldiers and dive-bomber attacks. Parachutists were dropped behind enemy lines the night before to destroy enemy positions and cut telephone wires. After this tactic was used in Poland in September 1939, the Polish armed forces were defeated, and again this tactic was used against other nations. These swift, surprise attacks meant the enemy wasn't prepared – and attacking in the same place meant the Germans could break through easily and give no time for the enemy to bring in reinforcements.

5.2A How should we remember Dunkirk?

PAGES 112–113

Over to You

1a The British government organised a huge rescue operation known as Operation Dynamo – the evacuation of troops to Britain using warships. They were helped by dozens of ordinary citizens in hundreds of small boats, paddle steamers, fishing boats, yachts, and even rowing boats.

1b Students may mention that the government was keen to report a good news story in a time of many Nazi victories; that the British public were behind the troops; that everyone was in it together against the Nazis.

2 Answers will vary, depending on opinion – but their opinion should be explained. 'I think this because…'

3 He is a little less enthusiastic about the evacuation and says that, while it was a victory of sorts, he points out that wars are not won by evacuations. He actually mentions the negative element of it.

Source Analysis

1 Some students might focus on the size of the well-dressed, well-armed soldier who is towering over a cliff – they might see the size as Britain's desire to become larger, well armed and equipped. His raised fist and stern look might be in defiance of the Germans, and the caption 'Very well' might suggest that they have accepted what is coming and will continue determinedly alone.

2 It was after the evacuation so was perhaps a morale booster to pull the nation together; a rallying call to the British people to show that they will stand up to the Nazis.

5.2B How should we remember Dunkirk?

PAGES 114–115

Over to You

1a As a battle that was the heaviest defeat for the British and French but a great victory for the Germans.

1b Answers will vary, but may reflect that it could be viewed both ways in that the British were in retreat, but getting so many soldiers home was a victory of sorts.

2a On page 113 the sources are largely reporting Dunkirk as a victory, whereas the evacuation is reported more as a defeat on the next two pages.

2b Because we are seeing British reporting on page 113 and a wider variety of sources from some different nations (Germany – the enemy) on the later pages. We are also seeing interpretations, which means the people have had time to reflect and weigh it up before coming to a conclusion and are not influenced by censorship or propaganda pressures of the time.

3a Answers may vary but may include a focus on boosting morale, censorship, propaganda.

3b Answers will vary.

3c Answers will vary but might reflect that it was a victory in getting soldiers and equipment back to Britain, but a defeat in that France was now part of the German empire.

Source Analysis

1 The broadcast says that Dunkirk was a military disaster – but almost immediately the British media began to turn it into a victory to boost the morale of the British public. And this created the 'Dunkirk myth' that the whole episode was somehow a type of victory, even though it was really a retreat/defeat.

2 Student answers will vary, but most will emphasise the fact that reports at the time were positive from a British perspective (they may use Source B as an example), despite the fact that the actual statistics show that it was a military disaster in terms of the retreat and the equipment the British left behind. This led to the creation of a 'myth' that the evacuation was some sort of victory, which was simply propaganda, when in fact the reality was different.

They will probably find the interpretation convincing.

5.3A Who were 'the Few'?

PAGES 116–117

Over to You

1 Answers will reflect Hitler's dominance of Europe and mention some of the countries the Germans had occupied as examples.

2a German secret plan to get German soldiers onto British soil by the end of August 1940. Troops were to launch a surprise attack from Ramsgate to the area west of the Isle of Wight. The British Navy would be attacked. Then troops would land in Britain. For Operation Sealion to have any chance of success, Hitler needed to destroy Britain's air force so it would be easier for German ships to transport soldiers over the English Channel to begin the land invasion of Britain.

2b Students will probably think 'yes' because of the overwhelming strength of Hitler's forces – e.g. Germany had 824 fighter planes and 1017 bombers in service. Britain only had about 600 fighter planes.

5.3B Who were 'the Few'?

PAGES 118–119

Over to You

1a Answers will reflect the figures.

1b Answers will vary, but students should explain their choice.

1c Possibly because it was sleek and beautiful, and it handled very well, while the Hurricane was slower and not as 'good looking'.

2 It shows pilots scrambling to get to their planes as bombers attack overhead.

3a It means that lots of people owe thanks to the few pilots who fought in the Battle of Britain.

3b Students' instructions will vary.

4 The figures agreed after the war are probably more accurate as they are not subject to the same censorship/propaganda influences as during the war.

Causation

1 Answers will reflect that both were important:
 • Radar: the British could detect enemy planes before they reached Britain – and the 51 radar stations could direct British fighters to the Germans in a matter of minutes, leaving them enough fuel to attack the German planes repeatedly.
 • Hitler's deadline: the decision to switch to bombing London meant that Hitler postponed the invasion. He decided to use his military forces to bomb London, rather than bomb airfields, so the Battle of Britain ended. He did not have the resources to do both. Students may add that they think one was more important than the other – and may add other reasons too (e.g. skilled pilots from all around the world; British spirit/determination; excellent aircraft; British production of planes was higher than Germans).

5.4 Soldiers of Empire

PAGES 120–121

Over to You

1a medals/bravery or leadership skills

1b submarines/Sydney Harbour

1c Victoria Crosses/Britain

2a Soldiers from Allied nations all marching together.

2b To show that Britain had allies around the world in the British Empire.

2c Issued in 1941, at a time when Britain 'stood alone' against Nazi-occupied Europe. Its aim was to reassure people that they had allies around the world in the British Empire.

3 Student answers will use examples from the map on page 121. For example, over 330,000 South Africans fought for Britain, and over 11,000 were killed.

Interpretation Analysis

1 Answers will vary, but students may pick out the fact that Britain was not truly alone in 1940–1941 and were helped out considerably by nations in the empire. So they may be 'convinced' by the interpretation.

5.5A Evacuation

PAGES 122–123

Over to You

1a Being taken from places at risk during war, such as cities, to safer places, such as the countryside.

1b Answers will vary.

2a Student inferences may vary but they may say it contains name, address, date of birth, destination etc.

2b Student inferences may vary but they may say clothes, book, photo of family etc.

2c Student inferences may vary but they may say helper/billeting officer.

2d Student inferences may vary but they may say they are queuing to get the train or to be seen by the helper. The boy may be out of line because he is lost, confused upset.

2e Answers will vary.

3 Answers will vary.

Interpretation Analysis

1 Answers will summarise 'Choose a child' and 'Hunt for a home'.

2 C says that they were last to find a home because the older boy

promised not to be separated from his sister, so they would have to be placed in a home big enough to house them, while D says that it may have been attitude to race at the time – they 'didn't have any coloured people there in those days'.

5.5B Evacuation

PAGES 124–125

Over to You

1a Answers will vary but students may think Rosie was scared because things are so unfamiliar/different (she whispers), the children had a poor background/were used to things being dirty (everything was so clean in comparison), they were not very hygienic at home (never cleaned teeth before).

1b Answers will vary but students might say cleaner, better facilities (hot water), better hygiene.

2a Examples include: Positive: from Interpretation E – cleanliness of new surroundings, from Source H – a loving, welcoming environment. Negative: from Interpretations C and D (on page 123) – difficulty finding a home; from Interpretation G – bullying at school.

2b Answers will vary, but will be based on personal experiences of both hosts and evacuees.

3 Student letters will vary.

Source Analysis

1 Hitler

2 Trying to get the evacuated mother to go back to the city – so he can bomb them.

3 Mothers should not put their children in danger. Hitler wants to bomb the cities so taking the children back puts them in danger and gives Hitler what he wants.

4 Answers will vary but will reflect that it is useful as it shows where the children went (out of the cities, shown

in the background) and why they went (to avoid what the Nazis/Hitler was doing to the cities). It also shows the effectiveness of the policy – that children were removed, but many were coming back, so the government acted to deal with it, which shows a level of policy making aimed at ordinary citizens.

5.6 The home front

PAGES 126–127

Over to You

1 When a war involves all of the people of a country in some way, not just soldiers fighting, but people 'at home'.

2 Students' talks or posters will vary but will reflect the content covered on the pages and should include the details listed.

3 Answers will vary but they might mention evacuation, bombing of cities and blackouts.

Change

1 Answers may include bombing from the air, a Women's Land Army, rationing.

2 Answers may include increased scale of city bombing, the Home Guard, evacuation.

5.7 How did the Second World War change health and medicine?

PAGES 128–129

Over to You

1 • Blood transfusions: Large blood banks were developed in both the USA and Britain in the years leading up to the Second World War, helping to save many lives during the war.
• Plastic surgery: Archibald McIndoe developed new ways to deal with the terrible burns that many pilots suffered when their

aircraft were on fire, using drugs in new ways to help control infections.
• Heart surgery: US army surgeon Dwight Harken developed ways to cut into beating hearts to remove bullets and shrapnel.

2a Answers may include the work of Archibald McIndoe in developing new ways to deal with the terrible burns that many pilots suffered. He simply may not have had the patients to work on if it were not for the war.

2b Answers may include the improvements made to fight poverty. The war highlighted the plight of some poor people and made the government more committed to tackling poverty. There were already moves made (e.g. Liberal Reforms) to tackle poverty, but the war sped up new moves and government intervention.

5.8 Penicillin and the war

PAGES 130–131

Over to You

1 A chemical substance that kills bacteria and cures infections.

2 Alexander Fleming: discovered penicillin could kill some germs. Florey and Chain: worked with penicillin as an antibiotic, secured funding, tested on animals, tested on humans. Albert Alexander: penicillin was first used on him when he got an infection. US government: funded the work of Florey and Chain, mass produced penicillin.

3 The growing number of wounded soldiers with nasty infections meant that more penicillin was quickly needed. In June 1941, Florey went to America to meet with the US government and the Americans realised what an important drug penicillin could be and agreed to pay several large chemical companies to make millions of litres of it.

4 Answers will include the initial work in the 1930s to make a list of all the substances that could kill germs, through to reading about Fleming's work, approaching British government, securing funding, experimentation (mice), then human (Albert Alexander), approaching US government (Florey) and securing funding for mass production.

Significance

1 Students should mention that the article says how dangerous even the smallest wounds could be before antibiotics, and then that the work of Fleming, Chain and Florey has not only given us the ability to treat infections, but it's made other medical procedures possible.

2 Answers will briefly outline the discovery – and then mention the work of Florey and Chain before describing the impact of penicillin in the Second World War and in today's world. Some students might reference that, at the time, little was done about Fleming's discovery, so the initial discovery did not make a great impact in the late 1920s and 1930s, and it was only when Florey and Chain began work that the real impact was shown.

5.9A Why is Sir Arthur Harris such a controversial figure?
PAGES 132–133

Over to You

1 Precision bombing is precise – it is carefully targeted bombing of specific locations such as docks, air bases and munitions factories. Area bombing is the release of bombs over a whole town or city – it is not precise.

2 Answers may include that Harris identifies Dresden as a centre of 'war industry' (Source D). Also, a military report from January 1945 reported that thousands of German soldiers were collecting in Dresden before being sent off to fight.

3 In October 1944, a detailed report by the British on Dresden concluded that the city was an 'unattractive target'.

Source Analysis

1 It shows British bomber planes dropping bombs on German factories in order to destroy them.

2 Student answers will vary but the purpose was to educate the public on Britain's tactics – and justify the bombings by explaining why they were taking place. The factories were targeted because that's where the manufacturing of Germans bombs took place.

5.9B Why is Sir Arthur Harris such a controversial figure?
PAGES 134–135

Over to You

1 Student opinions will vary, but should be backed up by evidence where possible.

5.10A Why is Winston Churchill on a £5 note?
PAGES 136–137

Over to You

1 • Blenheim Palace
 • war reporter
 • 1900
 • Prime Minister

2 Answers may vary but could include: to show he was tough and prepared to fight (the bulldog is a tough dog with fighting spirit, and he is pictured over the country to show protective instinct).

3 Answers will vary, but they may say they make you feel patriotic (to defend the hills and beaches etc.), perhaps worried (because of the 'struggle' and 'suffering' mentioned), encouraged that a leader was ready for the fight.

4 Answers may include that it shows he was aware and concerned of the plight of ordinary people, that he cared about their problems.

Knowledge and Understanding

1 Answers may include: determined, caring, defiant, tough, stubborn.

2 Students should mention that he became Prime Minister in 1940, and gave rousing speeches, rallied people in bombed out cities and inspired people with his determination and stubbornness to resist the Nazis.

5.10B Why is Winston Churchill on a £5 note?
PAGES 138–139

Over to You

1a Students will assess the sources and interpretations for strengths and weaknesses. For example, in Source I, Eisenhower mentions that one of Churchill's strengths was as an 'inspirational leader', whereas Source G says that one of Churchill's weaknesses was that he surrounded himself with people who said 'yes' to him all the time and that his colleagues feared him. This was a weakness because some people may not say the thing that would help the situation through fear of contradicting Churchill.

1b Answers may vary, but an example might be being single-minded and totally dedicated to winning the war. Often this would be seen as a quality, but sometimes it is important to know when to take advice from different sources to give you other views and options.

2 Answers will vary.

3 Student answers will vary, but they may say that opinions about events that people were involved in might change, as well as our perceptions of their actions.

Source Analysis

1 He didn't like it at all, it upset him.

2 It shows a negative view of him, he looks tired, old and worn out. It is very different to the image of Churchill as a great war leader.

5.11A The journey to the 'Final Solution'
PAGES 140–141

Over to You

1 Leading Nazis were informed of the plan to kill all the Jewish people in Europe by working them to death, using poison gas or shooting. The plan was called the 'Final Solution'.

2a antisemitism: the strong dislike or cruel and unfair treatment of Jewish people.

2b ghetto: a small, restricted area of a town where Jewish people were forced to live by the Nazis.

2c Einsatzgruppen: Nazi execution squads that went out into the countryside in mobile vans and shot or gassed as many Jewish people as they could find.

3 Answers will reflect the increasingly difficult laws and regulations, as well

as Kristallnacht and the introduction of ghettos.

4a To be cruel, to make their lives more and more difficult, to drive Jews away from Germany, because the Nazis increasingly wanted to persecute Jewish people.

4b They get harsher, more strict, crueler.

5.11B The journey to the 'Final Solution'
PAGES 142–143

Over to You

1a The commonly known name for the Nazis' attempt to wipe out the Jewish race.

1b Some have objected to this word, as it means 'sacrifice'. They argue that this implies that Jewish people were 'offering themselves' in some way.

2 Answers may include: Jews set up secret schools, theatres and places of worship in some ghettos. In 1943, Jews rebelled against the German soldiers in the Warsaw Ghetto in Poland. It took 43 days for the Germans to finally regain control. The Germans then arrested and executed all those involved, and burned down the ghetto. In the Treblinka death camp in 1943, one of the prisoners managed to get into the weapons store where he handed out guns and grenades. After setting the camp on fire, 150 prisoners managed to escape, killing 15 guards in the process. However, the Nazis soon regained control and many escapees were killed.

3a Answers will vary but may reflect that people might have wanted it destroyed to wipe out the awful episode, or to prevent it becoming a curious tourist attraction.

3b Answers will vary.

Change

1 Students may write that persecution before the war was designed to make the life of Jewish people uncomfortable and difficult, forcing them to leave their homes, jobs or even leave the country. When war broke out the Nazis increased the cruelty and rounded up Jewish people (in ghettos) and then began systematically exterminating them.

5.12 The war goes nuclear
PAGES 144–145

Over to You

1 Answers will vary, but may include: USA and Japan were rivals. Both wanted control over the rich lands of the Far East, containing coal, oil, rubber etc. Japan lacks natural resources and invaded other countries to get them. By attacking Pearl Harbor, Japan hoped to destroy the US fleet and take all the land it wanted. (50 words)

2a Answers will vary, but will reflect the information on these pages.

2b Student summaries will vary but should reflect four reasons: to end the war quickly; to get revenge (for the Japanese attack on Pearl Harbor in 1941 – and Japanese cruelty); to justify the expense of the nuclear weapons programme; to demonstrate power (particularly to the USSR).

2c To end the war quickly: despite the fact that Japan was close to defeat, the bombs were dropped to force a quick Japanese surrender.

3a • radiation sickness: illness as a result of exposure to very high levels of radiation. This can lead to burns, problems with the blood, and injury to many of the body's vital systems – even death.

- hibakusha: a person who has become ill as a result of radiation sickness from the atomic bombs.

3b Answers will vary but may include: didn't know much about it, so were unlikely to confirm what they didn't know; didn't want to admit to something so terrible; didn't want people near where the bombs had been tested (in the USA) to become alarmed.

5.13 A United Nations

PAGES 146–147

Over to You

1 Student responses will vary but should reflect the questions.
2 Answers will vary.
3 Blue was selected because it is rarely used by countries on the uniforms or equipment of their armed forces. The peace symbols (olive branches) are around the map of the world because the UN attempts to preserve peace around the world.

Knowledge and Understanding

1 The United Nations is an international organisation, founded in 1945, that attempts to maintain international peace and security, develop friendly relations among nations and promote social progress, better living standards and human rights through its various committees and organisations such as UNESCO, UNICEF and the WHO.

Chapter 5 Have you been learning?

Answers guidance

Chapter 5 Have you been learning?

Quick Knowledge Quiz

PAGE 148

1 **b** Blitzkrieg
2 **a** Dunkirk
3 **c** Operation Sealion
4 **c** India
5 **c** the Blitz
6 **b** penicillin
7 **a** Arthur Harris
8 **a** May 1940
9 **b** Pearl Harbor
10 **a** UNICEF

Literacy Focus

PAGE 149

Linking words

1 In 1936, two scientists from Oxford University read Fleming's article on penicillin. They were called Howard Florey and Ernst Chain. Florey was from Australia **and** Chain was a German-born Jew who came to Britain to escape the Nazis. Just days after the Second World War began, they got a small amount of money from the British government. **As a result** they began making small amounts of penicillin.

Firstly, in February 1941, they treated a policeman. The policeman was named Albert Alexander **and notably** he had developed a severe face infection **because** he had scratched his face on a rose bush. Alexander began to recover and his condition improved. **However**, supplies of penicillin ran out **and** he died. **Subsequently**, it proved the power of penicillin in treating humans.

Assessment summary

The assessments in this textbook have been carefully designed and tested with History teachers to support student progression throughout the course. This specific assessment is written to support Year 8 or Year 9 students in tackling questions relating to analysing interpretations.

1   Interpretations **A** and **B** give different views about Winston Churchill. What is the main difference between the views?

2   Suggest one reason **Interpretations A** and **B** give different views about Churchill.

3   How far do you agree with **Interpretation A** about Winston Churchill? Explain your answer, using both interpretations and your own knowledge of the historical context. (20)

▼ **INTERPRETATION A** Adapted from an article in the *Telegraph*, January 2015, by Boris Johnson. At the time, Johnson was the Conservative Mayor of London, and later became Prime Minister and leader of the Conservative Party – the same party that Churchill belonged to.

'His legacy is everywhere. He helped set up the modern welfare state, supporting unemployment insurance and other social protections in the years before the First World War. It was Churchill and Churchill alone who made sure that Britain continued to fight during the Second World War. It was Churchill who brought America in. If Churchill had not been Prime Minister in 1940, there seems little doubt that Britain would have let Hitler have his way, plunging Europe into darkness. No other politician at the time had the guts to do what he did; and it is to him that the world owes thanks for the eventual victory over Nazism, and the 70 years of peace that have followed.'

▼ **INTERPRETATION B** Annette Mackin was a journalist for the *Socialist Worker*, a publication that supported equality and working-class ideals and would be described as 'left-wing'. 'Right-wing' is the opposite and is usually linked to ideas that support traditions and keeping things the way they are. When Mackin refers to Churchill's 'class' in this article (published in January 2015), she is talking about the fact that he comes from a very old, rich, land-owning family.

'Racist and brutal – and against social progress. That is the way we should remember Winston Churchill. But the ruling class are desperate for us to celebrate a myth. Leading the charge is Boris Johnson who recently published a biography of Churchill. David Cameron has spoken of how Churchill is his "favourite" prime minister. They argue that through the power of his speeches he inspired the people of Britain to rise up against the Nazi threat during the Second World War. This is a lie. Churchill was not an anti-Nazi hero, he wanted to defend his class. What motivated many people to fight was vastly different from what motivated Churchill. He wasn't against Hitler because he was a Nazi. It was because he threatened Britain.

The truth about Churchill's role in many atrocities is slowly emerging. During the Indian famine in 1943 it is now estimated that over five million people died. The famine was a product of the Second World War. Churchill refused to send emergency famine relief. Instead he said Indians were used to starving. His racism didn't stop there. He waged a war at home against the working class in Britain. In 1911 transport workers walked out on strike for better pay. In response, Churchill sent in the military to help rail bosses. They opened fire on ordinary people in Liverpool.'

Students will start by looking at the content of the interpretations (Question 1) to find differences when considering opinions of Churchill. Then the focus will turn to the provenance to explain why those differences exist (Question 2). This will then allow students to write a structured answer explaining how far they agree with Interpretation A, using both interpretations and their own knowledge to help them make their judgement (Question 3).

Students are provided with sentence starters, scaffolding activities to help build answers, and questions to ask when evaluating the interpretations.

For the mark scheme, see page 123.

A note about the end-of-chapter assessments

There is an assessment for each Student Book chapter. Each is structured like a GCSE exam-style question, with scaffolding steps to support KS3 students. Each assessment has a total of 20 marks, and is designed to be completed in a typical lesson – each has been written with a time allowance of about 30 minutes.

There is a mark scheme for each assessment. You can choose how to give student outcomes: a mark out of 20; a percentage; a performance indicator (we use a three-stage indicator – 'Developing', 'Secure', 'Extending' – but you could adapt to match any performance indicators used in your school); or a GCSE grade indicator. To convert raw marks to a performance or GCSE grade indicator, use this table:

Raw marks			
0	1–6	7–13	14–20
GCSE grade (9–1) indicators*			
U	1–3	4–6	7–9
Performance indicator			
Ungraded	Developing	Secure	Extending

*Please appreciate that these are approximate grades based on grade boundaries from recent GCSE exam papers. If a student achieves a Grade 7 in one of these assessments, it is not the equivalent of a Grade 7 at GCSE. Instead it is an indicator of the grade the student could expect to get if they continue on their flight path through KS3 and GCSE. Please note:
  • the raw-mark boundaries are based on but do not match precisely those for recent GCSE exam papers: this is because our assessments are focused around one exam-style question, likely to be done at the end of a chapter (topic) rather than at the end of the course. Secondly, we provide carefully considered scaffolded steps to allow KS3 students to tackle high level questions and gain confidence through the deliberate practice of building up detailed answers.
  • the assessments for Student Book 3 are progressively more demanding in that they use higher-order command words and provide less scaffolded support – if you set one of them for Year 8 students, please take that into account when awarding GCSE grade indicators

Entering student outcomes into the Kerboodle Markbook

The Kerboodle Markbook records scores and percentages to allow for quick comparison of performance. If you want to use the Markbook to record student outcomes, you will need to enter the appropriate values given in the raw marks row of the table above.

Links to GCSE

By the end of KS3, students should be familiar with the History skill of comparing two or more interpretations. At GCSE, most exam boards specifically ask students to consider historical evidence to make a judgement on the most convincing or reliable account. For example:

AQA:

- How does Interpretation B differ from Interpretation A about... ? (4)
- Why might the authors of... have different interpretations about... ? (4)
- Which interpretation gives the more convincing opinion about... ? (8)
- How convincing is Interpretation C about... ? (8)

Edexcel:

- Study Interpretations 1 and 2... What is the main difference between the views... ? (4)
- Suggest one reason Interpretations 1 and 2 give different views about... (4)
- How far do you agree with Interpretation 2 about... ? (20)

OCR B:

- How far do [the interpretations] differ... ? (12)

Eduqas:

- Study the interpretations. Do the interpretations support the view that... ? (10)

Links to KS3 History resources

Student Book

This assessment question links to these lessons:

5.2A/B *How should we remember Dunkirk?*
5.9A/B *Why is Sir Arthur Harris such a controversial figure?*
5.10A/B *Why is Winston Churchill on a £5 note?*

Kerboodle

Support for this assessment question on Kerboodle:

TWI 5 *Assessment presentation: Interpretation analysis*
TWI 5 *Assessment worksheet (Core): Interpretation analysis*
TWI 5 *Assessment worksheet (Foundation): Interpretation analysis*

Curriculum and Assessment Planning Guide

Support for this assessment question in this guide:

5 *Assessment mark scheme – page 123*
5 *Assessment sample student answers – pages 124–125*

Student name: _____   Date: _____

Mark scheme

Assessment bands	Marks	GCSE grade indicators*	I have...
	0	Ungraded	
Developing	1–6	1–3	☐ identified one difference between the interpretations, but I have not included any supporting knowledge. ☐ written one reason why the interpretations differ, but I have not backed it up with any supporting knowledge. ☐ reached a basic judgment on whether I agree or disagree with Interpretation A, without any relevant supporting knowledge. Key words are not used correctly.
Secure	7–13	4–6	☐ identified one difference between the interpretations, and included some relevant supporting knowledge. ☐ written one reason why the interpretations differ, and I have backed it up with *either* a simple analysis of the interpretations *or* some relevant supporting knowledge. ☐ written a well-supported judgement on how far I agree with Interpretation A, and included some relevant supporting knowledge and comparison with Interpretation B. Some key words are used correctly. NOTE: Marks should only go above 10 if you have included both interpretations in your answer to Question 3.
Extending	14–20	7–9	☐ identified one difference between the interpretations, and included detailed, relevant supporting knowledge. ☐ written one reason why the interpretations differ, and I have backed it up with a detailed analysis of the interpretations *and* with relevant supporting knowledge. ☐ written a well-organised, well-supported judgement on how far I agree with Interpretation A, and included detailed, relevant supporting knowledge and comparison with Interpretation B. All key words are used correctly.

* IMPORTANT: These are approximate indicators devised using publicly available information on the new GCSE grades. They are designed to assist in the process of tracking and monitoring. They cannot and should not be used to replace teachers' professional judgement. Teachers should use their own discretion in applying them, taking into account the cumulative test scores of an individual student (rather than just one assessment point), and should refer to their institution's assessment policy.

Mark: _____

Comment:

Sample student answers

Assessment: Interpretation analysis

STUDENT BOOK PAGES 150–151

1 Interpretations **A** and **B** give different views about Winston Churchill. What is the main difference between the views?

2 Suggest one reason **Interpretations A** and **B** give different views about Churchill.

3 How far do you agree with **Interpretation A** about Winston Churchill? Explain your answer, using both interpretations and your own knowledge of the historical context. (20)

 ### Sample Developing band answer

1 The main difference is that Interpretation A says that Churchill helped to set up the early welfare state. Interpretation B says that Churchill was against making things better for workers.

2 One reason the authors have different views is that they support different political ideas. The writer of Interpretation A is a Conservative, like Churchill, but the writer of Interpretation B is not.

3 Interpretation A says that Churchill was a hero who saved Britain from the Nazis – I agree a little with this opinion about Churchill as he had been against appeasement.

 ### Sample Secure band answer

1 The main difference is that Interpretation A states that Churchill is responsible for the British victory over the Nazis. It suggests that Churchill was acting for Britain and its people. However, Interpretation B argues that Churchill was not an anti-Nazi hero. Mackin states that Churchill was more interested in helping the rich, and that he was not even against Hitler because he was a Nazi but because he did not want Britain's rich to be affected.

2 One reason the authors have different views is their personal politics. Johnson, the author of Interpretation A, is a Conservative, a right-wing party. He went on to become the Prime Minister – the same as Churchill. Mackin, however, is writing in the Socialist Worker a left-wing newspaper which is more interested in the working class and a more equal society. These different politics means they have different opinions about Churchill.

3 I agree with Interpretation A to some extent. Interpretation A says that Churchill was responsible for protecting Britain from Nazi invasion and that he was the only person courageous enough to defeat the Nazis. It is true that Churchill was against appeasement and stood up to Hitler and the Nazis. He did this consistently from the mid-1930s onwards. However, some people believe that Churchill was not a good leader, that he was just good at convincing people to believe him, and that he had different motives for standing up to Hitler. Interpretation B offers a different view, saying that Churchill was not the saviour of the British people but that he was thinking of his own class. This is supported by other accounts.

Sample Extending band answer

1   The main difference between the two views on Churchill is concerning his work on reform and improving society for all. In Interpretation A, Johnson states that Churchill helped to set up the welfare state and supported the unemployed even before the First World War. However, Interpretation B disagrees that Churchill did any good for poorer people. Mackin argues that he was only interested in protecting his class – the rich, land-owning class. She goes further to say that Churchill made life worse for some people; such as transport workers in 1911.

2   One reason the authors have different views is their political backgrounds. Johnson is a Conservative, like Churchill was, with ambitions to become Prime Minister, like Churchill. The fact that Johnson says that Churchill was responsible for protecting Britain shows that he greatly admires Churchill. Interpretation B, on the other hand, was written by Mackin, who is more left-wing. This means she does not support Churchill as he comes from a rich land-owning family. Mackin's article was also for the Socialist Worker, a paper produced for people who agree with her politics.

3   Interpretation A says that Churchill was the person responsible for getting America involved in the war and the person who made sure Britain continued to fight against the Nazis. I partially agree with this. Churchill was committed to fighting against Hitler even before he was in government. We know this because he was against appeasement. However, I do not agree with the idea that he was a keen social reformer. As is stated in Interpretation B there were many aspects of Churchill's character that were against reform and improving the lives of the poor. In fact, Mackin states that Churchill waged a war at home against the working class.
To conclude, I agree partly with Interpretation A. I know that Hitler was a good war leader and was a key motivator in the fight against the Nazis. However, as Interpretation B states he was not always interested in what was best for all, and he cared mostly about the rich.

Chapter 6 The post-war world

Links to KS3 History National Curriculum

Chapter 6 explores 'the creation of the Welfare State' and 'Britain's place in the world since 1945', both of which are given as examples of topics that could be covered in the latest KS3 History National Curriculum. Throughout the chapter, students are required to use key historical terminology appropriately, determine the significance both of key individuals and key events, and make connections between national and international history. This is particularly the case for the lessons on the Cold War, which look at early events such as the Berlin Blockade and the later case studies of Korea, Cuba and Vietnam. The supporting activities require students to read for meaning, think critically, weigh evidence, sift arguments and create their own structured accounts.

Throughout this chapter students are asked to analyse and evaluate sources and interpretations using inference and their own knowledge. The content covered will unequivocally help your students understand modern Britain, Europe and International Cooperation. Not only has this built on the understanding of government reform from Book 2: *Revolution, Industry and Empire 1558–1901 Student Book*, but it will also act as much-needed context when analysing Britain in the late twentieth and early twenty-first centuries in later chapters.

Skills and processes covered in this chapter

		Lesson/activity in the Student Book
History Skills	Knowledge and understanding	6.1A Over to You: 1, 2a, 2b; Knowledge and Understanding: 1, 2
		6.1B Over to You: 1a, 3
		6.2A Over to You: 1, 3a, 3b; Knowledge and Understanding: 1a, 1b, 1c, 1d
		6.2B Over to You: 1, 2, 3, 5a, 5b
		6.3A Over to You: 1, 2, 3
		6.3B Over to You: 1a, 1b, 1c, 1d; Knowledge and Understanding: 1, 2
		6.3C Over to You: 1a, 1b, 1c, 3
		6.4 Over to You: 1a, 1b, 1c, 1d, 4
		6.5B Over to You: 2; Knowledge and Understanding: 1
		Have you been learning? Quick Knowledge Quiz: 1, 2, 3, 4, 5, 6, 7, 8, 9, 10
	Interpretation analysis	6.1A Over to You: 4
		6.3B Over to You: 3a, 3b
		6.4 Over to You: 3a, 3b
	Source analysis	6.1A Over to You: 3
		6.1B Over to You: 1b
		6.2B Source Analysis: 1, 2
		6.3A Source Analysis: 1, 2, 3
		6.5A Over to You: 4a, 4b
		6.5B Over to You: 3
	Significance	6.5B Over to You: 1
	Cause and consequence	6.1B Over to You: 2a, 2b, 3
		6.2A Over to You: 2a, 2b, 3b
		6.2B Over to You: 4
		6.3A Over to You: 4

		Lesson/activity in the Student Book
		6.3B Over to You: 2, 4; Knowledge and Understanding: 2
		6.3C Consequence: 1, 2
		6.4 Over to You: 2a, 2b
		6.5A Over to You: 1, 2, 3
		6 Assessment: Causation: 1, 2, 3, 4
	Diversity/Similarity and difference	6.2A Over to You: 1
		6.2B Over to You: 2
		6.3C Over to You: 2
	Change and continuity	6.1B Change: 1, 2
Literacy and Numeracy	Literacy	**Have you been learning?** Literacy Focus: 1, 2
	Numeracy	

Lesson sequence

Lesson title	Student Book pages	Objectives
6.1A NHS: why we don't pay to see a doctor	pp 152–153	• Define the term 'welfare state' and explain its origins. • Outline how a report, written in the 1940s, still affects people in Britain today.
6.1B NHS: why we don't pay to see a doctor	pp 154–155	
6.2A Why was there a Cold War?	pp 156–157	• Define what was meant by 'Cold War'. • Explain why the allies of the Second World War became enemies.
6.2B Why was there a Cold War?	pp 158–159	
6.3A Cold War hotspots	pp 160–161	• Define the 'Truman Doctrine'. • Examine ways in which the USA tried to 'contain' communism. • Identify where Cold War conflicts took place around the world.
6.3B Cold War hotspots	pp 162–163	
6.3C Cold War hotspots	pp 164–165	
6.4 Cold War rivalry	pp 166–167	• Recall key events in the space race. • Examine how space, chess and sport were related to the Cold War.
6.5A A United Europe	pp 168–169	• Explain why the countries of Europe cooperated more and more in the second half of the twentieth century. • Outline which countries belong to the European Union and investigate when they joined.
6.5B A United Europe	pp 170–171	
Chapter 6 Have you been learning?	pp 172–173	• Choose the correct answer from the given options for a quick recap. • Ensure errors are corrected and events are placed in correct chronological order. • Improve sentences by adding specific factual detail.
Chapter 6 History skill: Causation	p 174	• Assess different causes relating to tension between East and West from 1945 to 1949.
Chapter 6 Assessment: Causation	p 175	• Construct an answer identifying specific reasons for tension between East and West from 1945 to 1949.

Links to the GCSE curriculum

This chapter provides some historical context to the following:

AQA: Conflict and Tension between East and West 1945–1972

AQA: Health and the People c1000–Present

AQA: Migration, Empires and the People c790–Present

Edexcel: Superpower Relations and the Cold War 1941–1991

Edexcel: Medicine in Britain c1250–Present

OCR A: The Changing International Order 1918–2001

OCR A: War and British Society c790–2010

OCR B: The People's Health c1250–Present

Eduqas: The Development of Germany 1919–1991

Eduqas: The Development of the UK 1919–1990

Eduqas: Changes in Health and Medicine in Britain c500–Present

Eduqas: The Development of Warfare in Britain c500–Present

WJEC: Changes in Health and Medicine c1340–Present

WJEC: The Development of Warfare c1250–Present

Exam-style questions covered in this chapter

Exam board	Lesson/activity question location	Command words	History skills/concepts
AQA	6.1A Knowledge and Understanding: 2	Describe…	Knowledge and understanding
	6.1B Change: 2	Explain two ways… different	Change and continuity
	6.2B Source Analysis: 2	How useful…	Source analysis
	6.3A Source Analysis: 3	How useful…	Source analysis
	6.3B Knowledge and Understanding: 2	Write an account…	Knowledge and understanding
	6.3C Consequence: 2	How far do you agree…	Cause and consequence
	6.5B Knowledge and Understanding: 1	Describe…	Knowledge and understanding
Edexcel	6.1A Knowledge and Understanding: 2	Describe…	Knowledge and understanding
	6.2B Source Analysis: 2	How useful…	Source analysis
	6.3A Source Analysis: 3	How useful…	Source analysis
	6.3B Knowledge and Understanding: 2	Write a narrative account…	Knowledge and understanding
	6.3C Consequence: 2	How far do you agree…	Cause and consequence
	6.5A Over to You: 1	Explain why…	Cause and consequence
	6.5B Knowledge and Understanding: 1	Describe…	Knowledge and understanding
OCR A	6.1A Knowledge and Understanding: 2	Describe…	Knowledge and understanding
	6.2B Source Analysis: 2	How useful…	Source analysis
	6.3A Source Analysis: 3	How useful…	Source analysis
	6.3C Consequence: 2	How far do you agree…	Cause and consequence
	6.5A Over to You: 1	Explain why…	Cause and consequence
	6.5B Knowledge and Understanding: 1	Describe…	Knowledge and understanding
OCR B	6.2B Source Analysis: 2	How useful…	Source analysis
	6.3A Source Analysis: 3	How useful…	Source analysis
	6.3C Consequence: 2	How far do you agree…	Cause and consequence
	6.5A Over to You: 1	Explain why…	Cause and consequence
Eduqas	6.1A Knowledge and Understanding: 2	Describe…	Knowledge and understanding
	6.4 Over to You: 1	Describe…	Knowledge and understanding
	6.5B Knowledge and Understanding: 1	Describe…	Knowledge and understanding
WJEC	6.1A Knowledge and Understanding: 2	Describe…	Knowledge and understanding
	6.2A Knowledge and Understanding: 1	Complete the sentences…	Knowledge and understanding
	6.3B Over to You: 1	Complete the sentences…	Knowledge and understanding
	6.4 Over to You: 1	Describe…	Knowledge and understanding
	6.5A Over to You: 1	Explain why…	Cause and consequence
	6.5B Knowledge and Understanding: 1	Describe…	Knowledge and understanding

A brief history

6.1A/B NHS: why we don't pay to see a doctor

In Chapter 5 students looked at the way politics can be rebuilt after war; this chapter starts with looking at the responsibility government has for the people. Students will look at the findings of the Beveridge Report and the action Beveridge suggested the government should take. This leads on to the different interpretations of the report. The lesson then takes students through all of the changes that occurred after 1945 from housing to free healthcare. Students will explore opinions of the NHS and then apply their knowledge by evaluating change and continuity of care in Britain.

6.2A/B Why was there a Cold War?

This lesson builds on students' understanding of 'communist' and 'capitalist' from earlier chapters by applying it to politics post-Second World War. Students gain some excellent context of the relationship between the USSR and the USA (the superpowers), and why their differences intensified after the war. The Marshall Plan, tension surrounding Berlin, NATO and nuclear testing all give a clear picture of increasing tension – one way to take this lesson further would be to create a tension/living graph as the students progress through the content. The activities allow students to complete sentences and analyse sources to consolidate their learning.

6.3A/B/C Cold War hotspots

This lesson develops students' understanding of tension between the USA and the USSR through the case studies of Korea, Cuba and Vietnam – all high points of tension between the superpowers during the Cold War. Students will explore cause and consequence of these key events and then will apply their contextual understanding by answering utility questions – a skill they have been developing throughout the previous chapters. The lesson culminates in an essay question that requires them to analyse the USA's attempts to contain communism. There are lots of excellent films, documentaries and songs that could enrich these lessons and develop cultural capital – for example, selected scenes from the film *Forrest Gump*, the PBS documentary *My Lai* or the song 'Fortunate Son' by Creedence Clearwater Revival.

Timeline

1942
The Beveridge Report is published.

1943
The Ministry of Town and Country Planning is established.

March 1947
US President Truman gives a speech outlining what became known as the 'Truman Doctrine'.

September 1947
Stalin sets up Cominform, the Soviet response to Marshall Aid.

1948
The Marshall Plan is enacted.
The NHS is founded.

June 1948
The Berlin Blockade.

1949
The USSR tests its first nuclear bomb.

June 1950
The Korean War starts.

1951
Six countries join to form the European Coal and Steel Community (ECSC).

1954
Vietnam is split into two – north and south. This leads to the Vietnam War.

October 1957
The USSR launches the first satellite, Sputnik, into space.

August 1961
The first part of the Berlin Wall is built, separating East and West Berlin.

October 1962
The Cuban Missile Crisis.

20 July 1969
Neil Armstrong and Buzz Aldrin walk on the moon.

1973
Britain joins the European Economic Community (EEC).

June 2016
Britain votes to leave the European Union (EU).

6.4 Cold War rivalry

Students will likely enjoy finding out more about the different ways in which the USA and the USSR competed with each other during the Cold War. The space race, chess and the Moscow and LA Olympic Games are excellent examples of the lengths both countries went to in order to outdo each other. Détente (the easing of tensions between the superpowers) is also explored in this lesson. Students will be expected to explain the importance of non-violent tensions for superpower relations and how they contributed to the Cold War.

6.5A/B A United Europe

Students should find this lesson fascinating as it shines a light on the history of the European Union, helping them make sense of the political situation surrounding Brexit following the UK referendum in 2016. Students will explore the different ways in which Britain became closer to other European countries and how this evolved throughout the late twentieth century. They will be expected to explain why countries wanted to join closer together. The map of member countries will help students to visualise the EU and its members; this – along with the timeline – will help them to understand the positives as well as people's reservations about the EU. Students will apply this knowledge by describing how the EU promoted stability after the Second World War.

Further reading and links

For teachers:

- *The Vietnam War* (BBC4, 2017) is an excellent series by documentary filmmaker Ken Burns. Watching this will give you more context about the war to help with answering student questions.

- The European Parliament website has some very useful information on the history of the EU as well as how it works today. With Brexit being such an important issue the students will definitely have lots of questions during lesson *6.5A/B A United Europe*. Go to europarlamentti.info/en and click European Union > History.

For students:

- Get students to search the cupboards in the History department and look at the different GCSE resources on the Cold War. This has been a compulsory unit in the past so there will be plenty for them to find. Encourage them to look at the cartoons to help develop source and interpretation analysis along with inference skills.

- Give more able students a copy of Ian Fleming's *From Russia with Love* (1957) to read. This will show them how the Cold War became part of Western culture, with the West being presented as 'good' and the East being presented as 'bad'.

Beyond the classroom

- A visit to the National Cold War exhibition at the RAF Museum Cosford would be a wonderful resource around which to build a scheme of work. If a visit is not possible, students could complete a research project on the Cold War, using the museum website, which is packed with useful information. Students can visit nationalcoldwarexhibition.org to find out more.

- The Cold War and the key conflicts of the 1960s inspired the emergence of an anti-war movement. Music was a big part of this movement, with some popular singers releasing anti-war songs. Get students to listen to some of these songs and then work with the Music department to develop their own anti-war song linked to the content covered in class.

- Ask students to plan a display about the EU and Brexit. They should provide context on the Cold War and the creation of the EEC.

Answers guidance

The answers provided here are examples, based on the information provided in the Student Book. There may be other factors which are relevant to each question, and students may draw on as much of their own knowledge as possible to give detailed and precise answers. There are also many ways of answering questions, including exam-style questions (for example, of structuring an essay). However, these exemplar answers should provide a good starting point.

6.1A NHS: why we don't pay to see a doctor

PAGES 152–153

Over to You

1 There was a basic system in place, e.g. free school meals and medical check-ups for poorer children, small pensions for over 70s etc.

2a The 1942 report about the most vulnerable people in society – the sick, the unemployed, low-paid workers and the elderly. It said that people all over the country had a right to be free of the 'five giants' (disease, want, ignorance, idleness and squalor) and suggested ways to tackle them.

2b Answers will vary but the basic idea is that the government should play a role in a person's welfare from the time they are born to the time they die.

3 The writer argues that people who have everything provided for them will never want to go out and get work.

4 Because the Labour Party promised to implement some of the ideas laid out in the Beveridge Report.

Knowledge and Understanding

1 A system whereby the state protects the health and wellbeing of its citizens with free healthcare, pensions, etc.

2 Answers will vary but they should emphasise the idea of 'the cradle to the grave', giving

examples of this from the diagram (A), as well as the idea of it helping to slay the 'five giants' that blighted people's lives.

6.1B NHS: why we don't pay to see a doctor

PAGES 154–155

Over to You

1a Government official who set up the NHS.

1b He refers to the fact that, before the NHS, seeing a doctor would cost money – and women in particular would go without treatment for illness in order to save money for the family's other needs.

2a They worried they would lose their independence because they would be working for the government and couldn't charge what they wanted.

2b By promising them a good salary and allowing them to have 'private patients' too.

3 Answers will vary but may include: cost, poor quality hospitals, lack of staff, overworked staff.

Change

1 Answers may include: Before the war some help was available: free school meals for poorer children, free school medical check-ups and treatment, small pensions for the over 70s, and basic sick and unemployment pay.

2 Answers may include: NHS set up to provide healthcare for everyone. This made all medical treatment free. This was different to before the war, when there were still fees for some of these services. School leaving age increased to give young people a better education (lower before the war). Schools also changed to be more adapted to individual needs.

6.2A Why was there a Cold War?

PAGES 156–157

Over to You

1 Answers will reflect the basic differences. Capitalist countries have private firms, two or more political parties to vote for, a free economy with businesses in competition with each other and great differences in wealth. Communist countries have companies controlled by the government with one party in control, and the wealth more equally shared. (47 words)

2a Students may outline the history of suspicion and mistrust between the Russians and the US in particular. Also, they should mention the disagreements over Germany and Berlin at the end of the war and Stalin's suspicions about the Marshall Plan.

2b Student choices will vary.

3a Money offered to European countries by the USA to repair war damage.

3b The Marshall Plan highlighted the differences between East and West. The USA claimed it offered the money to build up nations for trade, whereas Stalin thought it was a US plot to get more support and influence in Europe (and banned countries in the East from taking the money).

Knowledge and Understanding

1a superpower
1b the East
1c communist
1d the Iron Curtain

6.2B Why was there a Cold War?

PAGES 158–159

Over to You

1 Germany was divided into four zones, each one controlled by a different one of the four major winning countries – the USA, Britain, France and the USSR. It was also decided that Berlin, Germany's capital, should be divided into four.

2 The Blockade was when the USSR cut off all road and rail links between the Allied area of Berlin (West Berlin) and West Germany, in June 1948. The Airlift was the US supply of food and resources into the western part of Berlin by air.

3 NATO: North Atlantic Treaty Organisation was a military alliance linking 11 major Western powers. Warsaw Pact: linked the USSR with East Germany, Poland, Czechoslovakia, Hungary, Romania, Albania and Bulgaria.

4 It was not a 'hot war' with actual fighting. Despite the tension no fighting took place between US and Soviet troops. The term 'cold' relates to the relationship between the countries.

5a Answers will vary. An example is: MAD stands for Mutually Assured Destruction. It means that, as both the USA and the USSR have lots of nuclear weapons, they would not use them on their enemy as they know their enemy will use them in retaliation, resulting in both sides destroying each other. (46 words)

5b If one nuclear weapon is used, it might lead to others being used, which would result in an all-out nuclear war that could end mankind.

Source Analysis

1 The cartoon shows the USSR, represented by a bear, surrounding Berlin and only allowing a small gap for the Allies to get in and out of the city.

2 Answers should include that the source indicates that the USA felt that the Russians were strong (a bear) and well armed (claws) and were very protective of the city of Berlin, allowing only a small corridor for the Allies to get into the city.

6.3A Cold War hotspots

PAGES 160–161

Over to You

1 This was Truman's plan to stop communism from spreading from country to country.

2 After Japan's defeat in the war, Korea was split into two zones. The USSR occupied the north and the USA occupied the south. It was decided to use the 38th parallel (line of latitude) to divide the country.

3 • Korea is divided after the Second World War
 • China becomes a communist country
 • North Korean army invades South Korea
 • A United Nations army lands in Korea
 • China joins the war on the side of North Korea
 • A ceasefire is arranged

4 After the initial success of the North Korean army, UN troops gradually pushed them back out of South Korea and into North Korea. By October 1950, UN troops had captured most of North Korea and were close to the Chinese border. China, which had become a communist country in 1949, felt threatened by this and launched a massive invasion of Korea that forced the UN forces right back again.

Source Analysis

1 A capitalist system – 'based on the will of the majority, free elections, and freedom of speech and religion'.

2 Because 'it relies upon terror, a controlled press and radio, fixed elections and a lack of personal freedom'.

3 Answers should reflect that it shows that fear of communism went to the highest level of the US political system, and it was really a philosophical belief about the value of one system over another. The US placed considerable value on the capitalist system and saw no merit in communism at all. It shows historians the tactics used by politicians (the emotive language used) and the basis for US foreign policy.

6.3B Cold War hotspots

PAGES 162–163

Over to You

1a America
1b 1959
1c John F. Kennedy
1d Nikita Khrushchev

2 Cuba is within missile range of most major US cities.

3a D: Robert McNamara was so worried about what would happen that he believed it would be the last time he would be alive on a Sunday. E: Fyodor Burlatsky told his wife to get out of Moscow because he thought the USA had launched nuclear missiles.

3b Answers will vary but should focus on the fact that these men were very close to what was going on at the time and were in the 'inner circles' of power in both the USA and USSR – so if they thought it was close to all-out war, it must have been a very serious situation. As a result, they are very useful.

4 Answers will vary. Some may say that one side won more than the other (e.g. the USSR turned the ships around, so was beaten), but others may say both conceded, so no winners. Some may add that humanity won as there was no nuclear war.

Knowledge and Understanding

1
- Fidel Castro takes control of Cuba
- US invasion of Cuba fails
- The USSR begins to transport nuclear missiles to Cuba
- US spy planes spot more missiles being transported from the USSR to Cuba by sea
- Kennedy and Khrushchev begin negotiations
- Agreement is reached between the USSR and the USA

2 Answers will reflect what caused the crisis, the main events within the crisis, and how close the world came to nuclear war.

6.3C Cold War hotspots
PAGES 164–165

Over to You

1a Ho Chi Minh: Vietminh (Vietnamese communists) leader, who later ruled North Vietnam.

1b Ngo Dinh Diem: South Vietnam leader – hated communism, had spent a lot of time in the USA and knew many leading US politicians well.

1c Ho Chi Minh Trail: weapons and supplies route for the Vietcong through thick jungle; weapons and supplies came from China and the USSR.

2 The Vietminh were Vietnamese communists prepared to fight the French so they could be free of French control. The Vietcong were a communist group formed in the South after Vietnam was divided. The

Vietcong began a rebellion in the American-backed South.

3 The USSR supported North Vietnam and the Vietcong. It supplied weapons, ammunition and general supplies to the Vietcong and North Vietnamese forces, who were fighting the USA. Many of these supplies came via the Ho Chi Minh Trail.

Consequence

1 Students will summarise the key events.

2 Answers should mention both the Korean War and the Cuban Missile Crisis in relation to containment. The USA was not successful in containing the spread of communism to Cuba, but was successful in stopping its spread into South Korea. The USA was also unsuccessful in stopping its spread to South Vietnam.

6.4 Cold War rivalry
PAGES 166–167

Over to You

1a First human in space
1b First human on the moon
1c First woman in space
1d First living thing in space
2a Answers might include: they wanted to prove that their technology and way of life were the best; they wanted to explore outer space; or they wanted to perfect the technology that would let them send a nuclear warhead anywhere on the planet.
2b Answers will vary.
3a Chess players who competed in the 1972 World Chess Championship final. Fischer (from the USA) beat the reigning Russian world champion, Boris Spassky, ending 24 years of Soviet domination of the Championships.
3b He says it was not really just about chess – it was more

about politics. In the USSR, chess was very important and used to demonstrate the intellectual superiority of the Soviet communist regime over the West. He says that Spassky's defeat was crushing for the Soviets.

4 Answers will vary but should focus on the fact that the Olympic Games was a way for the two sides in the Cold War to compete at a very high level, but without resorting to actual shooting and warfare. It was an opportunity to demonstrate the superiority of their regimes.

6.5A A United Europe
PAGES 168–169

Over to You

1 They felt that future peace was far more likely if they put aside differences in language, culture and history, and worked together. Rather than compete as rivals, they could work together to increase wealth and ensure peace.

2 Britain had other world links – at this time Britain still had strong ties with the remaining countries (and former countries) of the British Empire. Britain was also closely linked with the USA.

3 Britain began to lose those links as their empire broke apart – and it was clear that the EEC was becoming an economic success.

4a Good answers should emphasise the factory and mine, the flags, the figures holding hands and the slogan.

4b Answers will focus on a show of unity and cooperation of the six countries of the ECSC, represented by the flags on the factory and the figures holding hands. The slogan reflects a bright future together.

6.5B Cold War rivalry

PAGES 170–171

Over to You

1 Students answers will vary, but they should justify their choices. For example: The Maastricht Treaty was an important development because it meant countries cooperated even further (in issues such as foreign affairs and security) – and this led to the EU being able to send help to the world's trouble spots, take part in peacekeeping efforts, or provide help to areas affected by war or famine.

2 Pro-Europeans are in favour of Britain remaining part of the EU and believe that the country benefits from the strong trade links and 'collective security' of its membership. Eurosceptics argue that Britain is unique and different from other European countries and should not be as strongly linked. They worry that Britain is losing its independence and identity and should be free to make all its own decisions.

3 Answers will vary but should reflect that the cartoonist is trying to show that the UK is free from 'interference' from other nations, but this means it is very much alone – and is now responsible for its destiny and cannot blame the EU for anything.

Knowledge and Understanding

1 Student answers might include the Common Agricultural Policy (CAP) which makes sure Europeans have enough food to eat and ensures a fair standard of living for farmers, as well as the EU's willingness to allow more countries to join so the European community is stronger, larger and more stable.

Chapter 6 Have you been learning?

Answers guidance

Chapter 6 Have you been learning?

Quick Knowledge Quiz

PAGE 172

1 **b** welfare state
2 **b** National Health Service
3 **a** Iron Curtain
4 **b** Warsaw Pact
5 **b** 1950
6 **c** Cuba
7 **a** Cambodia and Laos
8 **b** Neil Armstrong
9 **a** ECSC
10 **b** 2016

Literacy Focus

PAGES 173

Check and correct

1 At the end of the war, Germany was divided into **four** zones, each one controlled by a different one of the major winning countries – the USA, **Britain**, France and the USSR. It was also decided that Berlin, Germany's capital, should be divided into four.

In **1949**, the Soviet Union successfully tested its first nuclear bomb. Now both East and West had nuclear **weapons**, and both sides quickly began to make more and more.

Korea was divided in two after the Second World War. It was decided to use the **38th parallel** of the Earth as a dividing point – mainly because it divided the country **approximately** in half.

A potential nuclear war was avoided over Cuba in 1962 after US President **Kennedy** and USSR leader **Khrushchev** negotiated an agreement.

US President Nixon decided to end US **involvement** in the Vietnam War. He gradually reduced the amount of US troops fighting and, in March **1973**, the final US troops were removed from Vietnam.

Writing in detail

2 Answers will vary, but an example would be: The Beveridge Report was written by Sir William Beveridge in 1942 to try to tackle the problems people faced and to detail how those returning from war could have a better future. The report identified the 'five giants' of ignorance, want, squalor, idleness and disease, and suggested ways to improve people's lives through sick pay, pensions and free healthcare. This was the idea that the government should look after people from the 'cradle to the grave'. This was made possible by the Labour Party winning the General Election after the war. It had promised to follow Beveridge's advice. This all led to people being looked after by the creation of the NHS in 1948, the building of new towns with council houses, and benefits for the poor.

Assessment summary

The assessments in this textbook have been carefully designed and tested with History teachers to support student progression throughout the course. This specific assessment is written to support Year 8 or Year 9 students in tackling questions relating to causation.

 'The main reason for the increase in tension between East and West from 1945 to 1949 was the issue of Berlin.' How far do you agree with this statement? Explain your answer. (20)

The first stage of the assessment is for students to plan their answers by identifying the different causes of tension during the Cold War (Question 1). Then students must make a judgement on whether the cause in the statement was the most important cause (Question 2), or whether another cause was more important. Using this judgement, students will directly answer the assessment question (Question 3) and respond to the given statement. Finally, students will provide details to explain their response (Question 4) and write a conclusion.

Key event prompts, starter sentences and a mind map are provided to support students in this assessment.

For the mark scheme, see page 138.

A note about the end-of-chapter assessments

There is an assessment for each Student Book chapter. Each is structured like a GCSE exam-style question, with scaffolding steps to support KS3 students. Each assessment has a total of 20 marks, and is designed to be completed in a typical lesson – each has been written with a time allowance of about 30 minutes.

There is a mark scheme for each assessment. You can choose how to give student outcomes: a mark out of 20; a percentage; a performance indicator (we use a three-stage indicator – 'Developing', 'Secure', 'Extending' – but you could adapt to match any performance indicators used in your school); or a GCSE grade indicator. To convert raw marks to a performance or GCSE grade indicator, use this table:

Raw marks			
0	1–6	7–13	14–20
GCSE grade (9–1) indicators*			
U	1–3	4–6	7–9
Performance indicator			
Ungraded	Developing	Secure	Extending

*Please appreciate that these are approximate grades based on grade boundaries from recent GCSE exam papers. If a student achieves a Grade 7 in one of these assessments, it is not the equivalent of a Grade 7 at GCSE. Instead it is an indicator of the grade the student could expect to get if they continue on their flight path through KS3 and GCSE. Please note:
- the raw-mark boundaries are based on but do not match precisely those for recent GCSE exam papers: this is because our assessments are focused around one exam-style question, likely to be done at the end of a chapter (topic) rather than at the end of the course. Secondly, we provide carefully considered scaffolded steps to allow KS3 students to tackle high level questions and gain confidence through the deliberate practice of building up detailed answers.
- the assessments for Student Book 3 are progressively more demanding in that they use higher-order command words and provide less scaffolded support – if you set one of them for Year 8 students, please take that into account when awarding GCSE grade indicators.

Entering student outcomes into the Kerboodle Markbook

The Kerboodle Markbook records scores and percentages to allow for quick comparison of performance. If you want to use the Markbook to record student outcomes, you will need to enter the appropriate values given in the raw marks row of the table above.

Links to GCSE

By the end of KS3, students should be familiar with the History skill of causation. At GCSE, most exam boards specifically ask students to identify causes. For example:

AQA:

- Has… been the main factor/main way in…? Explain your answer with reference to… and other factors/ways. (16) (SPaG 4)

- Which of the following was the more important reason…

  - …

  - …?

  Explain your answer with reference to both reasons. (12)

- '…' How far do you agree with this statement? Explain your answer. (16) (SPaG 4)

Edexcel:

- Explain why…/what was important about… (12)

- 'The most significant reason/consequence/cause… was…' How far do you agree? Explain your answer. (16)

OCR A:

- Explain why… (10)

- '…' How far do you agree? (24)

OCR B:

- How far do you agree that…? Give reasons for your answer. (18)

- '…' How far do you agree with this view? (18)

Eduqas:

- Why was…? (12)

- Explain why… (9)

- Outline how… changed… In your answer you should provide a written narrative discussing the main causes… across three historical eras. (16) (SPaG 4)

WJEC:

- Explain why… (12)

- This question is about the causes of… To what extent has… been the main/most effective… over time? (16) (SPaG 4)

- How far did/Was… the main cause/reason…? Use your own knowledge and understanding of the issue to support your answer. (16) (SPaG 3)

Links to KS3 History resources

Student Book

This assessment question links to these lessons:

6.2A/B *Why was there a Cold War?*
6.3A/B/C *Cold War hotspots*
6.4 *Cold War rivalry*

Kerboodle

Support for this assessment question on Kerboodle:

TWI 6 *Assessment presentation: Causation*
TWI 6 *Assessment worksheet (Core): Causation*
TWI 6 *Assessment worksheet (Foundation): Causation*

Curriculum and Assessment Planning Guide

Support for this assessment question in this guide:

6 *Assessment mark scheme – page 138*
6 *Assessment sample student answers – pages 139–140*

Student name: _____   Date: _____

Mark scheme

Assessment bands	Marks	GCSE grade indicators*	I have...
	0	Ungraded	
Developing	1–6	1–3	☐ given a basic explanation of one or two of the causes of the increase in tension between East and West. ☐ written an answer that shows limited knowledge and understanding relating to the increase in tension between East and West.
Secure	7–13	4–6	☐ written a detailed explanation of several causes relating to the increase in tension between East and West, suggesting that one cause is more important than the others. I have reached a judgement that answers the question. ☐ written an answer that shows a range of accurate knowledge and understanding that relates to the question.
Extending	14–20	7–9	☐ written a well-developed explanation of several causes relating to the increase in tension between East and West, leading to a judgement that is backed up by reasons, and answers the question. ☐ included a wide range of accurate and detailed knowledge and understanding that is relevant to the question.

* IMPORTANT: These are approximate indicators devised using publicly available information on the new GCSE grades. They are designed to assist in the process of tracking and monitoring. They cannot and should not be used to replace teachers' professional judgement. Teachers should use their own discretion in applying them, taking into account the cumulative test scores of an individual student (rather than just one assessment point), and should refer to their institution's assessment policy.

Mark: _____

Comment:

Sample student answers

Assessment: Causation

STUDENT BOOK PAGE 175

'The main reason for the increase in tension between East and West from 1945 to 1949 was the issue of Berlin.' How far do you agree with this statement? Explain your answer. (20)

 ## Sample Developing band answer

The Cold War was when there was tension between America in the West and the USSR in the East. The main cause of this tension was the issue of Berlin. This was an important cause because it showed the two sides could not cooperate and that they had different aims in Europe.

Another cause of tension was nuclear bombs. During the Cold War both America and the USSR developed their nuclear weapons. This caused tension as both sides were scared of a nuclear attack.

 ## Sample Secure band answer

I agree that from 1945 to 1949 the issue of Berlin was the main cause of tension in the Cold War between East and West. The Cold War was a time in history when Europe was divided between the capitalist West and the communist East. In 1948 Stalin blocked off transport routes into Berlin so Western powers could not enter their zones of the city. His plan was to force the French, British and Americans to withdraw from their zones. This was known as the Berlin Blockade. However the Allied forces responded with the Berlin Airlift and in the end took back control of their zones. This increased tension as both sides no longer trusted each other.

Another important cause of tension was the Truman Doctrine. President Truman was worried that communism would spread so he stated in 1947 that America would give money and military help to any country that was in danger of being taken over by communism. This would mean that America would stop the spread of communism. This increased tension as Stalin reacted by creating Cominform, an organisation to support all communist countries.

Other causes of the tension were less important, for example, the development of nuclear weapons by both sides. This is because it was the mistrust caused by the issue of Berlin and the Truman Doctrine that led each side to develop these weapons.

Sample Extending band answer

I strongly agree with the statement that 'the main reason for the increase in tension between East and West from 1945 to 1949 was the issue of Berlin'. It is fair to argue that the Cold War actually started because of the Berlin Blockade in 1948. Both sides had been working together to manage Germany after the Second World War, and each controlled their different zones. However, when Stalin blocked off the Allies' transport routes into Berlin in June 1948 this resulted in a sharp increase in tension. Stalin had intended to force the Allies out of their zones in Berlin because they would not be able to survive there without food or fuel. Stalin had hoped that this would result in West Berlin coming under his control, but the Allies responded with the Berlin Airlift, when the Americans and British organised a constant supply of essential supplies such as food, fuel and medicine dropped by aircraft. The airlift was a success and Stalin ended the blockade in May 1949. This increased tension as the West saw the USSR's backdown as a victory.

Although Berlin was the most important cause of tension, there were also other causes, such as the Truman Doctrine. In 1947 Truman made a speech in which he made clear he wanted to contain communism, so it would not spread to other countries. Truman declared that America would offer money and military help to countries that were in danger of being taken over by communism. The Truman Doctrine led to Marshall Aid in 1947. This gave European countries money to help them rebuild after the Second World War. The USA hoped this would make them less likely to support communism. This further increased tension as Stalin thought that Marshall Aid was a US plot to get more support and influence in Europe. This increased tension as it led to Stalin creating Cominform which was an organisation to support and unite communist countries.

Another cause of tension was the development of nuclear weapons. In 1945 the USA dropped bombs on Hiroshima and Nagasaki, in Japan. The bombs had devastating effects. Although the development of nuclear weapons increased tension it did not lead to a lack of cooperation like the Berlin Blockade and the Truman Doctrine, which were evidence that each side was working against the other.

Chapter 7 From empire to Commonwealth

Links to KS3 History National Curriculum

Chapter 7 shows the sequence of learning that has taken place throughout the series. Students get to revisit knowledge and concepts from earlier chapters and books, but now they will be able to identify change and continuity in the British Empire over short and long periods of time. 'Indian independence and end of Empire' and 'social, cultural and technological change in post-war British society' are given as example topics in the latest KS3 History National Curriculum.

In this chapter, students are challenged to think carefully about historical concepts such as cause and consequence, continuity and change, and similarity and difference. They will also have to use a wide range of historical skills when analysing sources and interpretations. Students will have the opportunity to show how one event or change could lead to others: for example, the impact the world wars had on the decline of the British Empire. They will be required to explore and develop ideas as well as to organise and structure text in order to answer questions and write extended answers.

Students will get to focus on the role of people in shaping nations and identity; this is history at its best!

Skills and processes covered in this chapter

		Lesson/activity in the Student Book
History Skills	Knowledge and understanding	**7.1** Over to You: 1
		7.2 Over to You: 1, 2a, 2b
		7.3A Over to You: 1, 3
		7.3B Over to You: 1a, 1b, 1c, 1d, 1e, 2
		7.4 Over to You: 2
		7.5 Over to You: 2a, 2b, 2c
		7.6 Over to You: 1
		Have you been learning? Quick Knowledge Quiz: 1, 2, 3, 4, 5, 6, 7, 8, 9, 10
	Interpretation analysis	**7.3B** Interpretation Analysis: 1
		7.5 Interpretation Analysis: 1, 2, 3
	Source analysis	**7.1** Over to You: 4; Source Analysis: 1, 2
		7.2 Over to You: 3a, 3b
		7.3A Source Analysis: 1, 2, 3, 4
	Significance	
	Cause and consequence	**7.1** Over to You: 2, 3
		7.2 Over to You: 2c, 4
		7.3A Over to You: 2
		7.3B Over to You: 3
		7.4 Over to You: 1a, 1b
		7.5 Over to You: 1a. 1b, 1c
		7.6 Over to You: 2a, 2b, 2c, 2d
		7 Assessment: Causation: 1, 2, 3, 4

		Lesson/activity in the Student Book
	Diversity/Similarity and difference	
	Change and continuity	**7.2** Over to You: 2b
Literacy and Numeracy	Literacy	**Have you been learning?** Literacy Focus: 1a, 1b, 1c, 1d
	Numeracy	

Lesson sequence

Lesson title	Student Book pages	Objectives
7.1 The decline of the British Empire	pp 176–177	• Recall how Britain gradually lost its empire. • Examine the role played by the First and Second World Wars in the decline of the British Empire.
7.2 Independence for India	pp 178–179	• Recall key events in the campaign for Indian independence. • Assess factors that led to the partition of India in 1947.
7.3A Independence in Africa	pp 180–181	• Recall why so much of Africa had been colonised by 1901.
7.3B Independence in Africa	pp 182–183	• Explain how African nations regained their independence during the twentieth century.
7.4 Why did people migrate to Britain after the war?	pp 184–185	• Explain where Britain's immigrant population moved from. • Examine the reasons why they migrated to Britain.
7.5 Why should we remember the *Empire Windrush*?	pp 186–187	• Define the term 'Windrush generation'. • Outline the experiences and impacts of the 'Windrush generation'.
7.6 Multicultural Britain	pp 188–189	• Define the term 'multicultural Britain'. • Describe the benefits of immigration to British society.
Chapter 7 Have you been learning?	pp 190–191	• Choose the correct answer from the given options for a quick recap. • Write down the important words from sentences to practice note-taking.
Chapter 7 History skill: Causation	p 192	• Compare different causes for the decline of British Empire after the Second World War.
Chapter 7 Assessment: Causation	p 193	• Construct an answer that identifies specific reasons why the British Empire declined after the Second World War.

Links to the GCSE curriculum

This chapter provides some historical context to the following:

AQA: Power and the People c1170–Present

AQA: Migration, Empires and the People c790–Present

OCR A: Migration to Britain c1000–c2010

OCR B: Migrants to Britain c1250–Present

Eduqas: Austerity, Affluence and Discontent: Britain 1951–1979

Eduqas: The Development of the UK 1919–1990

WJEC: Austerity, Affluence and Discontent 1951–1979

WJEC: Changes in Patterns of Migration c1500–Present

Exam-style questions covered in this chapter

Exam board	Lesson/activity question location	Command words	History skills/concepts
AQA	**7.1** Source Analysis: 2	How useful…	Source analysis
	7.3A Source Analysis: 4	How useful…	Source analysis
	7.5 Interpretation Analysis: 3	How does Interpretation… differ…	Interpretation analysis
Edexcel	**7.1** Source Analysis: 2	How useful…	Source analysis
	7.3A Source Analysis: 4	How useful…	Source analysis
OCR A	**7.1** Source Analysis: 2	How useful…	Source analysis
	7.3A Source Analysis: 4	How useful…	Source analysis
	7.3B Interpretation Analysis: 1	Do you think this interpretation…	Interpretation analysis
OCR B	**7.1** Source Analysis: 2	How useful…	Source analysis
	7.3A Source Analysis: 4	How useful…	Source analysis

A brief history

7.1 The decline of the British Empire

Empire is one of the first order concepts that have been developed from the first chapter of Book 1: *Invasion, Plague and Murder: Britain 1066–1509 Student Book*. Students will now be able to see how this concept has changed over a span of 1000 years. Students will explore economic, political and social causes of the decline of the empire. This lesson gives an overview of the legacy of war both for Britain and its colonies to explain the decline of the empire. Students will be able to apply this knowledge while analysing the utility of a source about Britain's view of its empire at the turn of the twentieth century.

7.2 Independence for India

In Book 2: *Revolution, Industry and Empire 1558–1901 Student Book* students were given the opportunity to evaluate the impact of British rule on India. They now get to explore the change that takes place as the Indian people campaign for independence. Causation is a key concept in this lesson as students explore the various factors contributing to the independence campaign, such as: war, the role of the individual (Gandhi) and government. They will then learn about partition and the problems it created both short and long term. The activities allow students to evaluate change and continuity, causation and consequence.

7.3A/B Independence in Africa

This lesson provides vital knowledge to help students understand the changing identity of Africa – bursting some myths about the continent. Britain's role in Africa to 'civilise' and take raw materials is part of the uncomfortable history that we must share with our students so they can further evaluate the impact of the British Empire. Students will explore the factors of war, resistance and government to explain African independence. A way to extend this lesson would be to look at the positive and negative aspects of the Commonwealth. Finally, students will explore Africa today to see the different experiences of nations in this diverse continent.

7.4 Why did people migrate to Britain after the war?

Our story as an immigration nation is vital to help students understand British identity and British Values, and as a way to extend SMSC (spiritual, moral, social and cultural development). This lesson introduces the 'push' and 'pull' factors that explain why people would come to Britain; this is then applied to various

Timeline

1885
The Indian National Congress is formed to campaign against British rule in India.

1914–1918
The First World War takes place, with many 'Empire Troops' from India fighting for Britain.

1920s
Independence movement in India gathers momentum under Mohandas Gandhi.

1935
The Government of India Act is passed giving Indians the right to control everything except the army.

1939–1945
The Second World War.

1947
Partition sees the creation of two states – India and Pakistan.

1948
The *Empire Windrush* arrives in Tilbury Docks from the Caribbean.

1948
The British Nationality Act is passed.

1957
The British colony of the Gold Coast gains independence and becomes Ghana. This sparks many more African nations to declare independence.

1964
Notting Hill Carnival is celebrated for the first time.

countries and regions such as the Caribbean islands, Kenya, Uganda, Ireland and the rest of Europe. To explain why people came students must explore the factors of war, violence and government. They will combine their prior learning on the empire to make links with immigration and make judgements about the most important reason for immigration.

7.5 Why should we remember the Empire Windrush?

The arrival of the *Empire Windrush* will be an exciting part of twentieth-century British history to explore with your students, as for some it may link directly to their sense of identity and family history. It is also a story of young people, which students may relate to. The lesson will enable students to explain why people from the Caribbean came to Britain by exploring how this event linked to the war, the Commonwealth and Britain's need for workers. Reading about the different reactions to immigration and the experience of those who came will give them an insight into Britain in the 1950s and 1960s. Students will then develop their GCSE skills by comparing two interpretations of the immigrant experience.

7.6 Multicultural Britain

This lesson allows students to take what they have learned about empire and immigration across the series and evaluate the long-term consequences on Britain. Students will explore the cultural impact of immigration and the contribution those from other nations have made on the NHS and other institutions. Food, sport and music are also explored to give students enough content to explain what they think is meant by 'multicultural Britain'.

Further reading and links

For teachers:

- The spoken word poet Linton Kwesi Johnson has written a lot about life in Britain post-*Windrush*. His work gives an insight into multicultural Britain. Listen to 'Inglan is a Bitch' and 'Sonny's Lettah' on YouTube to explore the way black people were treated in the late twentieth century.

- Chimamanda Ngozi Adichie's novel *Half of a Yellow Sun* (Fourth Estate, 2006) is set during the Biafran War in Nigeria. Not only is it a great novel but it will also add context to your teaching of African history.

- The BBC 'IDEAS' video 'What would the UK be like without immigration?' presented by Jonathan Portes will offer some useful myth busters for class discussions around immigration. You could also use this to challenge higher ability students by asking them to evaluate why Portes has this interpretation of immigration. Search 'What would the UK be like without immigration?' on the BBC website to find the clip.

For students:

- 'The White Man's Burden' by Rudyard Kipling (1899) is a poem about a war between America and the Philippines – it gives an insight into the view of the coloniser. This would be a good poem for

students to analyse to test and consolidate their understanding of how Britain treated those in its empire.

- Students can search within the BBC website for the programme *Witness: Immigration, UK* (BBC2, 2011) to view clips that will develop their understanding of Britain after the *Windrush* arrived.

- *Partition Voices* (2017, BBC Radio 4) is a radio series that explores the experiences and opinions of British citizens who remember the partition of India. Students could listen to these programmes to develop their explanations of the legacy of the British Empire and partition. Search 'Partition Voices' on the BBC website.

Beyond the classroom

- Students could organise an assembly on the 'Windrush Scandal'. Researching this topic will also benefit them when evaluating change and continuity in Chapter 8.

- Religious differences and the division of India and Pakistan are considered in this chapter. Therefore, students could research the beliefs of Islam and Hinduism, finding out key facts about each religion, such as who they worship, the names of their religious scriptures, their places of worship, who their main prophets are, and so on.

- Get the students to create a 'British Values' display on what it means to be British. Encourage them to consider the diverse voices in multicultural Britain and also incorporate the Commonwealth.

- A tour of Dublin's Kilmainham Gaol would be a great opportunity not only for students to learn about the Easter Rising and the Irish independence movement, but also the Great Famine of 1845. The museum exhibition explores the role and responsibility of the British government, and the short- and long-term impacts of British control in Ireland. A trip here would be an excellent way to see the impact of the British Empire on one of its colonies.

- Students could collaborate with the Art department to deliver a presentation on the photography of British artist Vanley Burke. Burke documented life for the 'Windrush Generation' in Handsworth and the surrounding area of north Birmingham.

Answers guidance

The answers provided here are examples, based on the information provided in the Student Book. There may be other factors which are relevant to each question, and students may draw on as much of their own knowledge as possible to give detailed and precise answers. There are also many ways of answering questions, including exam-style questions (for example, of structuring an essay). However, these exemplar answers should provide a good starting point.

7.1 The decline of the British Empire
PAGES 176–177

Over to You

1   Answers will reflect the size and scale, e.g. containing approximately one quarter of the world's population and covering about one quarter of the world's total land area.

2   Britain's pre-war wealth was nearly all gone and it was now in debt. During the war, Britain had not been trading with lots of other countries because it had been concentrating on fighting and trying to win the war, so many countries had found new nations to trade with, or had developed their own industries.

3   Answers will reflect these themes: Ideas about democracy, freedom and nationalism spread around the world in the 1800s and many people in the colonies began to demand independence as a result. Africans and Indians who had fought for Britain felt they were fighting to defend freedom for Britain, but were getting increasingly frustrated that their own countries were not yet free; researchers and historians were showing how important the cultures and achievements of Africa and Asia had been before the Europeans had taken over.

4   The statue of Cecil Rhodes is being removed because he is a controversial figure – while working hard to expand the British Empire, which was seen as a good thing in the 1800s, he introduced laws that pushed people from their lands and increased taxes on their homes. He also thought that British people were superior to others.

Source Analysis

1   British Empire at beginning of the twentieth century. Britain is shown as a lion, surrounded with animals from different countries and areas within the empire. The various coats of arms of different areas are also shown.

2   Shows pride, as Britain produced the poster in the first place. Sees itself as the king (just as the lion is often known as the 'king of the jungle') and the other colonies (shown as animals) are at the lion's feet. The lion is also surrounded by a halo, implying that the British are a God-like presence in relation to the other colonies, and should be worshipped.

7.2 Independence for India
PAGES 178–179

Over to You

1   Victoria proudly called herself 'Empress of India', learned to speak and write in Hindi and Urdu, and had Indian food on most of her dinner menus.

2a   Many Indians fought alongside British soldiers in the war, and India gave Britain a huge amount of money, food and materials to help with the war effort. Nearly 64,000 Indian soldiers died in the war.

2b   Law-making councils were set up and over five million Indians were given the vote. However, the British government, based in London, still controlled taxation, the police, the law courts, the armed forces, education, and much more.

2c   Some thought it was a 'step in the right direction' and more than they had had before, while others felt it was rather limited.

3a   The British

3b   That the British exploit India for their own ends. They bring goods into India to sell, and take what they want.

4   There was tension between Hindus and Muslims living in India and severe violence had broken out between them. India was split into separate countries because the majority of people in India were Hindu and the majority of people in the area that became Pakistan were Muslim.

7.3A Independence in Africa
PAGES 180–181

Over to You

1   The time between 1880 and 1900 when more than 80 per cent of Africa was taken over by European powers.

2   Answers might include: to add to an already large empire; could sell British goods to the people who lived there; could take (or steal) valuable raw materials such as rubber, cotton, copper, gold and diamonds.

3   Britain as a 'mother country' – protected its colonies, helped them develop. France – similar role to Britain, but also wanted to turn Africans into French people. Belgium and Portugal ruled their colonies very harshly and were determined to hold on to them for as long as possible.

Source Analysis

1 Answers may say that there is only so much land in the world, so the British must get their share because it's important that in the future the world must be English-speaking and shaped by Britain.

2 Answers may vary but could say an African man is tied up while countries take the land.

3 That European countries are helping themselves to land in Africa and the Africans can do little about it.

4 Both are useful as they show Britain's arrogance and the fact it thought it was doing the right thing. They show how European nations did what they wanted at the expense of Africa.

7.3B Independence in Africa
PAGES 182–183

Over to You

1a Angola
1b South
1c Zimbabwe
1d Senegal
1e Uganda
1f The word spelled out is Ghana – the first British colony in Africa to get its independence. It was the Gold Coast until 1957.

2 An international association consisting of the UK and countries that were previously part of the British Empire.

3 Some countries have seen rivalries between tribes flare up into bloody civil wars; some new nations have struggled to create their own systems of government, build up their own industry and trade, and cope with differences between groups of people; also difficulties tackling poverty.

Interpretation Analysis

1 Answers will vary depending on students' viewpoints. However, many will probably highlight that European powers, including Britain, exploited their colonies in some way. They took their raw materials and used local people as a cheap workforce. Little attempt was made to understand the wishes or needs of the locals, so differences in race, language, culture and traditions were ignored.

7.4 Why did people migrate to Britain after the war?
PAGES 184–185

Over to You

1a Answers might include: Push – e.g. people from India and Pakistan came to Britain after partition in 1947 to escape violence; in the 1930s, around 60,000 German Jews came to Britain when the Nazis came to power. Pull – e.g. people from Jamaica, Barbados and Trinidad and Tobago were encouraged to come to Britain because of a shortage of workers after the Second World War; also after 1948, many West Africans moved to Britain to find jobs and get a better education.

1b Answers will vary.

2 Students should make a link between the fact that many immigrants came from countries within the British Empire as a result of, e.g., violence in countries after Britain withdrew (India and Pakistan), or being given British passports as a consequence of living in a former British colony (Hong Kong).

7.5 Why should we remember the *Empire Windrush*?
PAGES 186–187

Over to You

1a Answers may include: life was very hard in the Caribbean at this time; Jamaica had been devastated by a hurricane in 1944 and poverty and hardship were common; the Caribbean had not yet developed a tourist industry to provide jobs; the price of sugar was at an all-time low.

1b Answers may include: job opportunities – job shortages after the war; they actually had a right to move to Britain; they regarded Britain as the 'mother country'; they regarded themselves as British.

1c Answers may include: Parliament passed the British Nationality Act in 1948 – all the people of the empire (now called the Commonwealth) had full rights of British citizenship, which meant they could have a British passport and migrate to live and work in Britain.

2a A ship that brought the first generation (492 passengers) of what became known as the 'Windrush generation' to Britain in June 1948 from the West Indies.

2b The West Indian immigrants who arrived in Britain after the war, and the thousands of others who followed.

2c Answers will reflect the differences in experiences as outlined in the text, sources and interpretations.

Interpretation Analysis

1 He feels that the Britain he expected was not like the reality when he got here – and he was treated like an outsider (a 'foreigner').

2 He was offered five jobs as soon as he got here. He was here in the war and came back, and he was here to stay.

3 Answers will focus on the fact that one is a positive experience, while the other is not.

7.6 Multicultural Britain

Over to You

1 British society is made up of several cultural or ethnic groups each contributing part of their history, heritage, culture etc.

2a Answer might include: around 150,000 of the 1.2 million NHS employees were born abroad – around one in eight (12.5 per cent).

2b Answer might include examples of influences from around the world that are part of everyday food and drink, e.g.: Coca-Cola (USA), Sprite and Fanta (both Germany), pizzas (Italy) and kebabs (Turkey).

2c Answer might include the positive contribution that immigration has brought to sports teams, e.g. England cricket team.

2d Answer might include the positive contribution that immigration has brought to music.

Chapter 7 Have you been learning?

Answers guidance

Chapter 7 Have you been learning?

Quick Knowledge Quiz

1 **b** one quarter
2 **a** Indian National Congress
3 **b** 1947
4 **a** scramble for Africa
5 **a** Ghana
6 **c** Angola
7 **a** Commonwealth
8 **b** 1997
9 **c** *Empire Windrush*
10 **c** China

Literacy Focus

Note-taking

1a Africans & Indians – issues around independence. Fighting to protect countries from German occupation. What about their independence?

1b 1900 = some Indians want freedom. Indian National Congress 1885; meetings, demonstrations, but Britain ignored.

1c 1880 → 1900 = scramble for Africa by European powers (colonies). Early 1900s a few African countries – independent.

1d 1948 = British Nationality Act. All in Commonwealth (prev. empire) full British citz. This meant: British passport, live and work in Britain.

Chapter 7 Assessment: Causation

Assessment summary

The assessments in this textbook have been carefully designed and tested with History teachers to support student progression throughout the course. This specific assessment is written to support Year 8 or Year 9 students in tackling questions relating to causation.

> Which of the following was the more important reason why the British Empire declined after the Second World War:
> • the impact of two world wars
> • independence movements within the colonies?
> Explain your answer with reference to both reasons. (20)

The first stage of the assessment is for students to plan their answers by looking at the two given reasons for the decline of the British Empire (Question 1). Then students must make a judgement on which they believe to be the more important reason (Question 2). Using this judgement, students will directly answer the assessment question (Question 3), responding to the bullet points. Finally, students will provide details to explain their response (Question 4) and write a conclusion.

Key event prompts and starter sentences are provided to support students in this assessment.

For the mark scheme, see page 151.

A note about the end-of-chapter assessments

There is an assessment for each Student Book chapter. Each is structured like a GCSE exam-style question, with scaffolding steps to support KS3 students. Each assessment has a total of 20 marks, and is designed to be completed in a typical lesson – each has been written with a time allowance of about 30 minutes.

There is a mark scheme for each assessment. You can choose how to give student outcomes: a mark out of 20; a percentage; a performance indicator (we use a three-stage indicator – 'Developing', 'Secure', 'Extending' – but you could adapt to match any performance indicators used in your school); or a GCSE grade indicator. To convert raw marks to a performance or GCSE grade indicator, use this table:

Raw marks			
0	1–6	7 13	14–20
GCSE grade (9–1) indicators*			
U	1–3	4–6	7–9
Performance indicator			
Ungraded	Developing	Secure	Extending

*Please appreciate that these are approximate grades based on grade boundaries from recent GCSE exam papers. If a student achieves a Grade 7 in one of these assessments, it is not the equivalent of a Grade 7 at GCSE. Instead it is an indicator of the grade the student could expect to get if they continue on their flight path through KS3 and GCSE. Please note:
• the raw-mark boundaries are based on but do not match precisely those for recent GCSE exam papers: this is because our assessments are focused around one exam-style question, likely to be done at the end of a chapter (topic) rather than at the end of the course. Secondly, we provide carefully considered scaffolded steps to allow KS3 students to tackle high level questions and gain confidence through the deliberate practice of building up detailed answers.
• the assessments for Student Book 3 are progressively more demanding in that they use higher-order command words and provide less scaffolded support – if you set one of them for Year 8 students, please take that into account when awarding GCSE grade indicators.

Entering student outcomes into the Kerboodle Markbook

The Kerboodle Markbook records scores and percentages to allow for quick comparison of performance. If you want to use the Markbook to record student outcomes, you will need to enter the appropriate values given in the raw marks row of the table above.

Links to GCSE

By the end of KS3, students should be familiar with the History skill of causation. At GCSE, most exam boards specifically ask students to explain and analyse the causes of events and to make judgements on the most important cause. For example:

AQA:

- Has... been the main factor/main way in...? Explain your answer with reference to... and other factors/ways. (16) (SPaG 4)

- Which of the following was the more important reason...

  - ...

  - ...?

  Explain your answer with reference to both reasons. (12)

- '...' How far do you agree with this statement? Explain your answer. (16) (SPaG 4)

Edexcel:

- Explain why.../what was important about... (12)

- 'The most significant reason/consequence/cause... was...' How far do you agree? Explain your answer. (16)

OCR A:

- Explain why... (10)

- '...' How far do you agree? (24)

OCR B:

- How far do you agree that...? Give reasons for your answer. (18)

- '...' How far do you agree with this view? (18)

Eduqas:

- Why was...? (12)

- Explain why... (9)

- Outline how... changed... In your answer you should provide a written narrative discussing the main causes... across three historical eras. (16) (SPaG 4)

WJEC:

- Explain why... (12)

- This question is about the causes of... To what extent has... been the main/most effective... over time? (16) (SPaG 4)

- How far did/Was... the main cause/reason...? Use your own knowledge and understanding of the issue to support your answer. (16) (SPaG 3)

Links to KS3 History resources

Student Book

This assessment question links to these lessons:

7.1 *The decline of the British Empire*
7.2 *Independence for India*
7.3 A/B *Independence in Africa*

Kerboodle

Support for this assessment question on Kerboodle:

TWI 7 *Assessment presentation: Causation*
TWI 7 *Assessment worksheet (Core): Causation*
TWI 7 *Assessment worksheet (Foundation): Causation*

Curriculum and Assessment Planning Guide

Support for this assessment question in this guide:

7 *Assessment mark scheme – page 151*
7 *Assessment sample student answers – pages 152–153*

Student name: _____   Date: _____

Mark scheme

Assessment bands	Marks	GCSE grade indicators*	I have...
	0	Ungraded	
Developing	1–6	1–3	☐ given a basic explanation of one or two of the bullet points. ☐ written an answer that shows limited knowledge and understanding relating to the decline of the British Empire.
Secure	7–13	4–6	☐ written a detailed explanation of each bullet point. I have reached a judgement that answers the question. ☐ written an answer that shows a range of accurate knowledge and understanding that relates to the decline of the British Empire.
Extending	14–20	7–9	☐ written a well-developed explanation of each bullet point, leading to a judgement that is backed up by reasons, and answers the question. ☐ included a wide range of accurate and detailed knowledge and understanding that is relevant to the decline of the British Empire.

* IMPORTANT: These are approximate indicators devised using publicly available information on the new GCSE grades. They are designed to assist in the process of tracking and monitoring. They cannot and should not be used to replace teachers' professional judgement. Teachers should use their own discretion in applying them, taking into account the cumulative test scores of an individual student (rather than just one assessment point), and should refer to their institution's assessment policy.

Mark: _____

Comment:

Sample student answers

Assessment: Causation

STUDENT BOOK PAGE 193

> Which of the following was the more important reason why the British Empire declined after the Second World War:
> * the impact of two world wars
> * independence movements within the colonies?
> Explain your answer with reference to both reasons. (20)

 Sample Developing band answer

The British Empire started to decline in the twentieth century. There were lots of reasons. The impact of the two world wars was a key reason, as Britain was no longer in a position to control its colonies. Another key reason was the independence movements of its colonies, as when the countries decided to leave the British could not force them to stay.

 Sample Secure band answer

The British Empire was at its height during the reign of Queen Victoria. However, in the latter half of the twentieth century, the empire went into decline and many colonies were lost. There were many reasons for this decline.

On the one hand the two world wars were responsible for the decline of the empire. Britain was in a lot of debt after borrowing money from the USA to pay for the wars. Also, because Britain had focused so much on winning the First World War it had lost trading partners. This meant that Britain was no longer a world superpower as it had lost money and relationships. This made it harder to keep control of its colonies. Once the Second World War was over Britain no longer had the military or economic strength to hold on to the countries it controlled. Many of these countries had already been dealing with their own affairs and it became clear that they no longer needed to be part of the empire. Finally, some people in Britain felt that rebuilding Britain after the wars was more important that holding on to colonies around the world.

On the other hand, the independence movements in the colonies was a key factor as the people who lived there started to see things from a different perspective. By the start of the twentieth century many Indians, for example, had started to believe that India should be free from British control. This movement gathered support under Gandhi from the 1920s, and once the Second World War had ended the movement had shown the British that India should be independent. This desire for independence spread throughout the empire with many African nations demanding independence. This can be seen in the success of the independence movement in the Gold Coast in 1957 when it became Ghana.

To conclude, the two world wars were the most important reason for the decline of the empire as it was partly the frustration of empire soldiers fighting for Britain's freedom but not feeling free themselves that meant independence movements gained support.

Sample Extending band answer

The British Empire was at its height during the reign of Queen Victoria. However, in the latter half of the twentieth century, the empire went into decline and many colonies were lost. When looking at the reasons for this decline, I think that independence movements within the colonies was the most important reason, as this was down to the will of the people in the colonies. It is more important than the two world wars as they affected Britain's economy, power and ability to hold on to the colonies – but they were not the reason those in the colonies wanted independence.

On the one hand the two world wars are important as they left Britain bankrupt and no longer a superpower. The British had stopped trading with other countries during the First World War and this meant that when the war was over many countries had found alternative trading partners, or had started to produce good themselves. They no longer needed the British. On top of this Britain was in a lot of debt after borrowing money to fight the wars – mostly from America. In addition, many people from the colonies who had contributed to the war effort were frustrated that they had fought – especially in the Second World War – for British freedom, but that their own countries were not free. Many colonies also saw a rise in national pride and wanted to revive old traditions.

The wars, therefore, meant that the people who lived in the colonies were in a position to demand freedom. This point supports my judgement that independence movements were the main reason for the decline of the empire. The wars did not cause a desire for independence, they just created the right conditions for those in India and African colonies to demand independence. The independence movement in India had been going strong for many years with the National Congress being established in 1885. This movement grew from this point with Gandhi playing an important role from the 1920s. Independence movements in Africa gained strength throughout the latter half of the twentieth century.

To conclude, the most important reason for the decline of the British Empire after the Second World War is the independence movements within the colonies. Many countries had started to gain some freedom before the First World War, such as Australia, New Zealand and South Africa. This shows that there was a desire for countries to be independent before the world wars. Many people in the colonies wanted to celebrate their culture and revive their old traditions, and this could only be done if Britain left. It is clear that the world wars helped independent movements as Britain was weaker after them, but the movements existed long before both wars and the colonies had started to turn against the empire. The war just gave them more of a reason to fight.

Chapter 8 Into the modern world

Links to KS3 History National Curriculum

The lessons in this chapter, and the overall approach of a long-running group task, will get students to think carefully about the process of change, the diversity of society, and cultural, economic, military, political and social history in the years after the Second World War. Indeed, 'social, cultural and technological change in post-war British society' is specifically mentioned as a possible study topic in the latest KS3 History National Curriculum. This chapter clearly covers this, while giving students the opportunity to use a range of historical skills and develop their understanding of some key historical concepts.

Students will enjoy building on their context of the decades covered – especially the one they were born in. This focus on chronology, change and continuity, cause and consequence, significance and diversity will undoubtedly help students build a sense of British Values and SMSC, while building cultural capital. Be sure to play them as many songs and film and news clips as you can – they'll love it!

Skills and processes covered in this chapter

		Lesson/activity in the Student Book
History Skills	Knowledge and understanding	8.1 Over to You: 1a, 1b, 1c, 1d, 1e, 2
		8.2 Over to You: 1, 2
		8.3 Over to You: 1a, 1b, 1c, 1d, 1e, 2
		8.4 Over to You: 1, 2
		8.5 Over to You: 1a, 1b, 1c, 1d, 1e, 2
		8.6 Over to You: 1, 2
		8.7 Over to You: 1a, 1b, 1c, 1d, 1e, 2
		8.8A Over to You: 1a, 1b, 2, 3a, 3b
		8.8B Over to You: 1, 2
		Have you been learning? Quick Knowledge Quiz: 1, 2, 3, 4, 5, 6, 7, 8, 9, 10
	Interpretation analysis	8 Assessment: Interpretation analysis: 1, 2
	Source analysis	8.8B Source Analysis: 1
	Significance	
	Cause and consequence	8.8A Over to You: 2
		8.8B Over to You: 1
	Diversity/Similarity and difference	
	Change and continuity	8.1 Over to You: 2
		8.2 Over to You: 2
		8.3 Over to You: 2
		8.4 Over to You: 2
		8.5 Over to You: 2
		8.6 Over to You: 2
		8.7 Over to You: 2, 3
Literacy and Numeracy	Literacy	**Have you been learning?** Literacy Focus: 1, 2a, 2b, 2c, 2d, 2e, 2f
	Numeracy	

Lesson sequence

Lesson title	Student Book pages	Objectives
8.1 The fifties	pp 194–195	• Examine and assess key changes, developments, inventions and ideas in Britain in the 1950s. • Recall key political events and conflicts in the world in the 1950s.
8.2 The sixties	pp 196–197	• Examine and assess key changes, developments, inventions and ideas in Britain in the 1960s. • Recall key political events and conflicts in the world in the 1960s.
8.3 The seventies	pp 198–199	• Examine and assess key changes, developments, inventions and ideas in Britain in the 1970s. • Recall key political events and conflicts in the world in the 1970s.
8.4 The eighties	pp 200–201	• Examine and assess key changes, developments, inventions and ideas in Britain in the 1980s. • Recall key political events and conflicts in the world in the 1980s.
8.5 The nineties	pp 202–203	• Examine and assess key changes, developments, inventions and ideas in Britain in the 1990s. • Recall key political events and conflicts in the world in the 1990s.
8.6 The noughties	pp 204–205	• Examine and assess key changes, developments, inventions and ideas in Britain in the 2000s. • Recall key political events and conflicts in the world in the 2000s.
8.7 The twenty-tens	pp 206–207	• Examine and assess key changes, developments, inventions and ideas in Britain in the 2010s. • Recall key political events and conflicts in the world in the 2010s.
8.8A What is 'terrorism'?	pp 208–209	• Define the word 'terrorism' and analyse how terrorists operate in today's world. • Examine methods to combat terrorism.
8.8B What is 'terrorism'?	pp 210–211	
Chapter 8 Have you been learning?	pp 212–213	• Choose the correct answer from the given options for a quick recap. • Ensure correct spellings and chronological order of events. • Categorise historical vocabulary and check understanding.
Chapter 8 History skill: Interpretation analysis	p 214	• Explore how to compare interpretations.
Chapter 8 Assessment: Interpretation analysis	p 215	• Consider why two interpretations of Margaret Thatcher differ and explain whether you agree with either of them.

Links to the GCSE curriculum

This chapter provides some historical context to the following:

AQA: Health and the People c1000–Present

AQA: Power and the People c1170–Present

Eduqas: Changes in Health and Medicine in Britain c500–Present

Eduqas: The Development of the UK 1919–1990

Exam-style questions covered in this chapter

Exam board	Lesson/activity question location	Command words	History skills/concepts
AQA	8.8B Source Analysis: 1	How useful…	Source analysis
Edexcel	8.8B Source Analysis: 1	How useful…	Source analysis
OCR A	8.8B Source Analysis: 1	How useful…	Source analysis
OCR B	8.8B Source Analysis: 1	How useful…	Source analysis
WJEC	8.1 Over to You: 1	Complete the sentences…	Knowledge and understanding
	8.3 Over to You: 1	Complete the sentences…	Knowledge and understanding
	8.5 Over to You: 1	Complete the sentences…	Knowledge and understanding
	8.7 Over to You: 1	Complete the sentences…	Knowledge and understanding

A brief history

8.1 The fifties

This lesson will give much-needed context to students about how greatly life changed after the Second World War. Students will already have studied the change and continuity of transport, entertainment, technology and working life across many time periods and this lesson builds on their knowledge of those changes. The lesson has engaging pictures showing people and developments that will likely be familiar to the students – they will really get a sense of why this period was known as the 'fab' fifties! Students are introduced to an activity where they will work in groups to track change and continuity from the 1950s to the present day.

8.2 The sixties

The 1960s is usually an exciting topic for students. They will get to explore the causes and consequences of the changes that happened throughout the decade. They will start to see that the laws that were made then resemble our laws today. You could add to this lesson by playing songs and film clips from the decade, such as clips of screaming Beatles fans. The 1960s was a decade filled with different groups fighting for equality – it would be a missed opportunity if the plight and advances of women and black people were not highlighted. More able students should try to categorise the changes identified, for example into political, economic, social changes, etc.

8.3 The seventies

This lesson builds on some of the changes from the previous decade to shine a light on developments for workers, such as the Sex Discrimination Act and the miners' strike. The 'Winter of Discontent' is a cultural reference that students may come across again – this lesson offers the students context on this. The politics of the 1970s takes on a wider arena as Britain joins the EU. Students are again encouraged to analyse change; they could consider which areas have seen the biggest change, create links between different areas of change, and show how each decade influenced the next.

Timeline

1952
The first passenger jet takes holiday makers abroad.

June 1953
The coronation of Queen Elizabeth II.

1961
A Soviet astronaut named Yuri Gagarin is the first human to go into space.

1964
The Civil Rights Act is passed in America making discrimination illegal.

1966
The first InterCity electricity-powered train is used.

1969
US astronauts Neil Armstrong and Buzz Aldrin are the first humans to walk on the moon.

1970
The Equal Pay Act is passed in Britain.

1975
The Sex Discrimination Act makes it illegal to discriminate against women in employment, education and training.

1979
British people elect Margaret Thatcher as their first female Prime Minister.

1984
The miners' strike.

1989
World Wide Web invented by British scientist Tim Berners-Lee.

1994
Sony launches the first of its PlayStation consoles.

1998
The Good Friday Agreement is signed.

2001
9/11 terrorist attacks on the Twin Towers in New York.

2010
The Arab Spring begins in North Africa and the Middle East.

2017
Manchester Arena bombings.

8.4 The eighties

Students will be able to see why the 1980s are known as the technology decade. They will recognise some of today's big tech giants that developed and launched their first products in this decade, as well as the progress made with games consoles. It would be particularly engaging to show students what early video games looked like. They will continue to build on their understanding of issues regarding women, working life, politics and war. They will also develop the second order concepts of cause and consequence and should be able to start evaluating significance of events and developments from the 1950s onwards for women and workers, and people's leisure time.

8.5 The nineties

This lesson is likely to resonate with the students as some of their parents may have grown up in the 1990s, recent fashion trends link to this era, and the 1990s lifestyle resembles theirs more closely. However, it would be a missed opportunity if you did not treat the 1990s like the other decades and play the students music and film and news clips from the era. The categories explored are the same as previous decades but students should now try to analyse change over short periods of time – 1980s to 1990s – but also longer periods of time – from the 1950s to the 1990s.

8.6 The noughties

Students are taken back to the creation of social media and some of the tech companies that are a massive part of their lives today. They may have been born in this decade and will assume lots about it – it will be fun to give them more of a sense of context to the world they live in. The activities encourage students to make links between the different categories that they have explored. By now they will know that there were many changes from the 1990s to the noughties but can they explain how one category of change has influenced another? One way to take this further would be to give some students a different event, person or invention and then others a category and, using a ball of string, see if they can make connections between them.

8.7 The twenty-tens

This lesson will really encourage the students to read and interpret data properly. For example, it shows that while technology in general continued to advance in the 2010s, this progress reduced the use of some forms of technology, such as TV. This decade also introduces some new political issues and the civil rights issues of different groups are brought into focus. Once students have recorded their information they will be required to create a presentation on change from the 1950s to 2020. Students will have explained change over short and long periods, categorised changes and made links between them. They must now make a judgement on which category changed the most.

8.8A/B What is 'terrorism'?

Perhaps one of the most defining moments of the last 20 years was the 9/11 attacks on the Twin Towers in New York. Students have grown up in the shadow of this legacy. This lesson builds the narrative of the attacks and gives a clear account of who was involved and why. Students then see that terrorism is not something that is only carried out by Islamic extremists but by people all over the world from different religions, races and cultures. Students will be expected to define key terms and explain the various methods used by terrorists. This lesson would allow you to make links to British Values and SMSC.

Further reading and links

For teachers:

- The historian David Kynaston's series of books *Austerity Britain, Family Britain* and *Modernity Britain* (Bloomsbury, 2008, 2010, 2015) are great works that focus on accounts from ordinary people – an excellent way of putting people at the heart of history. The series will also provide some valuable sources for you to use.

- The Ken Loach television drama *Cathy Come Home* (1966) offers a different view of the 1960s, away from the music and fashion. This film could help you convey that there was still continuity for the poorest in society.

For students:

- Get students to read *The Secret Diary of Adrian Mole Aged 13¾* by Sue Townsend (1982) for some context of what life was like in the 1970s and 1980s. The book is not only very funny but it will also show students the experiences of people their age during the late twentieth century.

- BBC Bitesize has some videos that will help to consolidate students' learning on the periods covered in the chapter. Search online for 'BBC Bitesize Great Britain 26 class clips' to find the link to clips on the 1960s, computers, industry and social change.

Beyond the classroom

- Ask students to interview family members who remember the decades covered in this chapter. You could turn this into a group (or class) oral history project, asking groups to 'find' someone who was a teenager (or around the same age as the students are now) in the 1950s, 1960s and so on, and interview them about their lives. You could give students a set of questions to ask, for example:

  - How has the way you eat/travel/work changed?
  - How was life different before the Internet?
  - How have women's lives changed?
  - What was school like in that decade?
  - What have been the big developments in technology that have affected you?
  - Which political events do you remember most? Why?

- It would be fun for students to organise a theme day for one – or more – of the decades. They could work with another department such as PE and get them to teach or use resources that would have been available at the time. Working with the Food department would be a great way to explore previous decades with students using cookbooks from different decade.

- Working with the Citizenship, RE and Politics department students could plan an assembly on terrorism to educate and address misconceptions. This could be a good opportunity to link to British Values and SMSC.

- Students could organise a whole year *Dragon's Den*-style competition where they present the key technological advances of the decades and then decide which is the best. They should consider significance as a second order concept. Students should consider the 'wow' moment when the technology was invented – what did this mean for people and why was it remarkable or groundbreaking? Then they should analyse what it changed. Finally, they should explain the impact it has on our lives today to come to a conclusion about its significance. You could direct students to the diagram on page 26 of the Student Book for a useful guide on how to judge the significance of something.

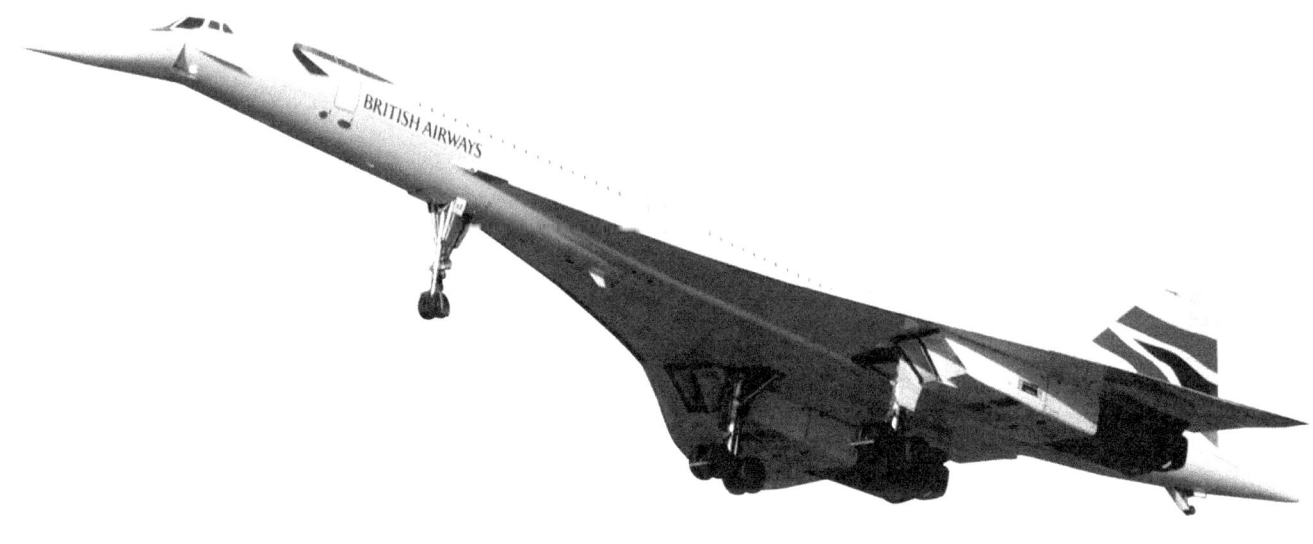

Chapter 8 Answers guidance

Answers guidance

The answers provided here are examples, based on the information provided in the Student Book. There may be other factors which are relevant to each question, and students may draw on as much of their own knowledge as possible to give detailed and precise answers. There are also many ways of answering questions, including exam-style questions (for example, of structuring an essay). However, these exemplar answers should provide a good starting point.

8.1 The fifties
PAGES 194–195

Over to You

1a one million
1b Korean War
1c Alec Issigonis
1d ten
1e 1959
2 Student notes will reflect the changes that have taken place in their chosen category.

8.2 The sixties
PAGES 196–197

Over to You

1 Answers will vary.
2 Student notes will reflect the changes that have taken place in their chosen category.

8.3 The seventies
PAGES 198–199

Over to You

1a ten million
1b three
1c Prime Minister
1d 1975
1e Vietnam
2 Student notes will reflect the changes that have taken place in their chosen category.

8.4 The eighties
PAGES 200–201

Over to You

1 Answers will vary.
2 Student notes will reflect the changes that have taken place in their chosen category.

8.5 The nineties
PAGES 202–203

Over to You

1a Channel Tunnel
1b service
1c 1992
1d Nelson Mandela
1e Harry Potter
2 Student notes will reflect the changes that have taken place in their chosen category.

8.6 The noughties
PAGES 204–205

Over to You

1 Answers will vary.
2 Student notes will reflect the changes that have taken place in their chosen category.

8.7 The twenty-tens
PAGES 206–207

Over to You

1a 33 million
1b London
1c European Union
1d climate
1e Spring
2 Student notes will reflect the changes that have taken place in their chosen category.
3 Presentations will reflect the key changes in each category from the 1950s to the present day. Students should focus on what the changes were, when the changes happened, reasons for the changes – plus any links between any of the changes; e.g. did changes in one category lead to changes in another? Also, which category changed the most… and the least?

8.8A What is 'terrorism'?
PAGES 208–209

Over to You

1a The use of violence and intimidation for political, economic, social or religious reasons.

1b A person who uses terror tactics.
2 • World Trade Center: answers may vary, but might include: large building, many deaths so big impact, publicity for their beliefs, to strike fear – if they can get a plane into the centre of New York, what else are they capable of?
   • Pentagon: answers may vary, but might include: centre of military, so strategic target, many deaths so big impact, publicity for their beliefs, to strike fear – if they can attack military base, what else are they capable of?
   • White House: answers may vary, but might include: symbol of US power/home to US President, to strike fear – if they can destroy White House, what else are they capable of?
3a al-Qaeda: terrorist group that attacked (among others) several US targets.
3b war on terror: an attempt by the US (and troops from other countries) to attack places where terrorists are harboured or trained.

8.8B What is 'terrorism'?
PAGES 210–211

Over to You

1 Answers may include: governments who want to control their own people through fear (as in Nazi Germany); groups who want control over different areas of land; people with their own personal beliefs or agenda (as in Oklahoma City in 1995); people with extreme religious beliefs.
2 Answers will summarise the information on page 211.

Source Analysis

1   Answers will focus on the insight the sources give us into terrorists' techniques, particularly bombs. Also, the sources provide insight into how seriously the terror threat is taken (the fact that there are public awareness posters), so the terrorists have clearly made a great impact on government policy. However, they only give insight into a few methods.

Chapter 8 Have you been learning?

Answers guidance

Chapter 8 Have you been learning?

Quick Knowledge Quiz

PAGE 212

1   a   Birmingham and London
2   b   Korean War
3   b   BBC2
4   c   Magnavox Odyssey
5   c   1979
6   a   Tim Berners-Lee
7   b   merry Christmas
8   b   2007
9   a   Brexit
10 c   11 September 2001

Literacy Focus

PAGE 213

Chronology and spelling

1   • **Millions** of people bought a TV set to watch the live broadcast of the coronation of **Queen** Elizabeth II.

• The Civil Rights Movement was at its **height** in America, calling for **equal** rights for black Americans.
• Glam rock and punk rock **were** the big new sounds in music. Disco **took** the world by storm too.
• Argentina invaded the Falklands, a group of **islands** in the South Atlantic Ocean **governed** by Britain.
• Iraq invaded **Kuwait** and the USA responded by sending in troops to fight Iraq in what became **known** as the Gulf War.
• Apple launched the hugely **successful** iPod, a portable music player. This was followed by the iPhone, a **smartphone**.

Vocabulary check

2b Answers may vary but students could say 'Rolls-Royce' as the others were best-selling post-war cars.

2c Answers may vary but students could say 'New Romantic' as others were styles of the 1960s – New Romantic was 1980s.

2d Answers may vary but students could say 'Virgin Atlantic' as others are linked to personal entertainment devices.

2e Answers may vary but students could say 'The Beatles' as others are groups from the 1990s.

2f Answers may vary but students could say 'Twitter' as the others were developed in the 1950s.

Assessment summary

The assessments in this textbook have been carefully designed and tested with History teachers to support student progression throughout the course. This specific assessment is written to support Year 8 or Year 9 students in tackling questions relating to analysing interpretations.

 Interpretations A and B both provide views on Prime Minister Margaret Thatcher. How do they differ, and what might explain the differences? (20)

▼ **INTERPRETATION A** David Cameron was Britain's Prime Minister from 2010 to 2016. He made this short speech shortly after Thatcher's death in 2013. He belonged to the same political party as Thatcher did – and actually worked for her, in 1988, in one of his first jobs.

> 'Margaret Thatcher didn't just lead our country – she saved our country. She took a country that was on its knees and made Britain stand tall again. We can't deny that Lady Thatcher divided opinion. For many of us, she was, and is, an inspiration. For others she was a force to be defined against [reckoned with]. But if there is one thing that cuts through all of this – one thing that runs through everything she did – it was her lion-hearted love of this country.'

▼ **INTERPRETATION B** David Douglass is a writer who worked as a coal miner in Durham and South Yorkshire. He was an important member of an organization called the National Union of Mineworkers that fought against the closing of coal mines by Thatcher's government in the 1980s.

> 'I will not be shedding any tears over her. I wouldn't normally take comfort in anyone's death, but the woman shed no tears over our communities or the poverty she caused. An entire generation was thrown on the scrapheap, and sons and grandsons are still suffering now. Thatcher's legacy has been unemployment, crime, poverty, low levels of life expectancy, heroin addiction – the list goes on in places where she ripped the heart out of the community… a lot of people have no idea of the damage that woman inflicted on this country…'

Students will start by looking at the content of the interpretations (Question 1) to find differences when considering views of Margaret Thatcher. Then the focus will turn to the provenance to explain why those differences might exist (Question 2). This will then allow students to write a structured answer explaining how and why the interpretations differ, using both interpretations and their own knowledge.

Students are provided with sentence starters, scaffolding activities to help build answers, and questions to ask when evaluating the interpretations.

For the mark scheme, see page 165.

A note about the end-of-chapter assessments

There is an assessment for each Student Book chapter. Each is structured like a GCSE exam-style question, with scaffolding steps to support KS3 students. Each assessment has a total of 20 marks, and is designed to be completed in a typical lesson – each has been written with a time allowance of about 30 minutes.

There is a mark scheme for each assessment. You can choose how to give student outcomes: a mark out of 20; a percentage; a performance indicator (we use a three-stage indicator – 'Developing', 'Secure', 'Extending' – but you could adapt to match any performance indicators used in your school); or a GCSE grade indicator. To convert raw marks to a performance or GCSE grade indicator, use this table:

Raw marks			
0	1–6	7–13	14–20
GCSE grade (9–1) indicators*			
U	1–3	4–6	7–9
Performance indicator			
Ungraded	Developing	Secure	Extending

* Please appreciate that these are approximate grades based on grade boundaries from recent GCSE exam papers. If a student achieves a Grade 7 in one of these assessments, it is not the equivalent of a Grade 7 at GCSE. Instead it is an indicator of the grade the student could expect to get if they continue on their flight path through KS3 and GCSE. Please note:

- the raw-mark boundaries are based on but do not match precisely those for recent GCSE exam papers: this is because our assessments are focused around one exam-style question, likely to be done at the end of a chapter (topic) rather than at the end of the course. Secondly, we provide carefully considered scaffolded steps to allow KS3 students to tackle high level questions and gain confidence through the deliberate practice of building up detailed answers.
- the assessments for Student Book 3 are progressively more demanding in that they use higher-order command words and provide less scaffolded support – if you set one of them for Year 8 students, please take that into account when awarding GCSE grade indicators.

Entering student outcomes into the Kerboodle Markbook

The Kerboodle Markbook records scores and percentages to allow for quick comparison of performance. If you want to use the Markbook to record student outcomes, you will need to enter the appropriate values given in the raw marks row of the table above.

Links to GCSE

By the end of KS3, students should be familiar with the History skill of comparing two or more interpretations. At GCSE, most exam boards ask students to consider differences in interpretations and to explain why these differences may exist. For example:

AQA:

* How does Interpretation B differ from Interpretation A about... ? (4)

* Why might the authors of... have different interpretations... ? (4)

* Which interpretation gives the more convincing opinion about... ? (8)

Edexcel:

* Study Interpretations 1 and 2... What is the main difference between the views... ? (4)

* Suggest one reason Interpretations 1 and 2 give different views about... (4)

OCR B:

* How far do [the interpretations] differ... ? (12)

Eduqas:

* Study the interpretations. Do the interpretations support the view that... ? (10)

Links to KS3 History resources

Student Book

This assessment question links to these lessons:

8.3 The seventies
8.4 The eighties

Kerboodle

Support for this assessment question on Kerboodle:

TWI 8 Assessment presentation: Interpretation analysis
TWI 8 Assessment worksheet (Core): Interpretation analysis
TWI 8 Assessment worksheet (Foundation): Interpretation analysis

Curriculum and Assessment Planning Guide

Support for this assessment question in this guide:

8 Assessment mark scheme – page 165
8 Assessment sample student answers – pages 166–167

Student name: _____   Date: _____

Mark scheme

Assessment bands	Marks	GCSE grade indicators*	I have...
	0	Ungraded	
Developing	1–6	1–3	☐ made some basic comments to analyse the interpretations. ☐ identified one difference between the interpretations. ☐ made some attempt to explain why they are different, but I have not backed up what I have written with examples or evidence.
Secure	7–13	4–6	☐ identified some key differences between the interpretations. I have also written a simple explanation of how they differ. ☐ given a reasonable explanation of at least one reason why they may differ. I have backed up what I have written with basic examples or evidence.
Extending	14–20	7–9	☐ written a detailed analysis of the differences between the interpretations. There is a well-written and well-supported judgement of how they differ. ☐ given a convincing and valid explanation of reasons why they may be different, and backed up what I have written with detailed examples or evidence. NOTE: If you introduce extra relevant knowledge or show understanding of related historical issues, you can be rewarded for this.

* IMPORTANT: These are approximate indicators devised using publicly available information on the new GCSE grades. They are designed to assist in the process of tracking and monitoring. They cannot and should not be used to replace teachers' professional judgement. Teachers should use their own discretion in applying them, taking into account the cumulative test scores of an individual student (rather than just one assessment point), and should refer to their institution's assessment policy.

Mark: _____

Comment:

Sample student answers

Assessment: Interpretation analysis

STUDENT BOOK PAGE 215

 **Interpretations A** and **B** both provide views on Prime Minister Margaret Thatcher. How do they differ, and what might explain the differences? (20)

Sample Developing band answer

One way that Interpretation A is different from Interpretation B is that A writes that everything Thatcher did was for a 'lion-hearted love of this country'. It is clear that the author of Interpretation A was a supporter of Thatcher. On the other hand the author of Interpretation B writes that Thatcher caused 'damage' to the country, showing that the author does not like Thatcher and does not think she made a positive contribution to the country. One reason the authors have different views is their political views. The writer of Interpretation A worked for Thatcher and shared the same political views as her. However, the writer of B was a member of the National Union of Mineworkers which protested against Thatcher's government.

Sample Secure band answer

One way that Interpretation A is different from Interpretation B is that A writes that Thatcher saved Britain. On the other hand, B writes that she damaged the country rather than saving it. Interpretation A focuses more on the economic impact that Thatcher had, saying she 'took a country that was on its knees and made Britain stand tall again'. However, Interpretation B focuses more on the social impact of her government by writing about generations that were 'thrown on the scrapheap'. Interpretation A also focuses on her impact at the time, whereas Interpretation B focuses on the legacy of her government on communities that 'are still suffering now'.

One reason the writers have different views is the jobs they did. The writer of Interpretation A was Prime Minister and leader of the Conservative Party – like Thatcher. This means that he is likely to agree with her policies. Furthermore, he worked for Thatcher during the 1980s just after the miners' strikes. However, the writer of Interpretation B was a miner and a member of the National Union of Mineworkers which fought against the mine closures brought in by Thatcher's government. This means he saw the impact of mine closures at the time but also experienced the long-term impact of mine closures on communities.

Sample Extending band answer

Interpretations A and B differ completely. One way that Interpretation A is different from Interpretation B is that Interpretation A presents Thatcher as someone who saved Britain and made the country better for everyone. On the other hand, Interpretation B blames her for ruining communities. Interpretation A states that Margaret Thatcher 'saved our country' but Interpretation B talks about the 'damage' that she 'inflicted on this country'. This clearly shows that the authors have different opinions on the impact Thatcher had on the country. Another way in which the two interpretations are different is that Interpretation A says Thatcher is an 'inspiration' – suggesting she is greatly admired by people. This is in direct contrast to Interpretation B, which argues that because of Thatcher's policies 'an entire generation was thrown on the scrapheap' – suggesting that she is hated. This is backed up by the comment from the author of Interpretation B that he 'will not be shedding any tears over her'.

One further difference is that Interpretation A mainly focuses on the economic impact that Thatcher had on the country. This interpretation writes that Thatcher saved the country when it was 'on its knees'. Interpretation B, on the other hand, focuses more on the social problems that communities still face as a result of the high levels of unemployment caused by Thatcher's policies.

One reason the writers have different views is their background. The writer of Interpretation A worked for Thatcher, and is a member of the Conservative Party and was Prime Minister, just like Thatcher. This means that he is likely to agree with her policies and was not working in an industry that was affected by her policies. However, the writer of Interpretation B worked as a miner, lived in a mining town that was directly affected by Thatcher's policies, and lost his job when the mines were closed. This means his views on Thatcher are based on the impact on his community rather than the impact she had on the whole country. Therefore, the interpretations differ completely as the writers view Thatcher from their own political viewpoint and do not give a balanced account of her and her policies.

Links to KS3 History National Curriculum

One key aim of the latest KS3 History National Curriculum is that students can understand change within and across time periods. This final chapter allows students to consider the changing twentieth and early twenty-first centuries while also building on the knowledge they have gathered since Book 1: *Invasion, Plague and Murder: Britain 1066–1509 Student Book*, starting in 1066.

A changing Britain is explored using different developments, discoveries and advances to show how factors influence each other. There are some particularly difficult abstract terms for young people to grasp in this chapter such as 'life expectancy' and 'communication', but the straightforward, logical route through the lesson, coupled with the activities, should allow students to demonstrate a number of historical skills and concepts. They will be given the opportunity to think carefully about cause and consequence, change and continuity, similarity, difference and significance. They will have to think for themselves, justify their opinions, weigh evidence and write structured accounts.

Skills and processes covered in this chapter

		Lesson/activity in the Student Book
History Skills	Knowledge and understanding	**9.1B** Over to You: 1a, 2
		Have you been learning? Quick Knowledge Quiz: 1, 2, 3, 4, 5, 6, 7, 8, 9, 10
	Significance	**9.1B** Over to You: 1c
	Cause and consequence	**9.1B** Over to You: 2
	Diversity/Similarity and difference	**9.1B** Over to You: 1d
	Change and continuity	**9.1B** Over to You: 1a, 1b, 1c, 1d; Change and Continuity: 1
		9 Assessment: Change: 1, 2, 3, 4
Literacy and Numeracy	Literacy	**Have you been learning?** Literacy Focus: 1, 2

Lesson sequence

Lesson title	Student Book pages	Objectives
9.1A How has Britain changed between 1901 and the present day?	pp 216–217	• Examine some of the key changes in British life since 1901.
9.1B How has Britain changed between 1901 and the present day?	pp 218–219	• Judge how far Britain has changed since 1901.
Chapter 9 Have you been learning?	pp 220–221	• Choose the correct answer from the given options for a quick recap. • Assess and find evidence to support different opinions about the twentieth century.
Chapter 9 History skill: Change	p 222	• Examine how to respond to questions on change.
Chapter 9 Assessment: Change	p 223	• Structure an answer which responds to a statement about the changes that took place in Britain between 1901 and the present day.

Links to the GCSE curriculum

This chapter provides some historical context to the following:

AQA: Power and the People c1170–Present

AQA: Migration, Empires and the People c790–Present

OCR A: The Changing International Order 1918–2001

OCR A: War and British Society c790–c2010

Eduqas: Changes in Crime and Punishment in Britain c500–Present

WJEC: Changes in Crime and Punishment c1500–Present

Exam-style questions covered in this chapter

Exam board	Lesson/activity question location	Command words	History skills/concepts
AQA	9.1B Change and Continuity: 1	Explain two ways…different	Change and continuity

A brief history

9.1A/B How has Britain changed between 1901 and the present day?

This lesson focuses on the lives of ordinary people, which will make it easier for the students to track change and continuity over the twentieth century through to today. Students will build on their group activity from the previous chapter, now showing how life changed from the start of the twentieth century up to the present. The lesson contains lots of dates and statistics so this would be a great opportunity to reinforce how to take notes and how to structure a spider diagram. Students are asked to give their opinion on when would be the best time to live; this can be descriptive but they must back it up with specific and relevant knowledge of the period. Students will answer an 'explain' style question, common on all GCSE specifications, which focuses on the changing lives of women.

Further reading and links

For teachers:

- George Orwell's *The Road to Wigan Pier* (1937) is a fantastic account of the British political landscape and social history of early twentieth-century Britain. It will give you some examples to enhance descriptions of life in Britain.

- *Milkman* by Anna Burns (Faber & Faber, 2018) is a coming of age novel set during the Troubles in Northern Ireland. It offers insight into what it was like growing up as a young woman in this period of turmoil.

For students:

- If you would like your classes to explore further the causes of terrorism and the methods deployed in the fight against terrorism, a Depth Study Student Book is available from Oxford University Press (*Terrorism: The Rise of Terror Tactics in the Modern World* by Aaron Wilkes; 2011).

- BBC Bitesize has a useful page on changes in twentieth-century society. Students could read this to consolidate their learning and find out more statistics and figures about the period. Go to bbc.co.uk/bitesize, and click Learn & revise > Secondary > KS3 > History > Modern World history (20th century) > Everyday life in the 20th century.

Timeline

1901
The population of the UK is 38 million.
Women do not have the vote.
News and important information is conveyed through word of mouth, newspapers/magazines, telegrams and letters.

1960s
The population of the UK is 52 million.
Women still have unequal pay to men.
News and important information is conveyed by through word of mouth, newspapers/magazines, letters, radio, telephone and television.

2020
The population of the UK is 66.5 million.
There have been two female Prime Ministers.
News and important information is conveyed through word of mouth, social media, newspapers/magazines, TV, email, telephone, radio and letters.

Beyond the classroom

- There are many motoring and transport museums around the country. Take your students on a trip to one of these so they can see the changing face of transport throughout the twentieth century.

- Get students to add to their oral history project from Chapter 8 and speak to the older men and women in their families, asking them about working life. They should compare how men and women were treated and what attitudes to school were like.

- Students could survey teachers in the school to see how they spend their free time. This would be a great exercise for them to compare how people spent their free time at the start of the twentieth century with how people enjoy their free time now. They should consider how much free time people have and the cost of activities.

Answers guidance

The answers provided here are examples, based on the information provided in the Student Book. There may be other factors which are relevant to each question, and students may draw on as much of their own knowledge as possible to give detailed and precise answers. There are also many ways of answering questions, including exam-style questions (for example, of structuring an essay). However, these exemplar answers should provide a good starting point.

9.1B How has Britain changed between 1901 and the present day?

PAGES 218–219

Over to You

1a Spider diagrams will reflect the information in the lessons, based on the categories shown (entertainment, population, position of women etc.).

1b Answers will focus on the key changes in different categories. For example: In 1901, the main forms of communication were word of mouth, newspapers/magazines, telegrams and letters. Many of these forms of communication remained in the 1960s, but radio, TV and the telephone were new developments. In today's world, email and social media are an important part of the way we communicate.

1c Answers will vary.

1d Answers will vary.

2 Answers will vary, but might reflect the fact that Britain is a democratic country with equal rights, with a decent standard of living for many, low infant mortality rates and a high average age of death etc.

Change and Continuity

1 Answers will vary, but here is a possible example. In 1901 it was very much a man's world – voting in elections for Parliament was for men only and many jobs (such as teaching) expected women to leave if they got married. Many people thought a woman's place was in the home, looking after the children and her husband. And even if women did the same jobs as men (such as factory work), they got paid less. In today's world, women's political rights are equal to men. Sex discrimination is illegal – so, for example, it's illegal to pay men and women different wages for the same job (although this still happens with some companies).

Chapter 9 Have you been learning?

Answers guidance

Chapter 9 Have you been learning?

Quick Knowledge Quiz

PAGE 220

1   b   Queen Victoria
2   b   150
3   c   4
4   a   increased
5   a   14
6   a   15
7   c   heart problems
8   a   NHS
9   c   90 per cent
10 b   40 per cent

Literacy Focus

PAGE 221

Weighing evidence

1

Evidence for destruction	Evidence for progress
Terrorist incidents	End of the Cold War
Unemployment in the 1930s and 1980s	Improved women's rights
War - for example the World Wars, Korean War and Vietnam War	Improved Civil Rights for minority groups
	Advances in medicine
The Holocaust	Space race

2 The twentieth century was both a century of progress and destruction. Throughout the century there were global wars that resulted in millions of deaths, including the Holocaust. Inequality grew around the world with nations in Africa and India that had been former colonies not having the same development as Britain and America. However, civil rights improved for all groups in countries like Britain, with women having more rights in the workplace and black people in America gaining equal rights. Also, by the end of the twentieth century, there had not been a global conflict for many years and an organisation (the UN) worked hard to prevent war and improve the world. Also, the Cold War had ended. This shows that the twentieth century was both a century of progress and destruction.

Assessment summary

The assessments in this textbook have been carefully designed and tested with History teachers to support student progression throughout the course. This specific assessment is written to support Year 8 or Year 9 students in tackling questions relating to change.

> How far do you agree that the way people communicate with each other has seen the greatest change between 1901 and the present day in Britain? Give reasons for your answer. (20)

Students will be expected to explain changes in communication over the time period, and then identify and explain other areas of change (Question 1). Then they must make a judgement on the area where the biggest change occurred (Question 2). Using this judgement, students will directly answer the exam question (Question 3) and explain how far they agree. Finally, students will provide details to explain their response and write a conclusion (Question 4).

To support students with this question we have provided sentence starters and tips to help them focus their ideas.

For the mark scheme, see page 174.

A note about the end-of-chapter assessments

There is an assessment for each Student Book chapter. Each is structured like a GCSE exam-style question, with scaffolding steps to support KS3 students. Each assessment has a total of 20 marks, and is designed to be completed in a typical lesson – each has been written with a time allowance of about 30 minutes.

There is a mark scheme for each assessment. You can choose how to give student outcomes: a mark out of 20; a percentage; a performance indicator (we use a three-stage indicator – 'Developing', 'Secure', 'Extending' – but you could adapt to match any performance indicators used in your school); or a GCSE grade indicator. To convert raw marks to a performance or GCSE grade indicator, use this table:

Raw marks			
0	1–6	7–13	14–20
GCSE grade (9–1) indicators*			
U	1–3	4–6	7–9
Performance indicator			
Ungraded	Developing	Secure	Extending

*Please appreciate that these are approximate grades based on grade boundaries from recent GCSE exam papers. If a student achieves a Grade 7 in one of these assessments, it is not the equivalent of a Grade 7 at GCSE. Instead it is an indicator of the grade the student could expect to get if they continue on their flight path through KS3 and GCSE. Please note:
- the raw-mark boundaries are based on but do not match precisely those for recent GCSE exam papers: this is because our assessments are focused around one exam-style question, likely to be done at the end of a chapter (topic) rather than at the end of the course. Secondly, we provide carefully considered scaffolded steps to allow KS3 students to tackle high level questions and gain confidence through the deliberate practice of building up detailed answers.
- the assessments for Student Book 3 are progressively more demanding in that they use higher-order command words and provide less scaffolded support – if you set one of them for Year 8 students, please take that into account when awarding GCSE grade indicators.

Entering student outcomes into the Kerboodle Markbook

The Kerboodle Markbook records scores and percentages to allow for quick comparison of performance. If you want to use the Markbook to record student outcomes, you will need to enter the appropriate values given in the raw marks row of the table above.

Links to GCSE

By the end of KS3, students should be familiar with the History skill of analysing change. At GCSE, all exam boards expect students to analyse change within and over long time periods. For example:

AQA:

- Compare… with… In what ways were they similar? Explain your answer with reference to both periods. (8)
- In what ways… Explain your answer. (8)

Edexcel:

- 'The main change… was…' How far do you agree? Explain your answer. (16)
- Explain one way in which… was different from/similar to… (4)

OCR A:

- Explain why… (10)

OCR B:

- How far do you agree that… ? Give reasons for your answer. (18)

Eduqas:

- Outline how… changed from… to… In your answer you should provide a written narrative discussing the… across three historical eras. (16) (SPaG 4)

Links to KS3 History resources

Student Book

This assessment question links to these lessons:

9.1A/B How has Britain changed between 1901 and the present day?

Kerboodle

Support for this assessment question on Kerboodle:

TWI 9 Assessment presentation: Change
TWI 9 Assessment worksheet (Core): Change
TWI 9 Assessment worksheet (Foundation): Change

Curriculum and Assessment Planning Guide

Support for this assessment question in this guide:

9 Assessment mark scheme – page 174
9 Assessment sample student answers – pages 175–176

Student name: _____   Date: _____

Mark scheme

Assessment bands	Marks	GCSE grade indicators*	I have...
	0	Ungraded	
Developing	1–6	1–3	☐ given a basic explanation of one or two areas of change in Britain between 1901 and the present day. ☐ written an answer that shows limited knowledge and understanding relating to the changes.
Secure	7–13	4–6	☐ written a detailed explanation of at least two areas of change in Britain between 1901 and the present day, suggesting that one change is greater than the others. I have reached a judgement that answers the question. ☐ written an answer that shows a range of accurate knowledge and understanding that relates to the question.
Extending	14–20	7–9	☐ written a well-organised answer with a well-developed explanation of three areas of change in Britain between 1901 and the present day, leading to a judgement that is backed up by reasons, and answers the question. ☐ included a wide range of accurate and detailed knowledge and understanding that is relevant to the question.

* IMPORTANT: These are approximate indicators devised using publicly available information on the new GCSE grades. They are designed to assist in the process of tracking and monitoring. They cannot and should not be used to replace teachers' professional judgement. Teachers should use their own discretion in applying them, taking into account the cumulative test scores of an individual student (rather than just one assessment point), and should refer to their institution's assessment policy.

Mark: _____

> **Comment:**

Sample student answers

Assessment: Change

STUDENT BOOK PAGE 223

 How far do you agree that the way people communicate with each other has seen the greatest change between 1901 and the present day in Britain? Give reasons for your answer. (20)

 Sample Developing band answer

In 1901 one of the main forms of communication was people talking to each other. People also wrote letters as a way to communicate. Telegrams could be sent to give important or urgent messages. However, this has changed a lot as now people can send emails, use social media and talk on the telephone. Another change from 1901 has been women's rights. Women have gone from having no vote to having had two female Prime Ministers by 2020. But I think that communication is where there has been the most change, so I agree with the statement.

 Sample Secure band answer

In 1901, the main methods of communication were word of mouth, letter writing and telegrams. Many people could not read well, and so did not read newspapers, but this changed in the middle of the century as newspapers become more widely available and literacy levels increased with better education. In the modern world there are many different types of newspapers and magazines, and people can access the news from their phones. Nowadays people hardly ever write letters as they can send emails or text messages, and many people keep in touch or find information through social media. So, the key changes in communication have been that we have more immediate forms of communication with the invention of the internet and smart phones.

There were other changes that were important too. One important area of change was in women's rights. In 1901, women were expected to be mothers and wives and it was rare for them to have careers; they didn't even have the vote. As the century progressed the suffragettes campaigned for women to have the vote and by 1928 women had the vote on equal terms with men. In the modern world, there have been two female Prime Ministers and women have equal access to education and employment. However, there is still work to be done to have true equality with men. So, the key changes have been that women have better opportunities and there is a more equal society than in 1901.

In conclusion I strongly agree that communication saw the largest change between 1901 and the present day in Britain, because everyone can communicate immediately and across the whole world using the internet and information travels faster than it has ever done.

Sample Extending band answer

I disagree that communication saw the largest change between 1901 and the present day in Britain. In 1901, the main methods of communication were by word of mouth, newspapers/magazines, letters and telegrams. Communication was slow and limited. Those who were able to read could write letters and telegrams, and read newspapers. Those who could not were limited to word of mouth communication only. However, as the century progressed more and more people could buy and read newspapers, and they could also take advantage of new technology such as the radio and the TV. Communication had become a lot quicker and easier to access due to this new technology. This is something that has continued. In the modern world technology has brought huge changes in communication as people can now send emails, write text messages and use social media to communicate. The internet means that news is instantly accessible across the world, and the vast majority of people are able to use this technology in their communications. So, the key changes in communication have been the speed and the accessibility to all.

There were other changes that were important too, such as health and medicine. In 1901 life expectancy was low for men and women, with some poorer cities having a life expectancy as low as 30. There were high infant mortality rates which saw 150 babies out of 1000 die by their first birthday. Most deaths were due to diseases such as heart disease and respiratory disease. However, as the century progressed and science and medicine developed, the lives of people massively improved. Many of these improvements were due to the establishment of the welfare state, started off by the Liberal Reforms of the early 1900s – these gave free school meals to children and sick pay to those who could not work. These reforms helped to improve the health of the nation. However, after the Second World War it was clear that more needed to be done. The Beveridge Report of 1942 led eventually to the creation of the National Health Service. The areas of welfare, health and medicine therefore saw the biggest change over the century. Today everyone is entitled to free health care. Life expectancy has increased in some areas to 80 and infant mortality has dropped to 4 deaths for every 1000 births. Furthermore, deaths from respiratory diseases have also reduced and are not the main cause of death, due to developments in vaccinations and treatment.

Yet another area of change was in women's rights. In 1901, women didn't even have the vote. As the century progressed the suffragettes campaigned for women to have the vote and by 1928 women had the vote on equal terms with men. Women carried on campaigning for equal pay, employment and education rights for women and now there have been two female Prime Ministers and women have access to education and employment.

In conclusion, I disagree that communication saw the largest change between 1901 and the present day in Britain. Women's rights changed a great deal, but the largest changes were in the areas of welfare, health and medicine. The establishment of the welfare state lifted many people out of poverty and gave them access to free health care. This then meant that people could demand a better living standard and more life chances.